CRIMINAL
JUSTICE
HISTORY

CRIMINAL JUSTICE HISTORY is an international forum for the history and analysis of crime and criminal justice. It annually publishes research and historiographical articles, comparative and interpretive essays, conference assessments, research notes, book review essays, and reviews. The annual encourages submissions from authors in any part of the world in disciplines such as history, law, anthropology, sociology, political science, and the criminal justice sciences that relate specifically to the history of crime and criminal justice and to its broader social, historical, legal, and institutional contexts in any geographical area or period.

Board of Editors

CRIMINAL
JUSTICE
HISTORY

AN INTERNATIONAL ANNUAL

Volume 14
1993

Greenwood Press
Westport, Connecticut • London

British Library Cataloguing in Publication Data is available.

Copyright © 1994 by Greenwood Publishing Group, Inc.

All rights reserved. No portion of this book may be
reproduced, by any process or technique, without the
express written consent of the publisher.

ISBN: 0–313–28736–8

First published in 1994

Greenwood Press, 88 Post Road West, Westport, CT 06881
An imprint of Greenwood Publishing Group, Inc.

Printed in the United States of America

The paper used in this book complies with the
Permanent Paper Standard issued by the National
Information Standards Organization (Z39.48–1984).

10 9 8 7 6 5 4 3 2 1

Contents

Preface

Prosecuting youthful offenders is a subject that has been with us since sixteenth-century Europe, whether in England, France, Germany, Italy, or the Low Countries. At times, "juveniles" have been seen as a threat to public order in the streets and neighborhoods of communities. Paradoxically, their activities have been regarded as reaching crisis proportions in some countries at the turn of the sixteenth, eighteenth, and nineteenth centuries; and some commentators would make the same argument for the turn of our own present century. Since World War II, relatively good crime statistics have been available from the industrial societies; for earlier times, hard evidence on youthful offenders has been difficult to attain. Two major chapters of this current volume attempt to address the evidentiary problem and suggest avenues for future research.

The origins of the problem in England is the subject of the work of Peter King and Joan Noel. They begin with the proposition that juvenile delinquency was not seen as destructive or threatening to society in general until the very late eighteenth and early nineteenth centuries. The history of juvenile offenders in the first critical period has yet to be adequately examined prior to committing them to their own hulks in 1823, prisons in 1838, and separate trials by summary process with national reformatories in the 1850s. The London Criminal Registers at the Old Bailey from 1791 allow the historian to develop a quantitative study of this phenomenon. The authors discover that the proportion of offenders under the age of sixteen increased four-fold from 1791 to 1820, in an era in which their percentage of society increased by only 2.5 percent and in which there were no major industrial, social, or demographic changes. The explanation is traced to a series of factors that would not surprise current American commentators: the creation of new offenses that targeted youthful offenders, increased vigilance in local communities and increased pay for prosecutors, the curtailment of serious punishments, and a "moral panic," which followed the end of the Napoleonic Wars.

By the late nineteenth century, juveniles had become an important element in the reform program of the urban middle class, who strove to bridge the class warfare of the century. The rise of youth street traders was perceived as the movement of a budding criminal generation. How this phenomenon was handled is the subject of Barbara Weinberger's work on policing juveniles in Manchester. The origins of street gangs can be traced to the 1880s and 1890s, and the response of reformers was to establish voluntary organizations such as Lads Clubs and school attendance officers who would attempt to keep these juveniles off the streets of urban centers. The reports of Manchester constables reveal that a "moral panic," similar to that which followed the end of the Napoleonic Wars, led to a dramatic rise in the arrests and prosecutions of juveniles in the years 1914–1916. The response of the reformers and the authorities, however, was different from that of the previous era and included the origins of the social welfare officer who served the often conflicting functions of policing and reformation. The interaction between the functions of social welfare and policing is also the subject of Alf Lüdtke's collected essays on the history of policing in Germany, reviewed here.

The foregoing and rather uncharacteristic function of policing can also be seen in the chapter by Jonathan Swainger, which examines the policing of a Canadian frontier settlement at Red Deer, Alberta, in the early twentieth century. With police constables, as well as justices of the peace, lacking in legal knowledge, it is little wonder that jails were used as hotels for overnight transients, that constables were ill-prepared for violence when it erupted, and that they did not make their offices their careers. Police Chief George Rothnie was confronted with a local drunk who pulled a gun on him, pointed it in his face, announced to Rothnie that he would "fix him," and pulled the trigger twice—each time without a discharge; one can easily understand the chief's resignation. Moral panics, moreover, could also occur with the slightest provocation, as witness the amusing story of Rocky Mountain House's James Oscar Triplett following his release from the Ponoka asylum. The local law-enforcement officials were hammered when they failed to apprehend him.

Policing in Britain and the Empire was traditionally viewed as prevention, arrest, and control—seldom as detection. The practice of having detectives in the employment of the state originated in the early 1840s, and Stefan Petrow provides a history of the early detectives in London in the period 1869–1914. The increase in their numbers is attributed to the garroting panic of the mid-1860s. Using a combination of the public records and personal memoirs, he examines their employment, training, organization, and profession. Petrow concludes that their increased use was paralleled by a wider latitude of action that enabled them to become semi-autonomous;

in turn, their autonomy gave rise to corruption, which came to match that of the Italians.

Moral panics have not always been initiated by people in the streets. As Kate Lowe and Eugene McLaughlin demonstrate in a study of the politics of penal reform in Hong Kong in the late nineteenth century, the state itself is capable of producing such results. Examining the governorship of Sir John Pope Hennessy, his attempt to install racial equality in the criminal justice system caused a virulent reaction from the small English contingent in the island that led to a moral panic in public debate and the press. Supported by the Colonial Office, his attempt to replace the "Rule of Iron" with deterrence, religious instruction, and reformative ideals was met with opprobrium. He attempted to eschew the older colonial policies of martial law, iron and chain, twenty-nine stripes, and capital punishment for indigenous peoples who threatened the tranquility of their conquerors; the history of his "reception" shows how fragile was the work of the reformers who have been studied by Randall McGowan (1987), Paul Cromwell (1989), and Christopher Adamson (1992) in previous volumes of *Criminal Justice History*. It also shows how entrenched these notions were in other colonies, as Greg Marquis discusses in his review of recent books on the history of crime and punishment in Quebec. Perhaps complementary studies of penology and philosophy have much to offer us in exploring the boundaries of capital punishment, as Tom Sorell notes in his review of Nigel Walker's *Why Punish?*

Policing a dominant culture is fraught with difficulties at the best of times. Reviewing several recent books on policing the empire and decolonization, Bernard Porter highlights the disparities and incongruities of the Victorians. Refusing to admit that their police often acted as a *gendarmerie* or as protectors of a free-market economy, they saw the police serving the function of social self-regulation of purely criminous acts. Thus it was also seen as readily exportable to places such as Canada, Hong Kong, South Africa, New Zealand, Australia, and the West Indies. This practice followed, after all, in the footsteps of the Justice of the Peace, who was deemed equally exportable to the same places, as discussed in a review essay on a recent three-volume history of the office. The difficulty was whether the police acted with "consent." While this was usually the norm in Britain, it was more problematic in the colonies, where the result was often a genuine hybrid of police institutions, particularly in Africa, New Zealand, and—as can be seen in this volume—in Canada. As Porter, and Richard Vogler's review of Philippe Robert's edited collection of essays on detention suggest, comparative policing is a topic waiting to be written.

Comparative history is also fraught with difficulties, of which language, culture, and institutions are paramount. In a wide-ranging and thoughtful essay on crime and criminality in the European countryside, Clive Emsley offers a number of suggestions for the study of comparative, local criminal

justice history. His starting point is the assumption that the growth of the
nation state since early modern times did not subvert the role of local
communities in dealing with law and order. He suggests that poaching could
be for commercial profit even in a non-industrial society, that rites of passage
were not necessarily class oriented, that bandits might indeed be real criminals, that the poor often stole from their own members, that the order
created by communities was not necessarily more "friendly" than that of
the state, and that often state intervention came at the behest of the
community.

What makes comparative history difficult, however, given the problem
of language, is familiarity with and access to the relevant scholarly literature.
In a document that challenges us to read it, Xavier Rousseau has prepared
a major bibliography of criminality and criminal justice history in Europe,
1250–1850. Focusing on the most recent work, and especially on that of
the last decade, he first introduces the methodological literature and then
provides sections on criminal justice and communal power in the Middle
Ages, criminal justice and monarchic powers in the early modern era, and
criminality and state powers in modern times. Covering the countries of
France, the Low Countries, the British Isles, Helvetic cities, Nordic countries,
Germanic areas, and Portugal, Spain and Italy, his selections suggest the
direction of both recent and current scholarship in criminal justice history.
Hopefully these directions will be explored in future writings.

CRIMINAL JUSTICE HISTORY

Crime and Criminal Justice in the European Countryside: Some Questions for Comparison

Clive Emsley
The Open University, Milton Keynes

Comparison is central to history. Historians make comparisons all the time; it is the way to demonstrate both the unique nature of individual historical events and change through time. Yet historians often also tend to shroud themselves in the cloaks of their specific "period" and the chosen country of their study. Serious cross-national comparison is difficult; it requires an attempt to master in depth the history of different countries and then to make meaningful comparisons and contrasts. Although this may be done employing only one language—and the policing studies of Wilbur Miller and Stanley H. Palmer are excellent examples[1]—more often than not the problem of different languages probably inhibits such research from the start. But language is a mechanical problem. Conceptual problems also exist, and they are not always as readily apparent.

Historians are brought up in different traditions, and their comparisons often have been conceptualised from within the traditions in which their work is rooted. Whether such a tradition is a single national experience or a set of assumptions about the process of history, the results of comparison made from such a starting point are likely to be limited and explain only how experiences differed from the model concept. A classic case is the question of why, in comparison with France in the 1790s and most of Europe in 1830 and 1848, there was no revolution in Britain at the end of the eighteenth century or during the nineteenth. Consciously or not the question draws on a Marxist tradition and rather presupposes that there ought to have been such a revolution; it also presupposes that all the social and political upheavals labelled revolutions in Europe during these years were the same kind of thing with the same kind of causes. In serious comparative history no single case can set the parameters for making comparisons. But serious comparative history can deepen our understanding of the particular and can force a recognition that the nation-state is, itself, a creation of history.

Much of the work suggesting directions for the study of crime in the countryside and in the small town emerged from the work of left-wing British academics who grew up in the interwar years and began to publish some fifteen years after World War II. Eric Hobsbawm's studies of "primitive rebels" and bandits first appeared, respectively, in 1959 and 1969.[2] They demonstrated what a historian with a wide grasp of languages and the courage to make cross-cultural comparisons could do. With a less broad perspective, again thirty years ago, George Rudé published his studies of French revolutionary and English Wilkesite crowds and also sought to make a comparative synthesis.[3] E. P. Thompson, while making no direct cross-cultural comparisons in his work, produced a profound analysis of the ideology of food rioters and their "moral economy," which has since been taken up by other academic disciplines;[4] he was also the inspiration behind the new studies of crime in eighteenth-century England. These three historians have encouraged a generation of graduate research into collective action, protest, and "social crime." During the last two decades a wide variety of monographs have appeared exploring these issues, but generally in individual national contexts.

The nation-state and high politics, so much the concern of academic historians in the first century of their professional existence, were often an irrelevance to peasants and plebeians, except when they made demands—notably, money for taxes or young men for the army. Sadly for the peasants and plebeians, the growth and increasing efficiency of the state made these demands more difficult to avoid and less likely to be alleviated in times of distress. But while the nation-state and high politics are peripheral to the prime concerns of the new generation of social historians, they still tend to determine the horizons of research. There are now studies of banditry, food riots, riots in defence of common rights, arson and poaching, and popular resistance to militia ballots and conscription.[5] This work, while overwhelmingly conducted in separate national contexts, has uncovered styles and patterns of crowd action providing a valuable point of entry into the lives and *mentalités* of these social groups.

Yet there remains much to be done. Hobsbawm's and Rudé's work particularly and much of the subsequent research have been rooted in a particular set of assumptions, a class-conflict model wherein the peasant was ranged against the landowner and/or the state and in which peasant protest appears as a precursor of labor protest. Peasant protest in this model is generally seen as reactive, part of a preindustrial world, subsequently to be replaced by the proactive labor movements and working-class politicians.[6] Dirk Blasius's pioneering work on nineteenth-century German criminality follows this line. He concentrates on the peasantry's protests against new patterns of ownership and the peasants' determination to maintain their right to wood for fuel, if needs be, by theft.[7] Yet, without detracting from the importance of Blasius's work, it has to be stressed that it was the urban artisans who contributed most to the emergence of labor organizations in Germany, not the peasants. Bob Bushaway's study of the folk customs and ceremonies of England's rural plebeians during the eighteenth and nineteenth centuries is, at times, open to similar criticism.[8] It is difficult to conceive of groups of men turning up in woods at the dead of night as always being poor laborers intent only on maintaining their right to fuel, especially when they came equipped with very large carts for carrying away the wood.

Poaching presents similar problems. Across Europe nongentry rural dwellers appear to have shared the view that animals, birds, and fish were put on earth for the use of all men and could not be the property of a privileged few. Some poaching, like some wood theft, probably was a form of resistance to the exactions of landlords.[9] But it is also clear that some poaching was conducted, not for the family pot in times of dearth or to provide a family treat, but for commercial profit.[10] This is not to deny that embryonic class conflict and consciousness might be found in all such activities, but increasingly, historians are finding it necessary to penetrate beyond, or else to refine, this model as an explanation. John E. Archer acknowledges that class perceptions played a part in arson, poaching, and animal maiming in East Anglia during the nineteenth century and that such activities could be consciousness raising, but not always in the sense defined by Marx. Young agricultural workers were fighting back with their criminal activities, but they were also leaving the land: "Many became conscious of the fact that, beyond the flat horizons, there was a brighter prospect than the glow of burning stacks." Archer's work also challenges the extent to which such offenses should be seen as a product of backwardness and a lack of working-class organization; arson, in particular, he suggests is timeless, and he draws a parallel with the activities of Welsh nationalists during the 1980s.[11]

Arson may be a timeless offence; class is a constantly evolving relationship between social groups. The more social historians have used class as an analytical tool, the more divisions and differing interests seem to emerge between those who, on an initial reading, might be lumped in the same class. Wood theft was a problem in the administrative district of Minden, Westphalia, during the early nineteenth century, but Josef Mooser shows that often there was little class solidarity among the nonnoble rural dwellers. Peasant proprietors were far more prevalent in the district he studies than were noble landowners; they were also the victims of wood theft by the increasing numbers of landless laborers. These peasant proprietors were more determined in their resistance to popular unrest than the nobles. They responded to theft by turning on the offenders through *charivaris*,[12] the destruction of their property, and even lynching. But they also employed other forms, more acceptable to authority, which suggests an increasing accommodation with the state and its elite.

They sometimes prosecuted the offenders; and they sought to establish institutions of control, like the Association of Respectability and Morality in Heepen, which aped those of the nobility.[13] Regina Schulte, while acknowledging that peasants accused of arson, infanticide, and poaching faced an essentially urban criminal justice, peels away at the layers of meaning which these offenses had in the villages of Upper Bavaria. Courts, and subsequent historians, may have concluded that men went poaching because they were poor and needed to support their families, because they enjoyed it, or because they were making some kind of sociopolitical statement; Schulte would not deny any of this. Yet, as she points out, village folklore suggests that for the young male participant, poaching also constituted some kind of *rite de passage*, while poaching denunciations often reflected conflicts within the village community.[14]

Banditry and brigandage are other forms of rural offense for which a class-conflict model figured prominently in much of the work that inspired recent research. Hobsbawm chose to focus on social bandits, "peasant outlaws whom the lord and state regard as criminals, but who remain within peasant society, and are considered by their people as heroes, as champions, avengers, fighters for justice, perhaps even leaders of liberation, and in any case as men to be admired, helped and supported." They were therefore different from "rural desperadoes who are not peasant by origin or allegiance, but impoverished gentlemen robbers," as well as from gangs drawn from "the professional underworld," "common robbers," and "communities for whom raiding is part of the normal way of life."[15] As lively and stimulating as Hobsbawm's essay is, there are so many caveats here that the reader may be excused from wondering what is left; especially as rather a lot of historical bandits seem to cross these different divisions. Jean Lamon the Elder, known as Pélot, certainly lived in his native Gascony in the early nineteenth century. But his robberies and rapes terrifed people; he was transformed into a "social bandit," a *bandit d'honneur*, years after his death, when the peasants who had not known him sought a mythical Robin Hood character with whom they could identify in opposition to the encroachments of the state and the towns.[16]

Increasingly, the new work is stressing the need for alternative definitions and interpretations. Uwe Danke has stressed that bandits in late seventeenth- and early eighteenth-century Saxony "were a good deal more modest a phenomenon than their legendary celebration has made them out to be." Moreover, Danke's bandits seem more the product of an early labelling process than "social bandits" or a potential reservoir for labor protest.[17] Marta Petrusewicz has challenged the class-conflict portrayal of southern Italian peasant brigandage, suggesting that anti-state rhetoric among the brigands was an effect rather than a cause of their behavior and that the growth of brigandage was the result of the increase in the number of occasions for conflict between peasants and the authorities brought about by an encroaching, modernizing state. Brigandage disappeared, in this analysis, not because of a recognition that there was no future in it, but because the state had the greater resources and the greater fire-power.[18] However, it has been forcefully argued that banditry in Sicily in the first half of the nineteenth century was less the result of conflict between peasants and the authorities, and stemmed more from resistance, by both traditional and new elites, to the centralization policies of the Bourbon monarchy. The armed bandits of Sicily emerged as instruments in this conflict, and were protected by their powerful patrons. In the north of Italy, in contrast, the banditry following the Revolution of 1848 was essentially "the poor stealing from the less poor, and often being pretty brutal about it."[19]

The Spanish guerrillas who fought Napoleon's armies and who were described by the French as bandits and brigands have acquired something of the heroic mantle of freedom fighters. Yet a harder look at the sources suggests that, like Pélot, they did not just live among the Spanish peasantry but sometimes lived off them and that they could be as brutal and burdensome to their own as to their enemies.[20] Later in the nineteenth century, Spanish bandits sometimes had close links with the local bosses, the *caciques*. They were employed to protect the property of one local boss and could be sent to attack the property of another. At the same time, probably because of their violent opposition to the distant state and its representatives, the *Guardia Civil*, local bandits could be romanticized into cultural heroes; they were the boys (*muchachos*), the horsemen (*caballeristas*), who practiced an identifiable trade (*negocios*).

Two disillusioned state officials wrote studies of Andalusian banditry in the late nineteenth and early twentieth centuries lamenting how local corruption, especially among those responsible for enforcing the state's law, fostered banditry.[21] Unlike the young rural workers of East Anglia described by John Archer, who instead of burning ricks could move to fill the demands of other, prospering areas of the Victorian economy, the tragic peasants of Andalusia had nowhere to go, and violence festered. Banditry had a variety of origins and took a variety of forms in different geographical areas and at different times. Furthermore, the word itself is loaded in the primary source material with a variety of different meanings depending upon who used it and it what context; indeed, it can be argued that much of what has come down to the historian as "banditry" or brigandage is the result of an early form of labelling process deployed by gendarmes, soldiers, and other state functionaries.[22] A new synthesis developing a broader theoretical thrust than Hobsbawm's would take courage and would not be easy, but it would yield dividends.[23]

While England gave the world the name and the myth of Robin Hood as the archetypal social bandit, large-scale banditry and brigandage is something England appears to have escaped. In his study of robbery in late seventeenth-century England, Alan Macfarlane has suggested that the reasons lay in the lack of a peasantry on the European model in England and in the long tradition of self-policing, within which there was little opposition between the traditions of local custom and the control of professional law-men and law officers.[24] England's general exclusion from the massive European wars of the seventeenth century, with the resulting escape from armies constantly crossing and recrossing her territory leaving deserters and stragglers, and the lack of internal customs barriers and tariffs were, perhaps, as much contributory elements to her lack of bandits as the social structure and legal system. A detailed study of eighteenth-century English smugglers may highlight a greater degree of brigand-style activity than has hitherto been assumed.[25] But then again there is the problem of assuming that because banditry existed elsewhere in Europe it was somehow in the natural order of things and that some explanation must be sought for the peculiarities of the English. Moreover, the implication of much of what follows here is that Macfarlane has underestimated the degree of self-policing and the use of litigation in peasant Europe.

Crime in the past was not simply the story of Robin Hoods, of the poor robbing the rich or the state or demonstrating against the rich or the state. Peasants were the victims of offenses as well as the perpetrators. Even in nineteenth-century England some rural dwellers sought out the local "cunning man" or "cunning woman" to investigate a theft before the local policeman.[26] A visit to a similar individual, the *znakhar*, in peasant Russia is, perhaps, more understandable.[27] French peasants consulted local sorcerers over a variety of problems, including thefts.[28] It seems likely that nineteenth-century Italian peasants visited their *strollica* for similar reasons and that Spanish and German peasants did also, but the question awaits investigation. Mooser shows the Westphalian peasant proprietors reacting ferociously toward some offenders when they were identified and caught, but he also notes in passing that other extralegal measures were administered by peasant community leaders, who punished thefts by ordering recompense by the offender to the victim.[29] In eighteenth- and early nineteenth-century France, thefts were commonly resolved in village communities by informal settlements between the victim and the offender negotiated by a third party—sometimes the *curé*, sometimes by a seigneurial official. Such settlements were favored not the least because they avoided the expenses of a trial, but also because they might bring the victim the restoration of his or her goods or reparations for damage or loss.[30] A physical assault by the victim on the offender to exact punishment might be tacitly authorized by the community provided it did not overstep recognized bounds of violence.

The general exceptions to these kinds of local settlement were cases in which the offender was an outsider to the village community.[31] The elders of the Russian commune were formally authorized to settle lesser offences.[32] Stephen P. Frank and Cathy Frierson have, separately, analyzed in some detail the way in which Russian peasants responded to being the victims of offenses during the nineteenth century.[33] They made an assessment of the offenses with reference to their interpretation of the scale of harm done and the motivation of the offender; they then inflicted summary punishment (*samosud*), following an identifiable code. An offending member of the village community could be punished by ritual akin to *charivari* (*vozhdenie vora*, "leading the thief," or simply *vozhdenie*). For offenders who would not play the game, or who had hurt the community significantly, the ritual could involve physical violence. The worst offenders, particularly, those coming from outside and especially horse thieves, were brutally killed. Some of the shaming punishments—a beating and, perhaps, shaving half of the offender's head and half of his beard—appear to have been similar to those inflicted in eighteenth-century France.[34] No doubt *samosud* had its equivalents throughout peasant Europe. In Sicily, where *malandrino*, a common Italian word for criminal, was often used to describe an individual noted for courage and verve, theft from the rich was not harshly condemned; but men who stole from their peers or from those poorer than themselves could be subjected to furious peasant justice and ignominious disposal.[35] Again it would be valuable to have some detailed comparative research and a synthesis attempting to draw together peasant notions and practices and addressing any notable regional variations. Such research will not be easy, but it will strengthen our understanding of the peasant *mentalité*, particularly with reference to the concepts of justice and honor.

Much of the recent work has served to highlight different concepts of "order": On the one hand is the concept of the state jurist, which is abstract and based upon the enforcement of a written code of laws; on the other is the community's perception, which appears to have been based essentially on the desire to maintain good neighborliness and a morality based on local opinion.[36] In this situtation a dispute might be settled, as noted in the case of France, by calling in a third party to resolve a conflict or a theft, without recourse to the law. The third party, generally some kind of functionary, a cleric, or even a local gentleman, might have some legal knowledge or expertise, yet this was not the prime reason for third-party involvement. In England the community perception of order was beginning to break down, at least in the early seventeenth century. Puritan evangelicalism made an important contribution to this change, as Puritan leaders within communities sought to use the institution of the state to legitimize their new code. Equally important was the growth of commercial enterprise in the towns and boroughs. This latter saw the advent of local lawyers becoming town and country officials and the rise of yeomen and gentlemen into the position of constables and foremen of grand juries. Lower-class unrest, which was itself a product of agrarian repression and the price revolution, was increasingly met with control, prosecution, and lawsuits and hence became publicly noted, written about, and debated.

At the same time some rural notables sought to distance themselves from their social inferiors and subscribed, increasingly, to the jurist's concept of order as outlined by men like William Lambard.[37] These notables were assisted by the parish constables, who were responsible for the maintenance of law and order in the community. An important study of the late Tudor and early Stuart constables shows them to have been drawn, usually, "from the more prosperous and more prominent sections of village society."[38] Our knowledge of who the constables were and what they did between the civil war and the early nineteenth century discussions on the need for a new professional police is sadly lacking.

But if the community perception of order was under pressure in the seventeenth century, it would be wrong to suppose that it had disappeared by the early nineteenth century. Negotiation is central in Thompson's description of the workings of the "moral economy," with crowds calling upon their social superiors to bring corn factors and farmers to market and to make them sell at a just price. In the seventeenth century, central government appeared to accept this behavior with its publication of the *Book of Orders* in 1631; constables and magistrates "negociated" with farmers and corn factors on behalf of angry crowds for more than a century afterward. By the corn riots of 1800, however, members of central government had become disciples of Adam Smith's free market, and they were greatly angered by gentlemen magistrates who continued to uphold the moral economy.[39] Even by the mid-nineteenth century and well after the creation of professional bureaucratic police in England, the community view of order was not dead. In rural Kent both policemen and magistrates appear to have turned a blind eye to *charivariesque* manifestations when they were directed at offending outsiders, while popular prejudice and community mores often influenced the discretion of these same officials.[40]

The same kind of duality in conceptions of order appears to have existed elsewhere in rural Europe until well into the nineteenth century, where it was probably much stronger than in England. *Charivari* and *samosud* are obvious examples of the peasantry imposing their own rational—if sometimes violent and brutal—adjudications on offenders. The peasants of Andalusia loathed the *Guardia Civil* and distrusted the state's courts, which were largely controlled by the *caciques*. It could be that their ready acceptance of political anarchism involved some incorporation of what might be considered the traditional peasant ideas of justice. Unfortunately, probably because of problems of access to the judicial files and the archives of the *Guardia Civil*, the detail of how Spanish peasants responded to crime and offenders remains largely unexplored. However, Ruth Behar's work on the peasants of Leon shows that community regulation thrived here well into the twentieth century. Andalusia was a land of increasing Latifundia, while northern Spain saw the continuing existence of peasant proprietors and tenants who clung steadfastly to their traditions and communal lands. The *concejos* of Leon, village assemblies made up of male householders, met weekly on Sundays after mass or whenever there was an emergency; bad behavior prohibited a man from participation. The *concejos* passed their own written ordinances, some of which went back to the sixteenth century. At the weekly meetings offenders against the community's regulations were forced to make a public confession and could be fined. Nineteenth-century reforms, particularly during the 1830s, deprived the *concejos* of their powers and bound villages together into more centralized administrative units; but the peasants continued to govern themselves by their traditional methods and their customary law.[41]

The peasants of the *mezzogiorno* had little time for the *carabinieri*. Around Naples and in Sicily their own systems of justice and honor, centered on family and local notables, became fierce rivals of the new Italian state and the new liberal economy eager to modernize "backward" areas. This rivalry fostered brigandage, which, as a parliamentary committee conceded in 1863, had a special meaning for the southern Italian peasant: "The brigand is not a murderer, a thief, a looter, but a man who knows how to use his force to render himself and others justice that the laws do not guarantee; a robber is transformed into a hero."[42] The problem for Italy was that subsequently the peasant systems spread to the center of the state itself and settled there as a corrupting influence. While the *caciques* were detested by the Andalusian peasant, similar rural bosses in Sicily, as noted above, became patrons and protectors. *Mafia* was the product of a particular set of social and economic relations unique to Sicily, especially the interior and western part of the island. But the small local notables who made up the competing groups known as *cosche* were not unique to Sicily and elsewhere in Europe. Often such men were entrusted with formal authority, including policing authority, by both the local lord and the developing nation-state: The *consuls* and *syndics* of the villages of *ancien régime* France, the village *Schulze* of east Prussia, and certain Tsarist police officials provide examples. However, our knowledge of precisely who these men were, how they sought to enforce order, the extent to which they were used by victims, and the extent to which their policies and practices changed over time is under-researched. What we do know has not been pulled together for cross-cultural comparison.

There is a danger that in concentrating on the two concepts of order the image of the rural community will be perceived as one of good neighborliness with a strict morality maintained by consent; manifestly, this was not the case. There were social divisions within the village; peasants abused each other and fought each other.[43] In many Mediterranean districts a stain on an individual's or a family's honor could be removed only with blood.[44] There were particular ways of formulating verbal abuse for the maximum effect in denigrating the honor and probity that peasants held dear.[45] Sometimes, and in some places, such insult could be pursued through the courts. Gossip and allegation in the village community could be one way of seeking

to bring to light the truth surrounding an incident; in southern Germany
during the eighteenth century it was common for any villager who did not
seek satisfaction for an allegation, by charging his accusers with slander
and taking the matter to court, to be assumed guilty.[46] Court action, however, was not necessarily indicative of a plaintiff's faith in state justice;
rather, it may have been perceived as merely an auxiliary weapon in settling
with a rival or continuing a feud. Richard Cobb has shown how feuds in
French villages took on a political hue during the Revolution as the opposing
factions sought to enlist external support to win the upper hand in their
long-term quarrels.[47] No doubt the law was often used in this way, especially
where courts were local and justice was cheap. It is probably also true that
over the last twenty years or so historians have been at fault in concentrating
too much on the criminal courts, when investigations into the archives of
the civil courts would probably enable a much better understanding to be
developed of the complexities and the frictions within peasant and plebeian
societies. It is also worth noting that, in eighteenth-century France, individuals could opt to settle some criminal offenses via civil proceedings.[48] Furthermore, the use of these courts by the peasants helped incorporate them
into the emerging political system. Maurice Agulhon has shown how peasants in the Var in the early nineteenth century employed traditional, illegal
methods against new forestry regulations, but how they also fought landowners in the courts. The lawyers who took on the peasants' cases were
often young and radical, and they used the opportunity of fighting the cases
for broaching their political ideas with their clients. Here, in Agulhon's
reading of the evidence, the courts and the legal process provided a means
of helping to transform peasants into Frenchmen, and radical Frenchmen
at that.[49]

Other courts would benefit from similar investigation where the surviving
archives will allow: Ecclesiastical courts have already yielded some useful
information, but there has been little investigation of the manorial and feudal
courts or of local courts connected with particular communities or local
trades. The assumption always appears to be that these courts gave way
before the pressure of more efficient state justice, but there could be other
reasons. The feudal courts of the *ancien régime* in France appear often to
have fallen into desuetude because of the expense of their upkeep rather
than pressure from the center. Many of the holders of seigneurial justice in
eighteenth-century France held on to the right largely for the status it gave
them. Under Louis XIV, the Crown sought to limit the rights of seigneurial
justice; but between his death and the Revolution, while little attempt was
made to curb the remaining vestiges of seigneurial justice, there were attempts, generally half-hearted and/or ignored in the implementation, to
make it more efficient.[50] Because they had to pay the cost of criminal prosecutions and even of a criminal's execution, some of the Junkers of East
Prussia did not always exert themselves in cases when they were not directly

involved. However, they took seriously the privileges of justice and police, which were rooted in their patrimonial courts. They successfully resisted the Gendarmerie Edict of 1812 on the grounds that "the police must not involve themselves in private and family relationships [i.e. the relationship between lord and peasant] unless those relationships collide with the state or its security." Eight years later they pressured the government in Berlin to reduce the new state police force, the *gendarmerie*, from 9000 men to 1300 men; they considered it an encroachment on their feudal authority.[51] Legislation during the nineteenth century gradually whittled away at the Junkers' authority; but they retained disciplinary authority over the un-married workers living on their premises until 1918. The courts of some Russian communes appear to have lasted into the twentieth century, with the village elders authorized to resolve quarrels and to dispense justice for the less serious offenses. Trade and community courts, like the Oystermen's courts in Essex and Kent and the courts of Load Manage on the Thames and Medway, remain largely unresearched. These probably declined because the admission of commercial instruments and juries of local businessmen in the Court of King's Bench, in the second half of the eighteenth century, enabled local processes to be incorporated into central courts with royal enforcement; there was also change in statute law especially in the second quarter of the nineteenth century and, of course, significant economic change.

In addition to the focus on the criminal courts, there has, perhaps, been rather too much emphasis on the impact of the capitalization of industry and on industrialization and urbanization in the study of criminal justice history in Europe since the eighteenth century. It is often forgotten that a high percentage of the population of Europe remained peasant up to and, indeed, beyond World War I. The problem has been compounded by the temptation to think in terms of linear development in history, with Britain, the first industrial nation, ahead during the nineteenth century and the others catching up at different rates. But as recent economic historians have stressed, there was more than one path to the twentieth century, even with the most advanced western economies. Without wishing to deny the im-portance of economic development and not intending to contradict my earlier suggestion of the need for exploring peasant culture across national boundaries with reference to criminal justice history in the eighteenth and nineteenth centuries, it is important to reconsider the significance of the developing nation-state and the significance of this state's use of law and law enforcement. As the nineteenth century progressed, the European nation state encroached more and more on the lives of its people in both town and country. With the state came reciprocal duties on its terms, of its definition, sanctioned and enforced by its law. The citizenry provided taxes and men for the army; the state promised security and the jurist's concept of order, and it dispatched the gendarme into the countryside who, more and more, was expected to enforce the reciprocal duties.[52] While there could be hostility and resistance to this internal colonization, manifested for example in the development of *mafia* in Sicily and anarchism in Andalusia, on occasion the peasantry elsewhere recognized that there were opportunities in using aspects of the new system, not the least the courts. Both responses can be explored with reference to different court records.

The extension of the state, and its law, poses another question which is, as yet, little explored: How did peasants learn about new laws and new systems? The traditional view, based generally on the reports of state officials, tended to label peasants as ignorant, stubborn, and obstructive. However, David Moon's study of Russian peasants and Tsarist legislation in the second quarter of the nineteenth century describes laws being read out publicly by parish priests and police officials who often lacked the literacy and knowledge to do this properly, laws interpreted by private intermediaries who misinterpreted them sometimes accidentally and sometimes deliberately in return for money while acting as scribes and unofficial attorneys, and laws spread by word of mouth and rumor. Moon also warns that peasants should not be seen as the passive receivers of information. He suggests some pointers of how information from the literate culture of official Russia was screened through the largely oral culture of the peasant and how misunderstandings of legislation identify some of the aspirations in the *mentalité* of the Russian peasant.[53]

When the historian plunges into the world of peasant *mentalité* and the process of change within the rural society of the pre-1914 European regimes, he or she loses the anchors of moments of change available to the historian of politics or administration. The creation of an administrative body, the passage of a law, or a change of government has a cause and an effect and constitutes a moment on which the question of change can be focused. Of course there were such changes that affected the peasant's community; the moment of abolition of serfdom is the most obvious example. But there were few such moments in the *longue durée* of the peasant's world. Court records offer the historian one way into this world. It would be useful now to explore further the increasing participation of peasants in the courts as they used the law for their own purposes; this, together with military conscription, better roads, and the development of railways, was probably one of the routes by which the peasant's notion of his or her *pays natal* was transformed into a perception of the much larger nation-state.

NOTES

1. Wilbur R. Miller, *Cops and Bobbies: Police Authority in New York and London, 1830–1870* (Chicago, 1977); Stanley H. Palmer, *Police and Protest in England and Ireland, 1780–1850* (New York, 1988).

2. E. J. Hobsbawm, *Primitive Rebels: Studies in Archaic Forms of Social Protest*

in the 19th and 20th Centuries (Manchester, 1959); Hobsbawm, *Bandits* (London, 1969).

3. George Rudé, *The Crowd in the French Revolution* (Oxford, 1959); Rudé, *Wilkes and Liberty: A Social Study 1763–1774* (Oxford, 1961); Rudé, *The Crowd in History, 1730–1848* (New York, 1964).

4. E. P. Thompson, "The Moral Economy of the English Crowd in the Eighteenth Century," *Past and Present* 50 (1971). This essay, together with Thompson's reply to his critics, is reprinted in his *Customs in Common* (London, 1991).

5. For the application of Thompson's "moral economy" notions to different European contexts see *La guerre de blé au XVIII siècle*, ed. Florence Gautier and Guy-Robert Ikni (Paris, 1988); and Manfred Gailus, *Strasse und Brot. Sozialer Protest in den deutschen Staaten unter der Berücksichligung Preussens, 1847–49* (Göttingen, 1990).

6. The notion of a shift from reactive to proactive action on the part of peasants and plebeians is also associated with the work of Charles Tilly; see, inter alia, Charles Tilly, *Collective Violence in European Perspective* (Washington, 1969); and Charles Tilly, Louise Tilly, and Richard Tilly, *The Rebellious Century, 1830–1930* (London, 1975).

7. Dirk Blasius, *Bürgerliche und Kriminalität: Zur Socialgeschichte Preussens in Vortäg* (Göttingen, 1976); idem, *Kriminalität und Alltag: Zur Konfliktgeschichte des Alltagslebens im 19. Jahrhundert* (Göttingen, 1978).

8. Bob Bushaway, *By Rite: Custom, Ceremony and Community in England 1700–1880* (London, 1982).

9. Rodney Bohac, "Everyday Forms of Resistance: Serf Opposition to Gentry Exactions," in *Peasant Economy, Culture and Politics of European Russia 1800–1921*, ed. Esther Kingston-Mann and Timothey Mixter (Princeton, 1991).

10. See, inter alia, P. B. Munsche, *Gentlemen and Poachers: The English Game Laws 1671–1831* (Cambridge, 1981); Marie-Renée Santucci, *Délinquence et répression au XIXe siècle: L'exemple de l'Hérault* (Paris, 1986), 162. There is no good, modern study of poaching in France, but a useful introduction can be found in the lively popular account of Marieke and Pierre Aucante, *Les braconniers. Mille ans de chasse clandestine* (Paris, 1983).

11. John E. Archer, *"By a Flash and a Scare": Arson, Animal Maiming, and Poaching in East Anglia 1815–1870* (Oxford, 1990), 254.

12. *Charivari* is a French term but has tended to be applied by historians to ritual mockery or hostility directed against individuals who had offended certain community norms. The whole ritual was generally accompanied by a cacophony on musical instruments real and improvised. See the essays surveying different European examples in *Le Charivari*, ed. Jacques Le Goff and Jean Claude Schmidt (Paris, 1981).

13. Josef Mooser, "Property and Wood Theft: Agrarian Capitalism and Social Conflict in Rural Society, 1800–50. A Westphalian Case Study," in *Peasants and Lords in Modern Germany*, ed. Robert G. Moeller (London, 1987). This is a translation of " 'Furcht bewahrt das Holz': Holzdiebstahl und sozialer Konflikt in der landichen Gesellschaft 1800–1850 an Westfällischen Beispielen," in *Räuber, Volk und Obrigkeit: Studien zur Geschichte der Kriminalität in Deutschland seit dem 18. Jahrhundert*, ed. H. Reif (Frankfurt, 1984).

14. Regina Schulte, *Das Dorf im Verhör. Brandstifter, Kindsmörderinnen und*

Wildere vor den Schranken des bürgerlichen Gerichts (Reinbek, 1989); see also idem, "Poachers in Upper Bavaria," in *The German Underworld: Deviants and Outcasts in German History*, ed. Richard J. Evans (London, 1988).

15. Hobsbawm, *Bandits*, 13–14.

16. José Ramón Cubero, *Pélot: "Bandit d' honneur"* (Paris, 1992).

17. Uwe Danke, "Bandits and the State: Robbers and the Authorities in the Holy Roman Empire in the Late Seventeenth and Early Eighteenth Centuries," in *The German Underworld*, ed. Evans, 100.

18. Marta Petrusewicz, "Society against the State: Peasant Brigandage in Southern Italy," *Criminal Justice History* 8 (1987): 1–20.

19. Giovanna Fiume, "Bandits, violence and the organisation of power in Sicily in the early nineteenth century," in *Society and Politics in the Age of the Risorgimento*, ed. John A. Davis and Paul Ginsborg (Cambridge, 1991); Paul Ginsborg, "After the Revolution: Bandits on the Plains of the Po, 1848–54," in ibid, 145.

20. Charles Esdaile, "Heroes or Villains? Spanish Guerrillas in the Peninsular War," *History Today* 38 (April, 1988): 29–35.

21. Henk Driessen, "The 'noble bandit' and the bandits of the nobles; brigandage and local community in nineteenth-century Andalusia," *Archives Européens de Sociologie* 24 (1983): 96–114; idem, "Heroes and Villains. Images of Bandits and Banditry in Eighteenth and Nineteenth-Century Andalusia," in *Bande armate, banditi, banditismo e repressione di giustizia negli stati europei di antico regime*, ed. Gherardo Ortalli (Rome, 1986). For the situation of the Andalusian peasants see Edward E. Malefakis, *Agrarian Reform and Peasant Revolution in Spain: Origins of the Civil War* (Yale, 1970).

22. Nicole Dyonet, "L'écho du brigandage dans les cahiers de doléances du Loiret et du Cher," in *Mouvements populaires et conscience sociale, XVIe et XIXe siècles*, ed. Jean Nicolas (Paris, 1985); John Dickie, "A Word at War: The Italian Army and Brigandage 1860–1870," *History Workshop Journal*, 33 (1993): 1–24.

23. *Bande armate, banditi, banditismo*, edited by Ortalli, is a collection of essays reviewing the manifestations of banditry in different countries and different geographical areas in Europe.

24. Alan Macfarlane, *The Justice and the Mare's Ale: Law and Disorder in Seventeenth-Century England* (Oxford, 1981).

25. I make this suggestion on the basis of the current work of my doctoral research student, Paul Muskett.

26. Clive Emsley, *Crime and Society in England 1750–1900* (London, 1987), 82.

27. Samuel C. Ramer, "Traditional Healers and Peasant Culture in Russia, 1861–1917," in *Peasant Economy, Culture and Politics of European Russia*, ed. Kingston-Mann and Mixter, 223.

28. Judith Devlin, *The Superstitious Mind: French Peasants and the Supernatural in the Nineteeth Century* (Yale, 1987), chap. 4.

29. Mooser, "Property and Wood Theft," 72.

30. Nicole Castan, *Justice et répression en Languedoc à l'époque des lumières* (Paris, 1980), chap. 1; François Ploux, "L'arrangement' dans les campagnes du Haute-Quercy (1815–1850)," *Histoire de la Justice* 5 (1992): 95–115.

31. See, inter alia, Daniel Hickey, "Crop stealing in the village community in the seventeenth and eighteenth centuries," *Proceedings of the Annual Meeting of the*

Western Society for French History 16 (1989): 145–52; Steven G. Reinhardt, *Justice in the Sarladais 1770–1790* (Baton Rouge, 1991), chap. 4.

32. Steven H. Hoch, *Serfdom and Social Control in Russia: Petrovskoe, a Village in Tambov* (Chicago, 1986), 149–53.

33. Stephen P. Frank, "Popular Justice, Community and Culture among the Russian Peasantry, 1870–1900," *Russian Review* 46 (1987): 239–65. Cathy Frierson, "Crime and Punishment in the Russian Village: Rural Concepts of Criminality at the end of the Nineteenth Century," *Slavic Review* 46 (1987): 55–69.

34. Iain A. Cameron, *Crime and Repression in the Auvergne and the Guyenne, 1720–1790* (Cambridge, 1981), 179.

35. Christopher Duggan, *Fascism and the Mafia* (New Haven, 1989), 64, 67.

36. Keith Wrightson, "Two concepts of order: Justices, constables and jurymen in seventeenth-century England," in *An Ungovernable People: The English and Their Law in the Seventeenth and Eighteenth Centuries*, ed. John Brewer and John Styles (London, 1980).

37. J. A. Sharpe, *Crime in Seventeenth-Century England: A County Study* (Cambridge, 1983).

38. Joan R. Kent, *The English Village Constable 1580–1642: A Social and Administrative Study* (Oxford, 1986), 150.

39. Thompson, "Moral Economy"; and see also John Bohstedt, *Riots and Community Politics in England and Wales 1790–1810* (Harvard, 1983); and Roger Wells, *Wretched Faces: Famine in Wartime England, 1793–1803* (Gloucester, 1988).

40. Carolyn A. Conley, *The Unwritten Law: Criminal Justice in Victorian Kent* (New York, 1991).

41. Ruth Behar, *The Presence of the Past in a Spanish Village: Santa Maria del Monte* (Princeton, 1986), especially Part 3.

42. Quoted in Petrusewicz, "Society against the State," 17, n. 3.

43. Keith P. Luria, "Conflict and the Construction of Moral Order in Old Regime Rural Society," *Proceedings of the Annual Meeting of the Western Society for French History* 16 (1989): 139–44, focuses on this issue in late seventeenth- and early eighteenth-century France. He argues, interestingly, that internal conflict helped to construct the moral order and at the same time was bounded by it.

44. Petrusewicz, "Society against the State," 5; Duggan, *Fascism and the Mafia*, 63–67.

45. Yves Castan, *Honnêté et relations socials en Languedoc 1715–1780* (Paris, 1974), 170–74; Nicole Castan, *Les Criminels de Languedoc: Les exigences d' ordre et les voies du ressentiment dans une société pré-révolutionnaire (1750–1790)* (Toulouse-Le-Mirail, 1980), 156–66.

46. David Warren Sabean, *Power in the Blood: Popular culture and village discourse in early modern Germany* (Cambridge, 1984), 148.

47. Richard Cobb, *The People's Armies: The armées révolutionnaires: Instruments of the Terror in the departments April 1793 to Floréal Year II* (Yale, 1987).

48. Reinhardt, *Justice in the Sarladais*, 75.

49. Maurice Agulhon, *La République au Village: Les populations du Var de la Révolution à la IIe République* (Paris, 1979), 253–54. English translation, *The Republic in the Village: The People of the Var from the French Revolution to the Second Empire* (Cambridge, 1982), 155–56.

50. J. Q. C. Mackrell, *The Attack on "Feudalism" in Eighteenth-Century France* (London, 1973), 67–71; Reinhardt, *Justice in the Sarladais*, 56–64.

51. Robert M. Berdahl, *The Politics of the Prussian Nobility: The Development of a Conservative Ideology 1770–1848* (Princeton, 1988), 61–62, 141–43; quotation at 143; Albrecht Funk, *Polizei und Rechsstaat: Die Entwicklung des staatlichen Gewaltmonopols in Preussen 1848–1914* (Frankfurt, 1986), 41.

52. Clive Emsley, "Gendarmes, Peasants and State Formation," in *National Histories: European Perspectives*, ed. Mary Fulbrook (London, 1993).

53. David Moon, *Russian Peasants and Tsarist Legislation on the Eve of Reform* (London, 1992), especially chap. 5.

The Origins of "The Problem of Juvenile Delinquency": The Growth of Juvenile Prosecutions in London in the Late Eighteenth and Early Nineteenth Centuries

Peter King
Nene College, Northampton

Joan Noel
Leicester University

The late eighteenth and early nineteenth centuries witnessed a sea-change in attitudes to the young offender.[1] Between the mid-seventeenth and the late eighteenth centuries, contemporary commentators rarely regarded young offenders as a separate, distinct problem. Early modern observers were well aware of the existence of young offenders and youth-related social problems, and particular attention was paid to the problems of youth during the years of rising anxiety about crime and vagrancy between 1560 and 1640.[2] However, while the Fieldings, Jonas Hanway, and other eighteenth-century writers gave some attention to young offenders and set up the Marine Society (which sent some of them to sea from the 1750s onwards), there is little indication in their writings that juvenile offenders were seen as a particularly distinctive or threatening subgroup. To quote John Beattie's recent authoritative work on the period before 1800, "Young offenders did not appear in the eighteenth-century courts in the numbers that were to become common in the nineteenth, nor were they isolated as they were then to be as a separate and crucially important criminal group."[3]

It was not until the nineteenth century that the authorities began to evolve special ways of responding to young offenders. In the eighteenth century juvenile offenders were tried before the same courts as adults, were confined in the same prisons, and subjected to the same range of sentences. Those under seven were exempt from prosecution, and those between seven and fourteen were sometimes able to claim similar immunity, but in general the criminal law made no formal provision for the separate treatment of juveniles. During the next century a radical transformation took place. "Juvenile delinquency" was established as a major social problem and a focus of great anxiety amongst the propertied. Separate modes of trial were gradually established, the acts of 1847, 1850, and 1879 being particularly important in formally transferring an increasing proportion of property crime cases involving juveniles to the summary courts. Separate penal policies and institutions were also set up. Hulks were established for juveniles alone in 1823. A large prison for boys was opened in 1838, and by the 1850s a nationwide system of reformatories had become the central plank of penal policy towards young offenders.[4] The existence of a major transition in attitudes to, and policies toward, young offenders is not therefore in doubt among historians. However, precisely when and why it occurred has yet to be fully established.

HISTORIOGRAPHY AND METHODOLOGY

Although several historians have recently published volumes on juvenile delinquency and "the youth problem" in the late nineteenth and early twentieth centuries,[5] and much work has also been done on youth groups, apprentice subculture, and attitudes to youth in the sixteenth and seventeenth centuries,[6] the intervening years, which witnessed the full emergence of "the problem of juvenile delinquency" (and the first use of that term), have been largely neglected.

The narrative of voluntary institutional experimentation and prison reform in relation to juveniles, from the Marine and Philanthropic Societies of the later eighteenth century through to the adoption of juvenile reformatories in the 1850s, has been laid out in the relevant sections of broader surveys by Leon Radzinowicz and Roger Hood and by Ivy Pinchbeck and Margaret Hewitt. However, precisely when, how, and for what reasons juvenile delinquency came to be constructed as a separate and urgent problem has not been adequately dealt with by these writers. Geoffrey Pearson's book *Hooligans* usefully traces the recurring cycles of fear among the propertied about youthful and violent crime back until the beginning of the Victorian era, but then becomes diffuse and chronologically unfocused when it attempts to explore earlier periods. Apart from this book, only three articles have attempted to address this problem.[7]

In the 1970s Margaret May argued that the flood of unofficial enquiries in the 1830s and 1840s "elaborated the first clear concept of juvenile delinquency," which was then fully expressed as a legal status for the first time in the 1850s legislation setting up separate institutions for the young offender. More recently Susan Magarey has argued for a less deliberate "invention of juvenile delinquency" in the later 1820s. By criminalizing, through the Vagrancy and Malicious Trespass Acts, forms of juvenile behavior previously ignored by the courts and by introducing new police forces with broader powers of arrest and a tendency to see juvenile offenders as easy targets, Peel's legislation helped to create a rising tide of juvenile convictions. This tide first became visible after 1838, when yearly statistics on the age structure of the prison population finally became available. Parlia-

ment, Magarey argues, therefore legislated juvenile delinquency into existence in the late 1820s and 1830s.

Peter Rush's new article provides perhaps the best analysis so far of the
ways juvenile delinquency was constructed as a social problem in the first
half of the nineteenth century. Moving beyond both historical narratives of
penal change that rely on the humanitarian struggle-for-reform perspective
and those "social control" accounts that are little more than a negation of
that perspective, Rush attempts not only to chart the emergence of a discourse on the increase in juvenile crime but also to describe its contours
and the key concepts around which it was formed. His article is certainly
a very useful, if brief, starting point for any attempt to analyze the rapidly
expanding printed debate on juvenile delinquency, which first reached substantial proportions in the Parliamentary reports of the 1810s and in the
"Report of the Committee of the Society for Investigating the Causes of the
Alarming Increase of Juvenile Delinquency in the Metropolis," published
in 1816.[8] However, because no systematic statistics were published before
the 1830s on the number of juveniles coming before the courts or on the
ways they were dealt with,[9] all these historians have had to construct their
theories about why, when, and in what forms juvenile delinquency came to
be perceived as a major social problem without any understanding of what
was happening in the courts of the time.

By detailed analysis of the records of the Old Bailey, which was one of
the few late eighteenth-century courts that systematically recorded the ages
of those indicted before them, this chapter begins the process of filling this
gap. Using a sample of 6,600 property offenders from the London Criminal
Registers, which first recorded the age of the accused in 1791, it has been
possible to answer two related questions. Did the number of juveniles reaching the courts increase rapidly between the early 1790s and the early 1820s,
and did juvenile offenders also form a rising proportion of indicted offenders
in those years? If so, our search for the origins of the problem of juvenile
delinquency will need to move back into the first two decades of the nineteenth century or beyond, a period largely ignored by the existing literature.[10]

The data presented in Figures 1 to 3 are not without problems, and before
interpreting them four specific issues need to be addressed. First, changes
in the number of offenders indicted at the Old Bailey cannot of course be
used as a guide to changing levels of actual law-breaking. Most victims
either failed to detect the offender or chose not to prosecute. Those who
wished to indict the accused were often prevented from doing so by the
committing magistrates, who preferred to deal with many cases at a summary level rather than send the offenders on for trial. However, changes in
the proportion of the accused falling within each age group are less difficult
to interpret. A rise in the proportion of the accused coming from a specific
age group will reflect either a relative increase in law-breaking by that group

or a relative increase in the willingness of prosecutors and magistrates to indict that group (or a combination of the two).

Second, as no systematic age information has yet been found for the lesser courts below the Old Bailey before 1793, this analysis is effectively confined to London's property offenders. Although some murder, rape, and riot cases were heard at the Old Bailey, the numbers involved are small, as are those for assault, affray, or misdemeanor. This study has therefore been unable to look at changes over time in prosecutions involving either youthful violence or affrays and joint recreational activities primarily involving the young. As the early nineteenth-century debate about the alarming increase in juvenile delinquency also focused primarily, although not exclusively, on property theft, this limitation does not pose major problems. Potentially greater difficulties are raised by the fact that some property crime indictments were not dealt with at the Old Bailey.

Because no systematic age information is available for the quarter sessions courts, changes in the distribution of cases between the Old Bailey, where almost all major property offenders were indicted, and the various general or quarter sessions courts that tried minor larceny indictments in the Metropolitan area[11] could therefore have affected both the overall pattern of indictments at the Old Bailey and the level of involvement of juveniles. The 1790s Criminal Registers do not, for example, contain information about those appearing before the Westminster or Middlesex sessions. If the proportion of all property crime cases being heard at the Middlesex sessions increased between 1790 and 1820, as it appears to have done over the previous half century, the 65 percent increase in the absolute level of Old Bailey indictments observable between 1791–93 and 1820–22 may considerably underestimate the extent of the change.[12] However, once again the proportion of juveniles within the accused would not have been affected by such intercourt transfers unless the type of indictment transferred included untypically large or small percentages of young offenders—and there is no evidence that this was the case. In Gloucestershire, where age information is available for both the quarter sessions and the assizes, the age structures of those indicted in each court follow much the same pattern. More important, if the age structures of those accused of simple larceny and of aggravated larceny at the Old Bailey are analyzed separately, it becomes evident that both changed in similar ways between 1790 and 1820.[13] Even if an increased proportion of simple, noncapital larcenies had been transferred to other courts by 1820, the overall age structure of all Old Bailey property offenders would almost certainly not have been significantly affected.

Finally, changes between war and peace have to be allowed for. The coming of war deeply affected the age structure of the accused. The proportion of young adult males reaching the courts was much lower throughout the period of the French wars (1793–1815) because many poor young

Figure 1
Old Bailey, Age Structure of All Property Offenders, 1791–93 and 1820–22

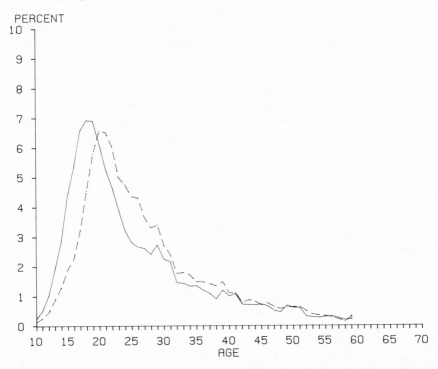

males were either pressed into the armed forces before they had an opportunity to commit offenses or handed over to the press gangs after they had
done so as an alternative to prosecution. Long-term changes in the age
structure of the accused can therefore be studied only by comparing peacetime periods. For this analysis two peacetime periods, October 1791 to July
1793 and October 1820 to July 1822, have been used. By choosing a later
sample period beginning half a decade after the end of the Napoleonic wars,
potential distortions in the age structure of the accused caused by the temporary effects of mass demobilization will be largely eliminated.[14]

What happened to juvenile prosecutions at the Old Bailey between the
early 1790s and the early 1820s? The results confirm that the period before
1820 did indeed see a decisive change in London (Figure 1). The age structure
of those accused of property crime at the Old Bailey peaked between twenty
and twenty-one in 1791–93. By 1820–22 the peak was reached between
seventeen and nineteen. The proportion of the accused under seventeen rose
from 7 to 16 percent, the proportion under twenty from 21 to 37 percent.
This pattern was much more pronounced among males, who constituted
about three-quarters of the accused,[15] than among females (Figures 2 and
3). The proportion of the male accused under seventeen rose from 8 to 18

percent between 1791–93 and 1820–22. The equivalent figure for females rose from 5 to 8 percent. Just as the early nineteenth century discourse about juvenile delinquency focused primarily on boys rather than girls, so too did the work of the major courts and the prisons.[16] As the absolute numbers of offenders coming before the Old Bailey rose by two-thirds in this period, the number of offenders under seventeen rose nearly fourfold and the number under twenty more than tripled. Thus the London courts experienced a flood of juvenile offenders before the legislative initiatives of the late 1820s that Magarey believes were responsible for the invention of juvenile delinquency, and well before the bludgeoning debate about juvenile reformatories in the late 1830s and 1840s that May identified as a key turning point.

JUVENILE PROSECUTIONS

Why did the number and proportion of juveniles reaching the courts rise so rapidly in this period? Until recently many criminologists and historians, following the example of almost all those who wrote about juvenile delinquency in the nineteenth century, explained the expansion of juvenile prosecutions visible in the statistics published from the 1830s onward by assuming that it reflected a real rise in the level of juvenile crime. This in turn was related to various economic, social, and demographic changes. It therefore seems appropriate to explore these potential links first.

Did the growth of juvenile prosecutions simply reflect a general rise in the proportion of the population who were juveniles? While this may have made some contribution, the increase in juvenile crime is much too substantial to be explained by changes in the general age structure of the population alone. Between the late 1780s and 1821 the proportion of the English population aged between ten and nineteen (after those aged nine and under have been excluded because all but a handful were immune from prosecution) rose by about 2.5 percent. The proportion of the accused in that age rose nearly 16 percent. No equivalents of Anthony Wrigley and Roger Schofield's estimates are available for London alone before the census of 1821, but preliminary calculations kindly made available by John Landers do not suggest that the proportion of the population in this age group grew any more rapidly in London than it did elsewhere. In 1821 about 24 percent of the London population over nine were aged between ten and nineteen, whereas nearly 37 percent of Old Bailey property offenders were in their teens.[17] Even if the proportion of teenagers in the capital grew slightly faster than the national trend between 1780 and 1820, which Landers's estimates suggest it did not, about 21 percent of both London's population and the Old Bailey accused would have been aged between ten and nineteen in 1791–93. In the early 1790s teenagers made a contribution to the Old Bailey accused roughly correspondent to their numbers in the general population. By 1820–22 their contribution was about 50 percent greater.

Can the growth of juvenile prosecutions be explained by reference to the general stresses caused by urbanization or industrialization? Many historians have certainly made such links in their analyses of the late eighteenth and early nineteenth centuries. Frank McLynn, for example, recently concluded that "there is a clear link between juvenile delinquency and the triumph of capitalism." In a more substantial discussion Sean McConville argued that "migration swamped the towns physically and administratively. Methods of urban finance, policing and administration . . . simply could not cope. Crime, social disorder, and urban distress increased at a rate far beyond that of the population. The swollen towns had a predominance of young people who faced difficult economic and social problems which they had to meet with few personal resources."[18] He then goes on to quote from *Crime and Industrial Society in the Nineteenth Century* by John Tobias. "Many young town-dwellers," Tobias concluded, "faced with these problems and receiving no assistance from their families or employers (if they had families or employers) or from the municipal authorities, found a solution by adopting the techniques, the habits and the attitudes of criminals. There was thus in London and the other large towns in the latter part of the eighteenth century and the earlier part of the nineteenth century an upsurge of crime which was the fruit of a society in rapid transition."

James Walvin's recent social history of childhood in this period follows a similar line. "Juvenile crime," he argues, "was but another manifestation of the growing pains of a new urban society."[19] This approach has proved equally tempting to some sociologists. Following the rhetoric of most propertied commentators in the early nineteenth century, many general criminological texts have also linked the growth of juvenile delinquency to the temporary breakdown of familial and institutional networks that is perceived to have accompanied the early stages of the industrialization process. In *Crime and Modernization*, for example, Louise Shelley argues that "juvenile delinquency has become a problem in developing countries only since the advent of urbanization and industrialization." She concludes that "the changes in criminality that were observed in Britain two centuries ago with the advent of the industrial revolution have been repeated time and time again as other societies have undergone similar transitions to modernity."[20] However, common though such analyses are, simplistic explanations relating the growth of juvenile prosecutions to industrialization or urbanization offer little assistance in explaining the London data presented here. London did not industrialize in the classic sense of the term in the later eighteenth and early nineteenth centuries. It was not a city of factories or huge workshops, and its industry remained generally small-scale in organization and traditional in technology. London was already a huge metropolis of nearly a million people in 1791. For centuries it had been a magnet for young migrants, and it continued to play much the same role and to be much the same kind of city in the thirty years that followed.[21]

Did London experience a major economic crisis or a period of over-rapid social and economic transition between 1790 and 1820 that might help to explain the sudden growth of juvenile prosecutions? The vast, complex, ambiguous, and unique nature of the capital's economy makes it difficult to generalize. London's growth arose from many specialized sources and sectors. However, as P. Garside has recently pointed out, "despite its chinese box character, a fundamental feature of London has been its stability and continuity." By 1820, she suggests, "London seemed poised on the verge of a new balanced completeness."[22] Long-term changes were, of course, occurring. While London's service-sector, luxury consumer-trades, and processing industries were expanding rapidly, parallelling the growth of its commerce, trade, and docklands, some of its mass-market handicraft industries, such as shoemaking, were beginning to move out to the provinces. Greater social segregation was gradually developing, and the heart of the metropolis, the city itself, was evolving into a mainly commercial rather than residential area.[23] Real-wage levels seem to have declined in London throughout the second half of the eighteenth century, and in that period London undoubtedly contained a large reservoir of casual unskilled labor.[24] However, although a number of industries suffered severe short-term difficulties during the changeover from war to peace after 1814, recovery was fairly rapid and was well underway by 1817–18. London's skilled and semiskilled artisans may have experienced great difficulties in the postwar period but there is no doubt that the capital remained a large and important center of both production and consumption throughout the first half of the nineteenth century. Indeed, it was still the greatest manufacturing center in the country in 1851, according to its foremost historian, Francis Sheppard.[25] London's population rose by nearly 40 percent between 1801 and 1821, and the period after 1815 witnessed an almost unbroken boom in the capital's building industry. Real wages, having reached rock bottom in 1800, began to rise fairly rapidly between 1810 and 1820 as prices fell. An overstocked labor market in a number of trades may have prevented some sectors of the workforce from taking advantage of this, and valuable perquisites may have been eroded in some industries, but overall the living standards of London's working population do not seem to have fallen significantly between 1790 and 1820.[26]

Given the lack of any major discontinuities in the economic and social history of London between 1790 and 1820, can the rapid growth of juvenile prosecutions be related to more specific changes in the forms of training, domestic supervision, or material support available to the young in this period? Apprenticeship, which was regarded as one of the key institutions that guided the capital's young men through the troubled years of adolescence, was undoubtedly in decline in the late eighteenth and early nineteenth centuries. Although Keith Snell's work is largely based on provincial rather than metropolitan data, it indicates that the proportion of apprentices who successfully completed their full seven-year term was falling in this period, as was the average age at which apprentices left their masters. The type of domestic arrangements that apprentices were subjected to was also changing. Outdoor apprenticeship, which did away with the requirement that the apprentice live in his master's household, was becoming increasingly common, and several early nineteenth-century commentators believed that the recent spread of this practice from the provinces into London was "a leading cause of juvenile delinquency."[27]

However, although the decline of apprenticeship was probably reinforced by Parliament's formal abandonment of apprenticeship regulation in 1814, the process was already very well advanced by 1790. In the early eighteenth century nearly half of London's labor force had entered into a formally indentured apprenticeship, but this figure may well have declined considerably by 1790. If Snell's Southern English data is any guide, the period between 1750 and the 1790s witnessed by far the most sustained fall in the proportion of apprentices who completed their full term.[28] Moreover, while contemporary attempts to link the growth of outdoor apprenticeship to a rise in juvenile crime were based on the assumption that indoor apprenticeship was more effective in providing the young with "moral restraint during the most dangerous period of their lives," in reality there is considerable evidence that this was rarely the case. As early as 1724 Daniel Defoe was complaining that "apprentices... so far are they from being subjected to their masters or to their family discipline... think it hard to have any enquiry made after them when they go out, and keep often times later hours than their masters. This insufferable liberty is not so much granted by the master as it is assumed by the apprentices... never was so many masters robbed by their apprentices as now." Half a century later Hanway observed, "There is scarce an apprentice boy turned fifteen years of age who... is not suffered to go abroad every night as soon as the shop is shut. These boys and young men challenge it as a kind of right." Francis Place's description of his London apprenticeship in the later 1780s fully confirms this picture. "During the whole of my apprenticeship," he wrote, "I was under no control so long as the work expected of me was done, I might go whenever I pleased and do as I liked and this was the case with many other apprentices." Place's account of the wild, unruly lives led by his circle of fellow apprentices and of the ways most of them stole from their masters or from others leaves little doubt that apprenticeship, whether indoor or outdoor, was no longer a major restraining influence by 1790, if indeed it ever had been.[29]

The problems experienced by the young in these years should not be underestimated. The parallel crises within both urban apprenticeship and rural living-in service that occurred between 1750 and 1850, coming at a time of rapid population growth, clearly had an impact on their prospects. As the population rose faster than the availability of secure and adequately paid employment, an increasing proportion of the young people brought

Figure 2
Old Bailey, Age Structure of Male Property Offenders, 1791–93 and 1820–22

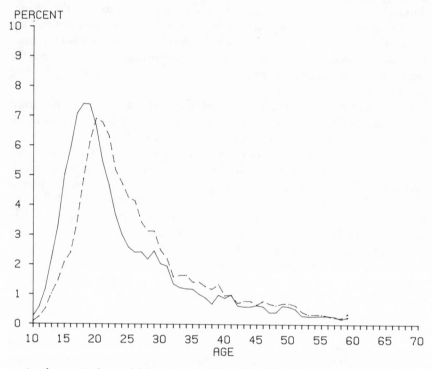

up in the capital would have come from families facing severe economic difficulties in the highly seasonal and volatile market for casual labor.[30] Young men may have been particularly badly affected. The decline of the predominantly male institution of apprenticeship and the gradual feminization of domestic service in London in this period would have severely curtailed their chances of obtaining work. Alternative sources of employment were particularly hard to find in London. In the 1851 census the percentage of Middlesex boys in employment was half the national average. However, given the very limited alternative employment available to women apart from domestic service,[31] it should not be assumed that these changes explain the relatively slow growth of juvenile prosecutions against females, compared to those against males (Figures 2 and 3). Too little is known about the precise timing of these institutional changes and how they affected both the migration of young men and women into London and about the deprivations, insecurities, employment problems, and appropriation opportunities they experienced once they were there to allow any broad conclusions to be made.[32] However, the decline of apprenticeship and of living-in service, the feminization of domestic service, and the rapid expansion of London's population were long-term processes that were well advanced by

Figure 3
Old Bailey, Age Structure of Female Property Offenders, 1791–93 and 1820–22

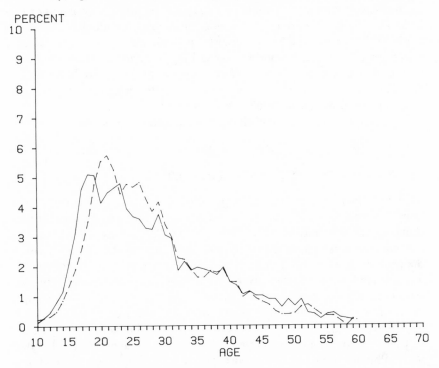

1790 and continued long after 1820. They cannot therefore provide an adequate explanation of the rapid growth of juvenile prosecutions in this thirty-year period.

Alternative explanations are not hard to find. A wide variety of very specific social and economic changes could have altered the lives of young Londoners in ways that would have made them more likely to commit crime, and contemporary commentators were not slow to make elaborate lists of them. The 1816 committee formed to investigate the "alarming increase of juvenile delinquency in the Metropolis" pinpointed, for example, "the improper conduct of parents, the want of education, the want of suitable employment, the violation of the sabbath and habits of gambling in the public streets" as the primary causes, before going on to name "the severity of the criminal code, the defective state of the police and the existing system of prison discipline" as "auxiliaries which . . . perpetuate the evil."[33] However, substantive links between these social and institutional problems and the increase of juvenile prosecutions were rarely made and never adequately proved by contemporaries. As there is no coherent evidence that these problems were any more acute between 1790 and 1820 than they had been for decades or even centuries, such analyses rarely shed light on the rapid growth of juvenile prosecutions in this period.

Thus the timing of the massive expansion in juvenile prosecutions in London between 1790 and 1820 undermines many of the generalizations made by historians and criminologists. Juvenile delinquency arrived as a major problem for the London courts long after urbanization and long before the city's economy was affected by anything that could be termed an industrial revolution.[34] It also came long after apprenticeship and the other institutions that governed the working lives of the young began to change, but long before those changes were completed.

TRIALS, CONVICTIONS, AND CONTEXTS

As it is difficult to explain the rapid growth of juvenile prosecutions in London solely by reference to the relatively limited social and economic changes that occurred between 1790 and 1820, it seems more likely that this increase was caused primarily, although not exclusively, by a rise in the proportion of juvenile offenders who were indicted in the courts. It is well known that juveniles received particularly lenient treatment from prosecutors and magistrates in the eighteenth century. In 1783, for example, the justices of the Whitechapel Rotation Office released Samuel Smith "a boy" on condition that he "be corrected at school" but committed his older codefendant for trial on a charge of theft. In the same period the London-based Philanthropic Society reported that "Children...carried before a magistrate for theft have been discharged not...in consequence of any doubt respecting their guilt but...through the unwillingness of the injured party to bring them to trial."[35]

Was this tendency to use informal sanctions or summary trial rather than formal indictment eroded between 1790 and 1820? The protection theoretically afforded by the notion of *doli incapax* to those between seven and fourteen certainly seems to have been undermined to some extent. Only 2.9 percent of London accused in 1791–93 were in that age group, but by the 1820s this figure was 6.5 percent. In contrast to the theory advanced by some historians that the eighteenth century witnessed "the discovery of childhood" and the development of an increased awareness of the need to treat children as separate from adults, at the beginning of the nineteenth century the courts were dealing with an increasing number of offenders seven to fourteen years old as if they were adults fully responsible for their criminal actions.[36] However, the main growth in juvenile prosecutions occurred in older groups that had no chance to claim such immunities. The proportion of offenders aged between fourteen and seventeen, for example, rose by more than 10 percent between 1790 and 1820. It is therefore necessary to look elsewhere in order to explain why fewer victims and magistrates became willing to use informal sanctions as an alternative to the prosecution of juveniles.

Perhaps the most obvious potential explanation was the impact of the transition from war to peace. What contribution did the moral panic about crime that accompanied demobilization at the end of the French wars make to the changes seen in Figures 1 to 3? The acute anxieties that accompanied the coming of peace in 1815 almost certainly increased the proportion of offenders that victims chose to prosecute and, along with the problems experienced by the poor in the overstocked labor market of the early peacetime years, this may account for much of the 63 percent rise in indictments observable in Middlesex between 1814 and 1817. However, following the end of the American War of Independence in 1783, the period from the mid-1780s to the early 1790s also witnessed a generalized moral panic about crime, a growth in unemployment, and a similar rise in indictment rates.[37] Why was the earlier moral panic of the 1780s not accompanied by a substantial rise in the contribution made by juveniles, whereas the later one in the years after 1815 was? Several related but separate lines of explanation can be tentatively offered at this point.

The first runs as follows. Unlike their counterparts in the 1780s, elite commentators in the late 1810s, faced with widespread popular agitation and radicalism, tended to see the rapid growth of crime as an indication of the deeper social and political alienation of the laboring poor whom they increasingly labelled as the "dangerous classes." As crime became the repository for more general fears about the consequences of rapid social change, so juvenile crime came to have a new and special significance within those fears. Juvenile offenders, as representatives of the future and mirrors of the broader society were seized on as a particularly significant manifestation of a larger problem—the insubordination and degeneration of a significant proportion of the working class. The need to reform and discipline the juvenile offender was inextricably mixed up with a broader desire to transform various elements of working-class life that were felt to be dangerous or lacking in respectability.[38] This broader context helps to explain the constant links made by contemporaries between "the alarming increase in juvenile delinquency" and other problems such as drunkenness, sexual vice, sabbath-breaking, idleness, cheap literature, gambling, or the lack of education, parental care, and employment. If this new perception about the significance and importance of juvenile delinquency had spread fairly widely through the propertied classes by 1820, it could have transformed the attitudes of many victims and magistrates toward cases involving juveniles. So long as, to borrow Rush's phrase, "the child was the embodiment of an innocence to be preserved" formal indictment and the period of pretrial imprisonment it entailed were rarely appropriate. Eighteenth-century victims and magistrates therefore tended to prefer other solutions. Once the juvenile offender was identified in the early nineteenth century as arising from, and representing, a potentially dangerous class and culture, formal indictment may have been seen as a much more appropriate option.[39] Prosecution and conviction would deter others while offering the opportunity to reform the life of the individual juvenile—providing, of course, that the prison reformers were successful in ensuring that young prisoners were kept separate from the contagious influence of the older offenders.

Although such comments recur at regular intervals throughout the history of delinquency and must therefore be treated with care, some contemporaries clearly believed that a major change in attitudes towards the indictment of young offenders was occurring in the early nineteenth century. The provincial J.P. Eardley-Wilmot, for example, commented in 1820 that

Crimes are now brought before the public, which formerly were passed over, if not without observation, at least without comment; the thoughtlessness of childhood does not now save a first offender being treated with all the rigour of the repeated offender, and the little wretch, who might by timely and judicious correction have become a valuable member of society, is hurried to associate with those who perfect him ... depredations on the public.

Such comments must, of course, be balanced against other evidence that indicates that some magistrates were still inclined to deal with most juveniles informally,[40] but if commentators like Eardley-Wilmot were correct and such a change of attitude had begun to occur by 1820–22, the proportion of juvenile offenders that were prosecuted in the major courts would have risen substantially. Given the huge size of the dark figure of unindicted crime, this alone would have been sufficient to explain the rapid increase in juvenile prosecutions.

However, such an explanation faces several problems. First, it remains doubtful whether a discourse about "the problem of juvenile delinquency" had developed sufficiently by 1820 to influence more than a small minority of victims and magistrates. The existence of one or two London-based societies committed to investigating and reforming juvenile offenders ensured that the matter was regularly brought up by witnesses before the select committees of the 1810s, and the second report of the 1818 committee contained detailed proposals and designs "for a penitentiary for juvenile depredators." However, no such penitentiary was opened until the late 1830s, and the handful of voluntary institutional initiatives begun before 1820 had mixed fortunes. Apart from a few individuals associated with the Philanthropic Society, the Refuge for the Destitute, the various asylums for female prostitutes, or the Warwickshire reformatory experiments, no coherent body of experts whose livelihoods or professional status depended on raising the profile of juvenile delinquents and offering ways of reforming them can be easily identified in the records.[41] Moreover, although it is possible to identify the beginnings of a debate about juvenile delinquency in this period, it cannot be assumed that this heralded the arrival of a new discursive formation. To understand the process by which one may or may not have led to the other, it is necessary to ask detailed questions about the language of the debate, the different explanatory frameworks being advanced, and who was trying to persuade whom, for what reasons and with what effects. So far historians have only looked at the parliamentary reports and well-publicized printed works published in the 1810s. Without a thorough study of newspaper reporting, judges and Home Office correspondence, contemporary diaries and other sources, it would be dangerous to assume that a powerful discourse about juvenile offenders capable of changing victims' attitudes had emerged by the early 1820s.[42]

A deepening debate about a more specific issue, the imprisonment of juveniles, had developed by 1820 as a major subtheme within the broader renewal of the prison reform movement that took place in the later 1810s. The influential 1816 Committee for Investigating the Alarming Increase in Juvenile Delinquency in the Metropolis, for example, was set up by prison reformers like Hoare and Buxton; and by 1818 they had renamed it the Society for the Improvement of Prison Discipline and for the Reform of Juvenile Offenders. By drawing attention to the large numbers of young offenders found in London's overcrowded and inadequately divided prisons, this debate undoubtedly focused increasing attention on juvenile delinquency, as the frequent references made to these problems in the parliamentary reports of the 1810s make clear.[43] Did this, in itself, produce an increased awareness of juvenile crime that began to overcome the reticence victims and magistrates often showed in presenting juveniles? It may have done so, but it appears equally likely that it had the opposite effect.

Certainly the reformers' attempts to separate juvenile offenders from other types of prisoner made relatively little long-term progress in the metropolis or elsewhere before the first limited steps to introduce classification were begun in 1823. The 1818 committee's survey of the London prisons concluded that "the greater part of these juvenile offenders... are mixed indiscriminately with old offenders of all ages."[44] Victims who wanted to reform rather than simply punish juvenile offenders would therefore have continued to be very reluctant to have them committed to prison awaiting indictment in the major courts. By itself, the publicity created by the reformers who worked to ensure that juveniles were properly separated from older prisoners would not necessarily have encouraged the public to ensure that a greater proportion of young offenders were taken to court. However, a related contemporary debate in which men like Buxton were also involved, the debate about the abandonment of capital punishment for property offenses, may, in combination with the growing belief that imprisonment could be used to reform the young,[45] have encouraged victims to do precisely that.

What impact did the decline of the capital sanction have on the level of juvenile prosecutions? In the 1780s, 43 percent of those convicted of capital crimes at the Old Bailey were actually hanged. Between 1791 and 1793, 32 percent suffered the same fate, including a small number of juvenile offenders. By the early 1820s only a very small minority of offenders were reaching the gallows, and none of the younger offenders sentenced to death were actually executed. A decade or more before Parliament repealed almost all the capital statutes relating to property offenses, the Judges had ensured that virtually no juveniles suffered the penalty of death.[46] There is considerable evidence that by the end of the eighteenth-century victims were particularly reticent about prosecuting juveniles in capital cases. As one early nineteenth-century report observed, "There is scarcely anyone of common humanity who would not shudder at taking away the life of a child under sixteen or seventeen. . . . Hence it is, that reluctance to prosecute, where the punishment is very severe, prevails more when the offender is in childhood, than when of more advanced age."

Those who had the misfortune to be successful in capitally convicting a young offender often faced communal censure and occasionally violence. When a ten-year-old postal employee was sentenced to death at the Essex assizes in 1800, the court dissolved into pandemonium and the judge was forced to drop heavy hints that a pardon would be forthcoming.[47] By 1820 victims were largely relieved of such fears because juveniles very rarely reached the gallows. Did the decline of hanging remove the previous taboo about felony prosecutions against the young and thus release a wave of juvenile prosecutions into the courts, which may in turn have created or reinforced a broader panic about "the alarming increase in juvenile delinquency" that had little to do with any actual increase in juvenile lawbreaking?

The evidence in relation to the picking of pockets and shoplifting, the two main offenses that parliamentary legislation effectively removed from the shadow of the death sentence between 1808 and 1820, suggests that it did. In 1808 the capital sanction was taken away in cases involving pickpockets. A dozen years later the value of the stolen goods necessary to make an act of shoplifting into a capital offense was increased sixty-fold, which virtually ended the use of capital indictments against shoplifters. Indictments for these offenses rose rapidly after the capital sanction was removed, provoking a heated debate amongst the supporters and opponents of reform.[48] Although the precise charge on which the offender was indicted is not always clear in the London Criminal Registers, indictments for these two offenses increased between ten- and fifteen-fold in the period between 1791–93 and 1820–22. More important the removal of the capital sanction coincided with a doubling in the proportion of these offenders who were under twenty (from 23 percent to 47 percent). In the early 1790s the registers suggest that only a handful of juveniles were indicted as shoplifters or pickpockets each year. By the 1820s nearly two hundred a year were accused of these crimes. As many of these types of offender were probably indicted for simple larceny in the 1790s, to avoid accusing them of a capital offense, the absolute growth of juvenile prosecutions caused by these statutory changes is greatly overstated by these figures. However, it seems clear that the removal of the capital sanction eroded victims' reluctance to prosecute juveniles much more than it did their reluctance to indict other offenders. As the judges continued to reduce the proportion of capital convicts who were actually executed through the first two decades of the nineteenth century and as they virtually put an end to the hanging of juvenile property offenders, their policies may well have caused a similar change in the prosecution practices of victims of other forms of aggravated larceny such as robbery or burglary.

Because aggravated and capital larcenies represented a minority of Old Bailey indictments throughout this period, the effects of these changes on the overall age structure of all property offenders might well have been relatively muted if these years had not also witnessed other changes in the administration of criminal justice that seem to have had a similar effect on indictments for less serious offenses. The number of juvenile offenders indicted for petty larceny could well have risen in response to the growth of expenses payments to prosecutors. The 1778 and 1818 acts and their increasingly liberal interpretation by the courts in the late eighteenth and early nineteenth centuries brought a substantial rise in the amount of expenses paid by the courts.[49] If this in turn increased victims' propensities to prosecute in minor larceny cases and if juveniles represented a higher proportion of offenders in such cases than in more serious ones (as seems likely), this change alone would have increased the proportion of the accused who were juveniles.

Changes in policing and in the distribution of rewards may also have had a similar, if more muted, effect. Although the Metropolitan Police was not established until 1829, limited improvements in both the parochial police and the watch were introduced in some parts of early nineteenth-century London, sometimes with the assistance of recently established prosecution associations, and the stipendiary magistrates introduced in 1792 may also have affected attitudes. As new policing agencies often picked on juveniles because they were relatively easy targets, this could have increased the proportion of prosecutions involving juveniles significantly; and at least one member of the 1816 committee was inclined to think that "the number of juvenile delinquents that appear on the books of the different offices proceeds more from the activity of the police in detecting them than from any real augmentation in the number of crimes." The ending of the reward system in 1818 probably reinforced this effect.

The 1816 committee investigating the increase in juvenile delinquency certainly believed that "blood money" had "a strong tendency to induce the officers to overlook the minor depredations of young thieves." "The practice of holding out rewards for the apprehension of criminals in proportion to the enormity of their guilt, stimulates the officer to overlook the minor depredations of the incipient thief," they argued, and, "often might the youth be early arrested in his course but for the principle on which it becomes the interest of the officer that the young offender should continue in iniquity until he attains maturity in crime." After 1818 thieftakers and police officers no longer had any incentive to ignore juvenile thieves until "they weighed forty pounds."[50] Although the criminal law reformers may have exaggerated the effect of such changes, this could only have increased the proportion of young offenders reaching the courts.

CONCLUSIONS

The indirect impact of changes in pardoning policies, in Parliament's use of the capital sanction, in policing, and in the financial incentives offered to both victims and detective agencies may therefore have played a much more substantial role in generating the flood of juvenile prosecutions than the more visible arrival of a new discourse or debate about "the problem of juvenile delinquency." More balanced and precise explanations of the rapid rise of juvenile prosecutions in London from 1790 to 1820 remain impossible until further work has been done on nonproperty offenders, on contextualizing certain types of juvenile offense (using the depositions, trial reports, etc.), on prison and bridewell records, on the summary courts, and on the various quarter sessions jurisdictions of London, as well as on the press and on the writings of other women and men who were involved in contemporary debates: the judges, the prison reformers, the philanthropic investigators, the criminal law reformers, and their opponents. It is hoped that the work of Paul Griffiths and others will also illuminate the extent to which previous periods such as the late sixteenth and early seventeenth centuries experienced similar short-term cycles of increased juvenile pros-ecutions and increased concern about juvenile crime. More detailed work on the Old Bailey criminal registers of the late eighteenth and early nine-teenth centuries could also answer important questions. For example, by analyzing the age structure of offenders in each year between 1790 and 1820, it might well be possible to pinpoint more clearly when the proportion of juveniles first began to rise substantially, which would in turn help to determine whether the heightened publicity about juvenile delinquency in the early nineteenth century created or was created by a wave of juvenile prosecutions in the courts. Equally important, parallel studies of the few provincial courts that recorded the ages of the accused in this period would answer a number of key questions by establishing whether the same changes occurred in rural areas, in provincial capitals or in the industrial areas of the North where the reformers were particularly worried that the new fac-tories were creating conditions in which juvenile crime would become rife.[51]

However, certain preliminary conclusions can be drawn at this point. First, somewhere within the complex and sometimes paradoxical set of changes that occurred in London between 1790 and 1820, juvenile delinquency as an accepted and feared social problem was born. Despite Radzinowicz and Hood's conclusion that "the concept of the young offender ... is a Victorian creation,"[52] the genesis of the problem of juvenile delinquency undoubtedly came at least two decades before Victoria reached the throne.

Second, neither urbanization nor industrialization was directly responsible for the rapid growth of juvenile property crime prosecutions in and around London between 1790 and the early 1820s, although contemporaries may well have been correct in assuming that the city's rapid growth led to an increase in the already considerable numbers of destitute children that could be observed in its streets in 1790. Nor can more specific economic, social, or demographic changes be seen as the prime movers behind the growth of juvenile prosecutions between 1790 and 1820. These changes were undoubtedly important. The dilution of skills in some London trades and the continued decline of apprenticeship and living-in service undermined the economic prospects of a subsection of the young in both London and southeastern England between 1790 and 1820, while simultaneously eroding the institutions that exercised some control over their domestic lives.[53] However, these processes had been going on for a considerable period before 1790 and were far too gradual in their effects to provide a complete explanation of the wave of juvenile offenders that hit the courts in this period.

On balance therefore it seems that the changing attitudes and actions of victims, magistrates, police, and prison reformers provide the main, although not the only, key to understanding the rise of juvenile prosecutions in this period. The late eighteenth and early nineteenth centuries witnessed a substantial rise in the proportion of juvenile offenders indicted in the courts because the behavior of those who were responsible for bringing offenders to justice was influenced both by general changes in the way society viewed juvenile delinquents and by more specific alterations in the ways criminal justice was administered. Prosecutors and magistrates were undoubtedly affected by the way that broader fears about the social consequences of economic change and urban growth were increasingly linked to anxieties about crime in general and about juvenile crime in particular. However, the declining use of capital punishment and the growth of the idea that imprisonment could reform the young, combined with more specific statutory changes in the financial incentives offered to prosecutors and policing agencies and in the use of the capital sanction in cases involving private stealing from shops or persons, probably had a more wide-ranging effect in eroding victims' reluctance to prosecute juveniles. Like the campaign against "habitual offenders" half a century later, the rising alarm about "the problem of juvenile delinquency" between 1790 and 1820 appears to have been more a creation of those who reacted to, investigated, or wrote about crime than a reflection of any substantial change in the nature or level of criminal activity amongst the young. As one highly exceptional contemporary observed in 1816, when asked a leading question about whether offenses by juvenile delinquents "have been very much augmented of late years," "I am inclined to think not so much as is generally supposed. I apprehend they are more known from being more investigated."[54]

NOTES

1. This work was supported by a Liverpool University research fellowship and by general financial assistance from the Nene College research committee. I would like to thank Randy McGowen and all the members of the Early-Modern European History Seminar at Cambridge University and of the G.E.R.N. Interlabo conference on juvenile delinquency held at the Open University in 1992 for their comments on earlier drafts of this paper. This article is dedicated to Joan Noel, research assistant at Nene College, who did all the computing work and some of the data collection that lies behind Figures 1–3. Her sudden and tragic death in the summer of 1992 has meant the loss of a loved and greatly valued friend and of a marvelous research worker.

2. Wiley Britton Sanders, *Juvenile Offenders for a Thousand Years: Selective Readings from Anglo-Saxon Times to 1990* (Chapel Hill, 1980), 7—175; Margaret Hewitt and Ivy Pinchbeck, *Children in English Society* (London, 2 vols., 1969–73), 1:91–125; John L. McMullan, *The Canting Crew: London's Criminal Underworld 1550–1700* (New Jersey, 1984), 32–33, 172; A. L. Beier, *Masterless Men: The Vagrancy Problem in England 1560–1640* (London, 1988), 54–56.

3. John Fielding, *An Account of the Origins and Effects of a Police* (London, 1758), 17–28, 43–45; S. Welch, *A Proposal to Render Effectual a Plan to Remove the Nuisance of Common Prostitutes* (London, 1758), 54–55; J. Hanway, *The Defects of Police* (London, 1755), 57–59, 241; Sanders, *Juvenile Offenders*, 51–56. Lean Radzinowicz and Roger Hood, *A History of English Criminal Law and Its Administration from 1750* (London, 5 vols., 1948–86), 5:133–35; John Beattie, *Crime and the Courts in England 1660–1800* (Oxford, 1986), 246–47. The other focus of the attention about young offenders before the late eighteenth century was prostitution and asylums for prostitutes. Anon., *An Account of the Rise, Progress and Present State of the Magdalen Hospital for the Reception of Penitent Prostitutes* (London, 1776). Although young offenders were subjected to the same overall range of sentences, they did attract proportionally more pardons, partial verdicts, and lighter punishments. Peter King, "Decision-makers and Decision-making in the English Criminal Law 1750–1800," *Historical Journal* 27 (1984):35–48.

4. M. May, "Innocence and Experience: The Evolution of the Concept of Juvenile Delinquency in the Mid-nineteenth Century," *Victorian Studies* 17 (1973):7–29; William Blackstone, *Commentaries on the Laws of England* (Oxford, 4 vols., 1765–69), 4:22–24; Radzinowicz, *History*, 1:11–13; 5:134–86; Phyllida Parsloe, *Juvenile Justice in Britain and the United States: The Balance of Needs and Rights* (London, 1978), 109–21; James Walvin, *A Child's World: The Social History of English Childhood 1800–1914* (London, 1982), 160; Jo Manton, *Mary Carpenter and the Children of the Streets* (London, 1976), 69–111; Hewitt and Pinchbeck,

Children, 2:431–81; John Muncie, *The Trouble with Kids Today: Youth and Crime in Post-war Britain* (London, 1984), 33–39.

5. Victor Bailey, *Delinquency and Citizenship: Reclaiming the Young Offender 1914–1948* (Oxford, 1987); John Gillis, "The Evolution of Juvenile Delinquency in England 1890–1914," *Past and Present* 67 (1975):96–126; John Springhall, *Coming of Age: Adolescence in Britain 1860–1960* (London, 1986); John Springhall, *Youth, Empire and Society: British Youth Movements 1883–1940* (London, 1977); David Smith, "Juvenile Delinquency in Britain in the First World War," *Criminal Justice History* 11 (1990):119–145; Stephen Humphries, *Hooligans or Rebels? An Oral History of Working Class Childhood and Youth 1889–1939* (Oxford, 1981); Harry Hendrick, *Images of Youth: Age, Class and the Male Youth Problem 1880–1920* (Oxford, 1990).

6. S. Smith, "The London Apprentices as Seventeenth-century Adolescents," *Past and Present* 61 (1973):149–161; N. Z. Davis, "The Reasons of Misrule: Youth Groups and Charivaris in Sixteenth-Century France," *Past and Present* 50 (1971):41–75; Bernard Capp, "English Youth Groups and the Pinder of Wakefield," *Past and Present* 76 (1977):127–33; Philippe Aries, *Centuries of Childhood* (New York, 1962), 25–29; John Gillis, *Youth and History: Tradition and Change in European Age Relations 1770–Present* (New York, 1974), 1–93; Keith Thomas, *Age and Authority in Early Modern England* (London, 1976); A. Yarborough, "Apprentices as Adolescents in Sixteenth-Century Bristol," *Journal of Social History* 13 (1979): 67–81.

7. Radzinowicz, *History*, 5:131–227; Hewitt and Pinchbeck, *Children*, 1:110–25; 2:419–80; May, "Innocence and Experience"; Geoffrey Pearson, *Hooligan: A History of Respectable Fears* (London, 1983). Emigration schemes for juveniles have received more attention. E. Bradlaw, "The Children's Friend Society at the Cape of Good Hope," *Victorian Studies* 27 (1984):155–77; E. Hadley, "Natives in a Strange Land: The Philanthropic Discourse of Juvenile Emigration in Mid-Nineteenth Century England," *Victorian Studies* 33 (1990):411–37.

8. May, "Innocence and Experience," S. Magarey, "The Invention of juvenile delinquency in early nineteenth-century England," *Labour History* 34 (1978):11–25; P. Rush, "The Government of a Generation: The Subject of Juvenile Delinquency," *Liverpool Law Review* 14 (1992):3–43. "Report of the Select Committee on the State of the Police in the Metropolis," *Parliamentary Papers* (henceforth *P.P.*) 15:510; "Second Report from the Select Committee on the State of the Police in the Metropolis," *P.P.* (1817) 7:288, 484; "Third Report of the Select Committee on the Police of the Metropolis," *P.P.* (1818) 8:423; "Report from the Select Committee on the Criminal Laws," *P.P.* (1819) 8:585; *Report of the Committee for Investigating the Causes of the Alarming Increase of Juvenile Delinquency in the Metropolis* (1816).

9. V. A. C. Gatrell and T. Hadden, "Criminal Statistics and their Interpretation," in *Nineteenth Century Society: Essays in the Use of Quantitative Methods for the Study of Social Data*, ed. E. A. Wrigley (Cambridge, 1972), 383–5.

10. The Criminal Registers are in the Public Record Office at Kew (henceforward P.R.O.) HO 26. The 1791–93 sample in Figures 1 and 2 are drawn from HO 26/1–2; the 1820–22 sample, from HO 26/26–28. The documents are not a complete register of all offenders indicted at every major court in London (unlike the registers in existence for other counties from 1805 onward in HO 27). The London 1790s

registers only include those tried as either Middlesex or City of London prisoners at the Old Bailey. By the 1820s those tried at the Westminster and Clerkenwell sessions are also included, but no age information is recorded for those individuals. Figures 1–3 are therefore based on Old Bailey trials alone. Systematic recording of the accused's age seems to have first developed in a few jurisdictions during the transportation crisis of 1775–1787. King, "Decision-makers," 34–35.

11. For the various general or quarter sessions jurisdictions within the Metropolitan area John Beattie, "London Juries in the 1690s" in *Twelve Good Men and True: The Criminal Trial Jury in England 1200–1800*, ed. J. S. Cockburn and Thomas Green (Princeton, 1988), 216–18; Peter Colquhoun, *A Treatise on the Police of the Metropolis* (London, 1797), 218–9, lists five jurisdictions: The City, Westminster, Middlesex, Tower Hamlets, and Southwark.

12. Ruth Paley, "The Middlesex Justices Act of 1792: Its Origins and Effects" (Doctoral dissertation, Reading University, 1983), 393; 1791–93 sample size = 2,514 (October 1791 to July 1793 inclusive); 1820–22 = 4,117 (October 1820 to July 1822); P.R.O. HO 26/1–2, 26–28.

13. Peter King, "Crime, Law and Society in Essex 1740–1820" (Doctoral dissertation, Cambridge University, 1984), 85. At the Old Bailey the proportion of non-aggravated larceny accused under seventeen rose from 20.7 percent to 36.0 percent, while the proportion of aggravated larceny accused rose from 17.7 percent to 38.9 percent. By 1828 all Middlesex indictments involving property over a shilling in value were sent to the Old Bailey for trial. "Report from the Select Committee on the Police of the Metropolis," *P.P.* (1828) 6:533, 165.

14. King, "Crime," 95; Peter King, "War, Judicial Discretion and the Problems of Young Adulthood 1740–1815," *Social History Society Newsletter* 9 (Spring 1984): 9.

15. P.R.O. HO 26/1–2 and 26–8. In 1791–93, 25.7 percent were female; in 1820–22, 21.1 percent were female. For an attempt to put this into the context of a long-term decline, see M. Feeley and D. Little, "The Vanishing Female: The Decline of Women in the Criminal Process 1697–1913," *Law and Society Review* 25 (1991).

16. *P.P.* (1817) 7:288, 484, 547–51, give statistics of the prisoners in four London prisons for the whole of 1816: Newgate, Clerkenwell, Cold Bath Fields, and Horsemonger Lane: 19.9 percent of felony prisoners were males under twenty, 4.4 percent were females under twenty. For all prisoners the percentages were 15.4 and 4.4. Precise definitions of the upper age of a juvenile varied from fifteen to nineteen or twenty. David Philips, *Crime and Authority in Victorian England: The Black Country 1835–60* (London, 1977), 161.

17. Calculated by comparing the 1786 national data with the 1821 census. King, "Decision-makers," 35–6; E. A. Wrigley and Roger Schofield, *The Population History of England 1541–1871: A Reconstruction* (Cambridge, 1981), 519 gives information only in five to fourteen and fifteen to twenty-four age groups. More detailed information was kindly supplied for 1786 by Roger Schofield. Personal Communication, John Landers. Figures obtained by applying a set of "model" age-specific mortality rates to the age-classified burials in the Bills of Mortality.

18. Frank McLynn, *Crime and Punishment in Eighteenth Century England* (London, 1989), 311; Sean McConville, *A History of English Prison Administration 1750–1877* (London, 1981) 1:217–18.

19. John Tobias, *Crime and Industrial Society in the Nineteenth Century* (London, 1972), 42; Walvin, *A Child's World*, 57.

20. Louise I. Shelley, *Crime and Modernization: The Impact of Industrialization and Urbanization on Crime* (Southern Illinois, 1981), 52, 137.

21. Iowerth J. Prothero, *Artisans and Politics in Early Nineteenth-Century London* (London, 1979), 2; P. J. Corfield, *The Impact of English Towns 1700–1800* (Oxford, 1982), 66–81; E. A. Wrigley, "A Simple Model of London's Importance in Changing English Society and Economy 1650–1750," *Past and Present* 37 (1967): 44–70; Francis H. W. Sheppard, *London 1808–1870. The Infernal Wen* (London, 1971), 2–5. There were, of course, variations in migration patterns but "the magnet of the metropolis" continued to be a dominant influence. *Migration and Society in Early Modern England* ed. Peter Clark and D. Souden (1987), 38.

22. Patricia L. Garside, 'London and the Home Counties', in *The Cambridge Social History of Britain 1750–1950*, ed. F. M. L. Thompson (Cambridge, 1990) 1:471–94.

23. Sheppard, *London*, 158–89; M. D. George, *London Life in the Eighteenth Century* (London, 1966 edition), 158–212; Corfield, *The Impact*, 69–81; L. Schwarz, "Social Class and Social Geography: The Middle Classes in London at the end of the Eighteenth Century," *Social History* 7 (1982):167–183.

24. L. Schwarz, "The Standard of Living in the Long Run: London, 1700–1860," *Economic History Review* 38 (1985): 24–41; George, *London*.

25. Prothero, *Artisans*, 62–68; George, *London*, 31–32; Sheppard, *London*, 158–59; Garside, "London," 471–491.

26. Peter Mathias, *The First Industrial Nation*, (2nd ed., London, 1983), 417; Sheppard, *London*, 96; Schwarz, "The Standard"; Prothero, *Artisans*, 62–67; Peter Linebaugh, *The London Hanged Crime and Civil Society in the Eighteenth Century* (London, 1991).

27. K. D. M. Snell, *Annals of the Labouring Poor: Social Change and Agrarian England 1660–1900* (Cambridge, 1985), 236–37 and 253; George, *London*, 268–69; John Rule, *The Experience of Labour in Eighteenth Century Industry* (London, 1981), 100; *P.P.* (1816) 5:510, 262.

28. Snell, *Annals*, 236–53; *P.P.* (1816) 5:510, 127; Rule, *The Experience*, 109; Linebaugh, *The London Hanged* (1991), 101. Linebaugh talks of a "crisis of apprenticeship" in the early eighteenth century (p. 15). Prothero, *Artisans*, 51–70.

29. George, *London*, 269–74; Rule, *The Experience*, 100–3; Daniel Defoe, *The Great Law of Subordination Considered* (London, 1724), 13; Hanway, *Defects*, 57, 241; M. Thale, ed., *The Autobiography of Francis Place* (Cambridge, 1972), 73–75.

30. Snell, *Annals*, 67–103, 228–269; Ann Kussmaul, *Servants in Husbandry in Early Modern England* (Cambridge, 1981), 120–7; on the seasonal and casual labor market's later development, Gareth Steadman-Jones, *Outcast London* (1971).

31. B. Hill, *Women, Work and Sexual Politics in Eighteenth-Century England* (Oxford, 1989), 128–29; P. Seleski, "The Women of the Laboring Poor: Love, Work and Poverty in London, 1750–1820" (Doctoral dissertation, Stanford University, 1989), 26–27; Peter Earle, "The Female Labour Market in London in the Late Seventeenth and Early Eighteenth Centuries," *Economic History Review* 42 (1989): 341–46; H. Cunningham, "The Employment and Unemployment of Children in England c 1680–1851," *Past and Present* 126 (1990):144–45.

32. For a preliminary exploration of these issues in relation to young adults, see King, "Crime," 82–148; and Peter King, "Female Offenders, Work and Lifecycle Change in Late Eighteenth-Century England," paper given to the American Social Science History Conference (Minneapolis, 1990).

33. Sanders, *Juvenile Offenders*, 104. Magarey, "The Invention," 17.

34. The Parisian experience may have been very similar. Recent work on mid-nineteenth century Paris concluded that broken or overburdened families, and failure to adapt to a new urban environment were unimportant in explaining delinquency in the French capital. Lenard R. Berlanstein, "Vagrants, Beggars and Thieves: Delinquent Boys in Mid-Nineteenth Century Paris," *Journal of Social History* 12 (1979).

35. P.R.O. HO 42/2/99 27 Jan. 1783; *An Account of the Nature and Present State of the Philanthropic Society Instituted in 1788* (London, 1804), 8; Peter King, *Crime, Justice and Discretion Law and Society in Essex and South-Eastern England 1740–1820* (forthcoming), chaps. 2 and 4.

36. Magarey extends this by suggesting *doli incapax* fell into increasing disuse and disrepute 1820–50, Magarey, "The Invention," 19; Lawrence Stone, *The Family, Sex and Marriage in England 1500–1800* (London, 1979), 254 and for a critique Linda Pollock, *Forgotten Children: Parent-Child Relations from 1500–1900* (Cambridge, 1983), 110.

37. *P.P.* (1819) 8:585, 140; Douglas Hay, "War, Dearth and Theft in the Eighteenth Century: The Record of the English Courts," *Past and Present* 95 (1982); Beattie, *Crime*, 223–25; King, "Crime," 64–73; Michael Ignatieff, *A Just Measure of Pain: The Penitentiary in the Industrial Revolution 1750–1850* (London, 1978), 82.

38. Ignatieff, *A Just Measure*, 156–162; V. A. C. Gatrell, "Crime, Authority and the Policeman-state" in *The Cambridge Social History*, ed. Thompson, 3:244–52; Pearson, *Hooligan*, 182; Rush, "The Government," 11–12.

39. Sanders, *Juvenile Offenders*, 51–112; Rush, "The Government," 23–24.

40. Sanders, *Juvenile Offenders*, 111, 122; *P.P.* (1816) 5:510, 262.

41. Ignatieff, *A Just Measure*, 156–57; Sanders, *Juvenile Offenders*, 70–112; Radzinowicz, *History*, 5:133–36; Hewitt and Pinchbeck, *Children*, 2:414–40.

42. Rush, "The Government" is not primarily concerned with the process by which "the discourse on juvenile delinquency," as he terms it (p. 26), emerged nor with the timing of that process. For an interesting discussion of changing ways of seeing the treatment of juvenile offenders, see Muncie, *The Trouble*, 35–6.

43. Ignatieff, *A Just Measure*, 153–173; Sanders, *Juvenile Offenders*, 106. *P.P.* (1917) 7:484, 328–541.

44. *P.P.* (1817) 7:484, 329. The 1823 Act was only a small step forward. Ignatieff, *A Just Measure*, 168.

45. Radzinowicz, *History*, 1:478–566; Randall McGowen, "The Image of Justice and Reform of the Criminal Law in Early Nineteenth-Century England," *Buffalo Law Review* 32 (1983):89–125; and McGowen, "A Powerful Sympathy: Terror, the Prison and Humanitarian Reform in Early Nineteenth-century Britain," *Journal of British Studies* 25 (1986):312–34.

46. *P.P.* (1819) 8:585, 138–39; Walvin, *A Child's World*, 160.

47. Sanders, *Juvenile Offenders*, 111; Radzinowicz, *History*, 1:13. For examples

of attacks on successful prosecutors see Clive Emsley, *Crime and Society in England 1750–1900* (London, 1987), 139.

48. Radzinowicz, *History*, 1:497–554.

49. R.P.O. HO 26/1–2, 26–8. David Philips, "A New Engine of Power and Authority: The Institutionalization of Law-Enforcement in England 1780–1830," in *Crime and Law. The Social History of Crime in Western Europe Since 1500*, ed. V. A. C. Gatrell, Bruce Lenham, and Geoffrey Parker (Oxford 1980), 170; King, "Decision-makers," 32–33.

50. David Philips, "Good Men to Associate and Bad Men to Conspire: Associations for the Prosecution of Felons in England 1760–1860," in *Policing and Prosecution in Britain 1750–1850*, ed. Douglas Hay and Francis Snyder (Oxford, 1989), 146–48. R. Paley, "An Imperfect, Inadequate and Wretched System? Policing London before Peel," *Criminal Justice History* 10 (1989):113; Radzinowicz, *History*, 2:57–82; *P.P.* (1817) 7:484, 430–37, *P.P.* (1816) 5:510, 169–70.

51. P. Griffiths, "Some Aspects of the Social History of Youth in Early Modern England with Particular Reference to 1560–1640" (Doctoral dissertation, Cambridge University, 1992); Ignatieff, *A Just Measure*, 156.

52. Radzinowicz, *History*, 5:133.

53. Snell, *Annals*, 322.

54. Jennifer Davis, "The London Garrotting Panic of 1862: A Moral Panic and the Creation of a Criminal Class in Mid-Victorian England," in *Crime and the Law*, ed. Gatrell et al., 209–20; Emsley, *Crime*, 133–5; *P.P.* (1816) 5:510, 169.

Policing Juveniles: Delinquency in Late Nineteenth and Early Twentieth Century Manchester

Barbara Weinberger
University of Warwick

Evangelicals, philanthropists, educationalists, and progressive liberals took center stage in the late nineteenth-century debate on the incorporation of the mass of the working class into civic life. A wide variety of middle-class reformers, it appeared, wished to reestablish closer relations and gain working-class acceptance for a new, bourgeois-led moral order.[1] The profound class division of the early Victorian era had given rise, after the class confrontations of the 1840s and the economic strains and stresses of the 1860s, to a strong desire on the part of the middle class to try to bridge the gap. In place of class war there was to be negotiation and accommodation, as witnessed by the extension of the franchise and the legalization of the trade unions. Social harmony would replace class antagonisms, and the whole would be cemented by philanthropy and moral reform.

In this debate, the attention given to the activities and behavior of juveniles not only accompanied, but in many ways overtook a parallel attention being directed at the adult urban slum population in Britain. The present chapter charts some of the processes involved, taking Manchester as its example, but in contrast with most work on this topic lays stress on juveniles in relation to the middle-class reformist enterprise. In the remaking of social relations between the classes that took place at the end of the nineteenth century, historians have underplayed the place of juveniles as an expression of that new relationship. Nevertheless, it is clear that concern about the desired behavior of juveniles was a crucial element in the reformist program. From the time of the 1870 Education Act, discussion on the relationship between school and paid employment and on the regulation of leisure offered reformers scope to inaugurate policies to encourage the relations of dependency and control that they favored. Juveniles absorbed so much reformist energy precisely because they presented the ideal arena in which to demonstrate the preferred form of social relations between the classes.

JUVENILES ON THE STREETS

It was after the mid-nineteenth century that concern over the children of the streets gathered pace. An immense weight of moral and legal attention came to be focused on youth—and in particular on juvenile offenders—both as the harbingers of a budding criminal generation and as the most receptive part of the underclass for reclamation and reform. Generally speaking, this was a field in which private effort preceded and remained well to the fore of official involvement, in a period that has been called "the heroic age of charity." Private agencies largely set the agenda and staffed the institutions initially established to deal with the prevention of juvenile crime and the aftercare of juvenile offenders. It was the men and women who ran these agencies who became the acknowledged experts, who gave evidence to parliamentary inquiries, and whose opinions were canvassed by magistrates and town councillors. The organizations that they set up, ranging from rescue homes to lads' clubs, constituted a major drive to oversee, influence, and direct the lives of inner-city juveniles. However, public authorities were also involved. With the establishment of compulsory education from the 1870s and the regulation of juvenile street trading, the state—in the form of school attendance officers and the police—joined forces with voluntary agencies to monitor the presence of juveniles in the streets.

The remarkable feature of the conjunction of public and private institutions is the extent to which the work of these separate agencies interlocked. The voluntary organizations soon turned to the state for more comprehensive provision and support than they themselves could offer singlehandedly, while state agencies frequently took on the viewpoint and criteria of the voluntary sector. A cooperative relationship was established whereby the magistrates would discharge juveniles into the care of charitable refuges instead of inflicting punishment. The police informed school attendance officers of cases needing their attention, while these officers would hand over to the police juveniles who contravened local authority regulations. In sum, these philanthropic, educational, and corrective agencies formed different parts of a totality that, from the 1870s onwards, was based on a perceived need for the training and disciplining of children from the lower ranks of the working class.

The upsurge of charitable activity concerning juveniles in the 1870s and 1880s gained impetus from the growth in economic opportunities for young school dropouts. In Manchester, the intensification of commercial activity in the central zone gave rise at this time to a host of jobs for youths that took them onto the streets as messenger, van, or newsboys. Indeed, it was this use of the freedom of the streets by the city's youth, rather than the poverty and squalor of the conditions in which they and their parents lived, that charitable workers found most distressing and which the authorities found difficult to curb. As John Gillis has noted in his seminal essay on adolescents in the period, "The model adolescent became organised youth, dependent but secure from temptation, while the independent and precocious young were stigmatised as delinquent."[2] For the authorities, the presence of the children of the streets stood both as a reproach to their parents and as a sign of the breakdown of family discipline and morality; it was on this basis that intervention in the lives of these children was publicly justified.

Official concern was aroused by juveniles whose leisure pursuits brought them to the city center streets. Here the warring street gangs of the late 1880s and early 1890s were prominent, and indeed notorious, as they defended their territory against opposing bands (often in an Irish/Protestant divide). But in the debates surrounding the moral panic over "scuttlers," as the Manchester gangs were called, more concern was expressed about their freedom from adult control than about the actual effects of the warfare.[3] A common feature, in the three cities of Manchester, Birmingham, and Liverpool that were best known for their gangs, was the demand for juvenile labor; and court evidence shows that gang members were usually in employment.[4] In Manchester, where the demand for boy labor continually exceeded the supply, it was said that any boy on leaving school could find employment within two hours.[5] In consequence, according to the local expert on the city's youths, a boy left school early to earn a wage. His wage made him feel independent, and he was pandered to by his parents in order not to drive him from home. The result, it was said, was that young men came to lack discipline and control.[6] In addition, their strong economic position and relatively high wages allowed young people to take charge of their own lives and to spend their leisure as they wished—which, in the absence of countervailing attractions, was frequently on the streets and occasionally in gang warfare. Youth workers were in no doubt as to the nature of the problem. These youths had been hanging about the streets in their free time since leaving school. The remedy was to provide alternative attractions, and here lads' clubs provided the best answer.[7]

The city council, while largely in agreement with this diagnosis, was happy to leave the implementation of such a recreational policy to private initiative and preferred to stick to more direct and traditional methods for dealing with the public-order problem caused by the gangs. The Watch Committee reacted by increasing the number of police posted to the fairly confined area of the city where gang warfare took place. However, the police, who bore down heavily not only on gang warfare but on other expressions of youthful exuberance, were clearly perceived to be only one of several agencies central to the fight against juvenile crime and delinquency. Thus, by the 1890s a 25 percent drop in the number of juveniles appearing before the courts was ascribed to the effect of the Education Act by the Recorder of Manchester, who told the grand jury of 1891:

There were reasons for this diminution of crime. . . . the School Board had taken the children of the city under its guidance and protection, had kept them off the streets, and had disciplined them and taught them the advantages of industry. The fruits of that system appeared to him to have become ripe about 1883, and they had continued to be enjoyed down to the present time.[8]

In short, other agencies apart from the police were actively involved in monitoring the activities of children and juveniles on the streets and helping to bring about a diminution in juvenile crime. School attendance officers scoured the streets and brought offending children and their parents before their own tribunals. However, it was the work of the industrial school officer that most clearly overlapped with that of the police. Manchester appointed two such officers, whose task was to look for neglected, homeless, and semicriminal children and, where necessary, to secure their entry into industrial schools. Close liaison with the police was essential. The following example of two boys charged with sleeping out illustrates the process, in which the industrial school officer reported as follows:

The Police Inspector sent me their names and addresses and, as both were well-known to me, I attended court and informed the Bench that both lads would be better in Industrial Schools. They were accordingly committed as vagrants.[9]

PROBLEM ADOLESCENTS

Although the school provided the obvious socializing agency for children of school age, ways to oversee the post-school adolescent were not so readily at hand. For this generation, clubs provided the most widely supported alternative to leisure time spent on the streets. The idea of these clubs had originated in the city police courts, where large numbers of working lads were brought for minor offences because they had no place other than the streets to spend their leisure hours. The result, it was said, was that there were few working lads who had not been in the hands of the police for some trifling offense against public order in the late decades of the nineteenth century.[10] But the clubs also had the more positive purpose of providing healthy and "manly" activities that would extend the public school virtues of *esprit de corps* and muscular Christianity to working-class youths as part of a program of "character building."[11] By 1913, it was estimated that there were over 12,000 boys attending lads' clubs in the Manchester district.[12] Together with Boy Scouts and the Boys Brigade (formed with the object of "advancing Christ's Kingdom among boys and promoting habits of obedience, reverence, discipline, and self-respect"),[13] these accounted for around 24,000 club members. It seems fair to conclude that by the turn of the century the majority of inner city youths had been successfully enrolled in one or another of these clubs. The leisure time they spent on the streets was lessened, not only because of the clubs and the public provision of parks and playing fields,[14] but also through the extension of commercial outlets in the form of cinemas and dance halls.[15]

A parallel but greater worry was over juveniles whose work brought them on to the streets and required different measures for its containment. Concern was focused on those who lived by street hawking and selling, a concern that came to assume enormous proportions. This was quite out of scale with the numbers involved, as only 2 percent of school leavers in the 1890s became newsboys or hawkers. Nevertheless, strenuous efforts to eradicate juvenile street trading involved the broad spectrum of those engaged in dealing with children and adolescents, because the image of the child street trader had resonance as a symbol of parental neglect and as precursor to a life of crime and prostitution.

The school board was the earliest to concern itself with the problem, because of reports by the industrial school officer that many of these children were growing up as criminals.[16] The influential charity organization, the Boys and Girls Welfare Society (BWGS), would have preferred that juvenile street trading be prohibited and campaigned for parliamentary legislation to this end, receiving strong local support. However, a comprehensive Employment of Children Act was not passed until 1903.[17] In the meantime, a local act assigned the supervision of its juvenile street-trading regulations to the school board, and Manchester was given the powers to license its own juvenile traders in 1901. It soon became a model of what could be achieved by such methods.[18] The scheme was run by the watch committee, which dealt with offenders against the regulations[19] and appointed five plainclothes police officers, whose full-time task was the surveillance of juvenile street traders. In parallel, a private and charitable Police-Aided Clothing Association was inaugurated, of which the mayor declared:

the vital part of the proposal was the cooperation of the police . . . mutual confidence between the police and the children would be evoked, and instead of a reign of terror there would be a reign of sympathy.[20]

All in all, there was general approval for the way in which the police dealt with child traders, while any difficulties that arose were not so much practical as conceptual. In making a case against juvenile street traders, reformers and public authorities had always argued that such work led youngsters into moral degradation and crime. But not all youngsters. Those living in the suburbs and from artisan families were not adversely affected; on the contrary, they were earning a useful addition to the family budget. However, those whose parents relied to a much greater degree on their earnings and who could make more money selling newspapers than they might in factory employment were said to be on the way to ruin.[21] Similarly, girl traders outside a one-mile radius of the town hall could trade with impunity, whereas it was said that those trading close to the center would, without doubt, become prostitutes. The police inspector dealing with street-trading juveniles categorically told the Employment of Children Act Committee:

The children trading in the centre of the city have got poor homes and come from worthless parents. When a child does earn money in the centre of the city it looks after itself first and what it has left it takes home to its parents.... With regard to the children on the outskirts, the money there earned is put to good use ... it is used more for the clothing of the children than for anything else.[22]

Where girls were concerned, the chairman of the Watch Committee, Alderman Rawson, claimed that:

We are quite certain that the trading by girls in the streets leads them to a loose life.... The selling of newspapers and matches by girls in the streets is often a mere cloak for solicitation.[23]

But the view that only the children of respectable parents could withstand the harmful effects of trading in the streets led to some awkward questions. Regarding the dangers of prostitution, Alderman Rawson, who thought only respectable girls should be licensed to trade in the streets, was asked:

If the employment is so bad and so degrading as it certainly has been presented to us, would it be a desirable thing to allow respectable girls to go into it? ... Might it not, as a matter of fact, be less harmful for girls who come from bad homes to do it... suppose the girl coming from a very bad home is making something by selling newspapers in the streets.... You stop her getting her livelihood in this way. Is there not in that case a danger?[24]

Similarly, the chief constable who wanted to prevent the children of known thieves from trading in the streets was asked:

In that case you would prevent this boy, who is the child of thieves, of his only way of getting a living? ... you say this life is very bad, but you would bring into it the respectable boys and take it away from the boys who have no other means of earning their livelihood.[25]

The replies to these embarrassing dilemmas show that the primary interest of the authorities was not so much to regulate juvenile street trading as to encourage an approved way of life. They chose to punish those who did not conform by withholding a licence to trade and, through the power of inspection granted to the police, kept a close eye on all juvenile traders, especially those from suspect families.

STATISTICS OF JUVENILE CRIME

There remains the question of the policing implications of the juvenile crime statistics. Unlike the criminal statistics for adults, the level of juvenile crime in the early postwar period was not dramatically lower than its level in the last decade of the nineteenth century. There was, however, an extremely steep rise in juvenile offenses during the war years at the national as well as local level. Nationally, the number of proceedings against juveniles in the courts jumped from 36,929 in 1914 to a peak of 51,323 in 1917 before slowly subsiding back to the 1914 figure by 1920.[26] Manchester parallels this trend almost exactly, except that the peak in juvenile court appearances there was reached somewhat earlier, in 1916 as shown in Figure 1. How can we account for these variations? I would suggest that statistical trends in offense rates reflect public consciousness and the implementation of public policies rather than a true picture of a rise or fall in the number of offenses actually committed. The declining and then static trend in the last decade of the nineteenth century may be seen as a measure of a changing and more child-centered attitude towards juvenile transgressions in the period before ameliorative legislation concerning juveniles had been enacted.[27]

The work of the charitable homes and refuges was certainly instrumental in keeping down the number of juveniles who might otherwise have appeared in court. The BGWS, for example, declared an active interest in juvenile offenders and believed that it had helped to gradually bring the law into harmony with the public conscience. In its own words, the voluntary agencies had educated the state.[28] They had campaigned for the Employment of Children Act (1903), which gave magistrates the power to remand any person under sixteen to a voluntary home instead of a prison,[29] while the Children Act (1908) saw the culmination of this campaign through its statutory establishment of juvenile courts, the abolition of imprisonment and the death sentence for children under sixteen, and the "permissive" appointment of voluntary workers by the courts as probation officers. Paradoxically, the trend in juvenile court appearances began to rise quite consistently after the 1908 Act had done away with the harshest penalties and reached a peak in 1916.

While the more interventionist role of private and state agencies "in the best interests of the child" may thus help to account for this upsurge in the last few years before the war, the extraordinary wartime rise in juvenile offenders probably has a different genesis and bears all the hallmarks of a moral panic. Family life was disrupted by the war: Men were away in the services, women were out at work, and children were out of control. Matters were not helped by the fact that there were few places where children could expend their energies, as clubs and parks had been closed because of the lack of personnel to run them. At the same time, restricted street lighting encouraged thefts from shops, street, and market stalls.[30]

The upsurge in the juvenile offense rate was on a national scale, causing the Home Office to become alarmed, while the local chief constable declared that "children today have neither regard nor respect for their elders, nor any fear of the law. They are well aware they will be treated leniently, with

Figure 1
Juveniles before the Courts in Manchester 1890–1930

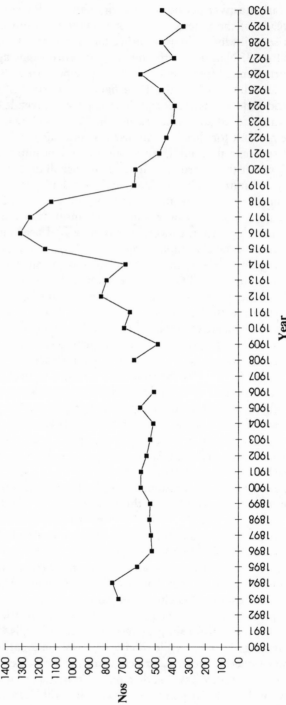

Relevant legislation: Employment of Children Act 1903
Children Act 1908
Education Act 1921
Manchester Corporation Act 1901 (juvenile street trading)
City of Manchester Bye-law 1922

Year

Nos

Source: Chief Constable's Annual Reports
(reports for 1890-1892, 1907 missing)

no serious punishment."[31] The Manchester educational authorities were equally concerned and set up an enquiry into the causes for the increase in juvenile crime.[32] Its report found that nearly all the heads of families it investigated were in casual employment, which it believed consigned many of the children to casual and unsettled employment as adults. The remedies suggested included the removal of children from the custody of incompetent parents, "in order that the right ideal of family life should be maintained"; the supervision of certain types of children out of school hours, such as those living in the central areas of the city and those who traded in the streets; and the organized provision of recreation.[33]

PHILANTHROPIC POLICIES AND THE STATE

We are back to the scenario confronting the philanthropic agencies when they started their work in the 1870s. Juvenile crime was due to the lack of supervision and control over the children of the streets, and the remedy was a closer watch and the provision of organized recreational facilities. The difference was in the degree to which the parents were now held responsible and the greater willingness of the state to intervene on behalf of the child, at least in theory. The Home Office responded to the rise in the juvenile offense rate by encouraging magistrates to revive the work of the boys clubs,[34] and by promoting the appointment of local committees to coordinate juvenile welfare work. These local committees were to be affiliated to a central Juvenile Organisations Committee (JOC) appointed by the Home Secretary in December 1916.[35]

With this official seal of approval, lads' clubs came into their own as an effective branch of public policy, with the local JOCs taking on a growing role in tackling the problem of school leavers who escaped the influence of any organization. Clubs were ascribed almost automatic powers in solving social problems involving adolescents, to the extent that the Home Office applied for the early release of men from the armed services who had experience of work in Boys Clubs and Brigades. In its view:

the work done by these clubs is one of the most effective ways of checking juvenile delinquency and in view of the change in industrial conditions it is especially important to maintain the work of these organisations.[36]

In the era when peace was reestablished, we enter a world where the ideals and policies of the Victorian charitable organizations for the rescue and rehabilitation of juveniles had become official practice. The charitable organizations themselves were flourishing and tightly enmeshed with the public agencies dealing with destitute and delinquent juveniles. As the BGWS annual report for 1923 noted:

for forty-four years the BGWS watched a great revolution in social service, has taken a prominent part in its accomplishment and rejoices that we are serving, and being served by, practically every social agency and church in the city and borough.[37]

With the necessary legislation and support systems in place, it seemed that the authorities were no longer unduly alarmed by unruly behavior in juveniles. Although the offense rate remained moderately high in comparison with the prewar rate, when public concern was so much greater, it now elicited little comment.

The police, however, never deviated from the class-control element in their policing policy, even though they were careful, as far as juveniles were concerned, that this should be given benevolent form. The chief constable had long been at pains to stress the welfare aspects of the police role, while at the same time warning of the criminogenic effects of any loss of police control. The additional duties undertaken by the police, including the licensing of juvenile street traders and the work of the police-aided clothing association, he suggested, "should tend to create a better feeling between the police and the public."[38] The welfare service role of the police was strongly emphasized, and constables were encouraged by the chief constable to engage in social and charitable work in their spare time. But parallel with this benevolent stance ran the need to maintain control. The chief constable expounded his views on what was required to reform young criminals, whom he equated with juvenile street traders. Children had to be prevented from running wild in the streets without restraint or legitimate outlet for their energies; and he would have liked legislation to give him greater powers in this field as, in his view, the child trader drifted naturally into the hooligan, the thief, and far worse.[39] Welfare work and the power of arrest were thus two sides of the same coin, dedicated to the surveillance and control of a suspect and potentially dangerous section of society in the form of juveniles on the streets. But the long period during which the police had exercised this control, in cooperation with their voluntary helpmates, meant that by the 1920s, when public attitudes and policies had become much more sympathetically youth-centered, they were able to discard some of their previous strong-arm tactics in favor of softer policing methods that had greater public support.

NOTES

1. See Gareth Stedman Jones, "Working-class culture and working class politics in London 1870–1900: Notes on the remaking of a working class," *Journal of Social History* 7(4) (Summer 1974): 460–508.
2. John Gillis, "The Evolution of Juvenile Delinquency in England 1840–1914," *Past and Present* 67 (May 1975): 96–126. But for a critique of the view that independent youth *was* widely stigmatized as potentially delinquent, see Harry Hen-

drick, *Images of Youth: Age, Class and the Male Youth Problem 1880–1920* (Oxford, 1990), 141 fn 109.

3. For a description of the scuttling gangs, see Geoffrey Pearson, *Hooligan: A History of Respectable Fears* (London, 1983), 94–96.

4. This contrasts with twentieth-century evidence linking youth gangs with unemployment, especially in the interwar period, as rival groups sought to exclude others in the competition for jobs and other resources. See Stephen Humphries, *Hooligans or Rebels? An oral history of working-class childhood and youth 1889–1939* (Oxford, 1981), chap. 7.

5. Evidence of C. E. B. Russell to the Employment of Children Act Committee, *Parliamentary Papers* (hereafter PP XLIV) (1909). See also C. E. B. Russell, *Manchester Boys: Sketches of Manchester Boys at Work and at Play*, (Swinton, 1984 reprint). Charles Russell began a long and distinguished career in youth work at the Heyrod Street Lads' Club, and as secretary of the Boys Brigade and chairman of the Manchester and Salford Playing Fields Society. His educational work at Heyrod Street was taken over as a Continuation School by the Education Committee in 1907. He was also chairman of the Borstal Committee, and in 1913 he was appointed as Chief Inspector of Reformatory and Industrial Schools in England and Wales. For a summary, see *C. E. B. Russell: For Remembrance 1866–1917* (London, 1917).

6. *Board of Education: Special Reports on Educational Subjects, Supplement to Vol 8*. Report on the School Training and Early Employment of Lancashire Children, by E. T. Campagnac and C. E. B. Russell, *PP* Cd. 1867 (London, 1903), 8.

7. *Manchester City News* (hereafter *MCN*), 6 September 1890, quoting H. C. Devine, who with his brothers was deeply involved in the Boys' Club movement in Manchester. H. C. Devine was the first secretary of the Openshaw Lads' Club; Walter Devine started the Hulme and Chorlton-on-Medlock Working Lads' Club and Gym, and the Hugh Oldham Lads' Club in 1886, while the best known of the brothers, Alexander Devine, founded the Police Court Mission to Lads and the Gordon Boys Home. Dedman states that Alexander Devine was the inspiration for the development of working-lads' clubs in the Manchester area as a preventive measure against juvenile crime. See M. J. Dedman, "Economic and Social Factors affecting the development of Youth Organisations for Civilian Boys in Britian 1880–1914" (Doctoral dissertation, University of London, 1985), 266.

8. *MCN*, 12 December 1891. The Recorder repeated these views when he chaired a meeting of the Gordon Boys' Home and Police Court Mission to Lads, where he also included "the better provision of places of recreation" as contributing to the decrease in crime. *MCN*, 13 June 1891. As regards the Recorder's comments on the effect of the Education Act, it is worth noting that attendance was not made compulsory until 1880.

9. *Industrial Schools Sub-Committee Minutes*, Vol. III. Quoted in M. Beetham, "Education and Social Welfare in late 19th Century Manchester, with special reference to the work of the Manchester School Board" (M.A. thesis, University of Manchester, 1974), 48.

10. A. Devine, *A "Brief" for the Boys: A Record of the Police Court Mission to Lads and the Gordon Boys Home* (Manchester, 1889); article by H. C. Devine, "How the Lads Live," *MCN* 1 April 1893. Devine wrote that "the authorities are

so pestered with complaints that they often lock up or summons members of a gang simply for standing together in the street."

11. For an extended discussion, see John Springhall, *Coming of Age: Adolescence in Britain 1860–1960* (Dublin, 1986), chap. 4.

12. Figures from M. Harrison, "Social Reform in Late Victorian and Edwardian Manchester with special reference to T. C. Horsfall" (Doctoral dissertation, University of Manchester, 1987), 332.

13. *The Boys Brigade* (January, 1902), Manchester Central Library Archives Department. The 1st Manchester Battalion Church Lads Brigade, founded in 1895, had similar aims and about 1,000 members by the end of the decade. See *Manchester Faces and Places*, Vol. 8 (Manchester, 1897).

14. Here, as elsewhere, the clubs were in the forefront of the movement for the provision of playing fields, buying or renting land for use as football and cricket grounds in advance of municipal provision, which also placed onerous restrictions on the activities allowed in its parks. As late as 1930, the Council voted to prohibit the playing of games in public parks on Sunday. *MCN*, 5 July 1930.

15. But see Andrew Davies on the maintenance of a vigorous street life among working-class youths up to the time of World War II. A. Davies, *Leisure, Gender and Poverty: Working Class Culture in Salford and Manchester 1900–1939* (Buckingham, 1992), 97, 170.

16. Beetham, "Education and Social Welfare," 54.

17. Employment of Children Act (1903). The Act regulated the age of employment and hours below and between which juvenile employment was illegal and permitted local authorities to make bylaws restricting street trading by children under sixteen.

18. A committee appointed by the Home Secretary in 1909 to see what further legislation was required with regard to juvenile street trading cited Manchester as the best example of what could be achieved under a regulatory system, as opposed to total prohibition, which the committee recommended. Public Record Office (hereafter PRO) H045 10630/200493/19, November 1910.

19. In its first year the subcommittee granted 2,845 licenses, cautioned 489 traders, revoked sixty-four licenses, and sent twenty cases to the magistrate's court. Licenses could be revoked if the licensee were convicted of an offense, used the license as a cloak for immorality or begging, or failed to notify the police of a change of address. The majority of juveniles brought before the subcommittee, however, were charged with failing to wear their badge or carry their license. *Manchester Watch Committee Minutes*, Street Trading Report, May 1903.

20. *Watch Committee Minutes*, 12 December 1901. The mayor stressed the independence of the Association from the Corporation, since it was to be entirely privately funded.

21. Charles Russell stated that newsboys could make from 10s to 14s a week, or even more, whereas a factory lad working for twelve hours a day might earn about 13/- a week. Interdepartmental Committee on the Employment of School Children. Special Report No. 22, *PP XXVI* (1902), 1001.

22. *PP XXVII* (1910), Q. 3046, Q. 3052.

23. Departmental Committee on Employment of School Children, *PP XXV* (1902), Q. 7896.

24. Ibid., Q. 7927–31.

25. Ibid., Q. 8070, Q. 8089.

26. "Fourth Report on the Work of the Children's Branch," Home Office Library (London 1928), 108. Data from "Persons proceeded against in juvenile courts 1913–1927." Reproduced in Bailey, "Delinquency and Citizenship."

27. See, for example, the spate of correspondence in the letter pages of the *Manchester Guardian* in 1891, and the *Manchester City News* campaign against police harrassment of juveniles for minor transgressions, that made "Criminals under Our Local Acts" (*MCN*, 31 May 1891).

28. *BGWS Annual Report* (1911).

29. Ibid. (1903). The report notes that in the previous year 141 children were handed over to the Society on remand.

30. See C. Leeson, *The Child and the War* (London, 1917), 37–45, on these points.

31. PRO, HO 45 10790/301145/6, and 10, 21 March, 11 April 1916.

32. "Juvenile Crime" by Spurley Hey, Director of Education. Paper read to the National Special Schools Union Conference held at Manchester, October 1916.

33. Spurley Hey, "Parental Neglect and Juvenile Crime," Education Office, Manchester, January 1919.

34. For example, the magistrates in the large towns were asked by the Home Office to ask probation officers to try to persuade lads coming before the court to join one of the local organizations, 31 May 1917. PRO, HO 45 10962B/349554.

35. See Victor Bailey, *Delinquency and Citizenship: Reclaiming the Young Offender 1914–1948* (Oxford, 1987), 11.

36. Letter from the Home Office to the War Office, 22 March 1919, PRO, HO 45 16515/375684/6.

37. *BGWS Annual Report*, 1923.

38. *MCN*, 30 September 1905.

39. Chief Constable Robert Peacock's address to the *Third International Congress for the Welfare and Protection of Children* (London, July 1902). Quoted in *MCN*, 19 July 1902.

"An El Dorado of Riches and a Place of Unpunished Crime": The Politics of Penal Reform in Hong Kong, 1877–1882

Kate Lowe

University of Birmingham

Eugene McLaughlin

The Open University, Milton Keynes

In every part of the world where his countrymen have settled an Englishman finds something special to be proud of. Whether the country be desert or densely peopled, whether the population be savage or civilized, the colonizing and governing instinct of the race is sure to prove equal to the occasion.

The Times, 30 August 1882

This chapter will focus on Hong Kong in the period of the controversial governorship of Sir John Pope Hennessy, 1877–82,[1] and will concern itself with the colonists' virulent reaction to his attempts to reform an extremely severe penal regime. Hennessy's "tampering" with the apparatus of law and order provoked one of the most serious moral panics in the history of the colony. In the editorial columns and letters pages of the colony's English-language newspapers[2] and in public debates, the colonists gave vent to their fears and racist beliefs about the Chinese. As a consequence of the clearly articulated differences between the governor and the colonists, the Colonial Office found itself embroiled in a highly charged and racially informed debate about whose interests should be represented and prioritized by the colonial administration. In order to understand the degree of conflict provoked by the reforms, it is first of all necessary to consider both the wider imperial setting and the more particular fractious histories of Hong Kong and Sir John Pope Hennessy.

In the course of the nineteenth century, Britain, more by default than design, acquired one of the most diverse and decentralized of the world's modern empires. As L. H. Gann and Peter Duigan note, there was no overall administrative center or uniform pattern of governance.[3] So, for example, protectorates such as British East and Central Africa initially came under the jurisdiction of the Foreign Office. Possessions such as Malta, Gibraltar, and Bermuda had governors appointed by the War Office. Sarawak was governed by a White Rajah, while the Indian subcontinent was administered by the Indian Civil Service. Self-governing colonies enjoyed full autonomy, whereas the colonial empire was a diverse group of colonies run by the Colonial Office.

One of the few common features of this empire was the potential for or actual racialized conflict between settler and native for, as Lord Roseberry noted, "What was Empire but the predominance of race."[4] The white settler's highly developed sense of racial superiority over subjugated native populations was accompanied by obsessive fears about native conspiracies and uprisings and corresponding moral panics. In the colonial "mind" there was a straightforward connection between native crime and conspiracy. As David Arnold has argued, "Serious crime was an implicit defiance of state authority and a possible prelude to rebellion."[5] In this context, extremely severe law-and-order policies were a common feature of imperial governance. In many parts of the empire any attempt by the home authorities, by enlightened governors, or by the more tolerant members of their communities to introduce liberal criminal justice reforms were viewed by settlers and colonists as fundamentally threatening to the fragile social and racial stability. Such fears and beliefs inevitably led to instances of overreaction to, and brutal suppression of, the natives. In 1865 in Jamaica, for example, the authorities' and settlers' response to what they perceived to be a black rebellion led to 350 executions, 600 floggings, and the burning of 1,000 dwellings.[6] The meaning and lessons of incidents such as the infamous Morant Bay Rebellion were also quickly absorbed into the racialized belief systems and folk memories of "vulnerable" colonial communities in other parts of the empire, such as Hong Kong.

The island was seized by the British in 1841, in the aftermath of the controversial First Opium War.[7] The form of government replicated that of other principal crown colonies.[8] A governor was normally appointed by the Colonial Office for a five-year period and was assisted in his rule by an Executive Council. He also presided over a Legislative Council comprised of official and unofficial community representatives who were nominated by the crown. Although governors of crown colonies were accountable to the Colonial Office rather than to the colonial community, the former encouraged governors to take account of local circumstances and to work with the Executive and Legislative councils in implementing policy circulars from the home government.

In Hong Kong this meant paying close attention to the wishes and interests of the powerful taipans, the men in control of the prominent merchant houses, most significantly "the princely hong" of Jardine, Matheson, and Co.[9] Thus, while the Colonial Office had the role of authorizing or vetoing a governor's actions, given the need to be sensitive to the wishes of colonial society, individual governors had considerable autonomy and latitude. In the short term, therefore, policy was effectively decided by the governor, not least because of the geographical distance involved.[10] If a conflict arose between a particular governor and the colonists, there was also a Colonial Office tendency to support the governor, particularly if the wider imperial interest was involved.[11] However, in the long term, time was on the side of the colonists, who normally managed, if necessary, to reverse the unwanted policies of unpopular governors. The other salient feature of government in Hong Kong was the lack of Chinese representation. Although both communities were mutually dependent on the China trade, liaison between them was minimal. Cultural difference were compounded by practical language difficulties and the colonists' belief in the racial inferiority of the Chinese. In 1858 Governor Bowring noted that "the separation of the native population from the European is nearly absolute; social intercourse between the races wholly unknown."[12] Three decades later a visiting journalist noticed among the colonists "a distinct abhorrence for the Chinese. They speak of them as if they were beasts."[13]

The political outcome of apartheid was that a numerically insignificant elite of colonists attempted to maintain control over and govern ever-increasing numbers of Chinese. This was achieved by a variety of indirect and direct means because British rule was initially founded on two bases: British law should be applied wherever possible, but Chinese social customs "were respected except where they conflicted with local ordinance."[14] Hence it was the numerous triad societies, neighborhood associations, district watch committees, guilds, and temples committees that provided the infrastructure of Chinese social order in the colony.

The formal criminal justice system operated on the premise that the Chinese, as a race, were impervious to forms of punishment used in Britain and that harsh measures had to be utilized in order to deter the Chinese criminal class. A manifestly deterrent penal regime was believed to be especially necessary because of the extreme barbarity of punishments meted out by the authorities in mainland China.[15] It was argued that if the Chinese criminal class was ever given the slightest impression that Hong Kong had a more lenient penal regime than that which operated on the mainland, every villain in South China would make for the colony. Allied to this, the European colonial communities along the south China coast, as in other parts of the Empire, also held that there was a conspiracy to drive them from China, and this conviction generated anxieties about increasing Chinese lawlessness and criminality. These beliefs generated demands for more repressive measures to regulate and control the native population.

THE HONG KONG CRIMINAL JUSTICE SYSTEM, 1841–1877

Capital punishment, public flogging, the cangue,[16] deportation, branding, cutting the "queue" (pigtail), and curfews, in the form of the "light and pass law,"[17] were the favored means of formally controlling the Chinese and were used in various combinations. These methods were viewed by the colonists as combining the virtues of maximum deterrence and minimum cost.

Such measures did not go unnoticed in England. The Colonial Office refused in 1845, to sanction an ordinance for the suppression of triad and other secret societies[18] because it permitted the authorities to brand criminals on the cheek.[19] In 1846 the question of excessive use of public flogging in Hong Kong was debated in the British parliament. This debate resulted from an incident on 25 April 1846, when 54 men were flogged, had their queues cut off, and were deported for being in the colony without registration tickets. During the debate it was reported that "the use of flogging was habitual in the Colony of Hong Kong... and the extent to which the lash was used was almost incredible. The Chinese, for the most trivial offenses, were publicly scourged."[20]

In 1847 a House of Commons Select Committee, appointed to inquire into the condition of the nation's commercial relations with China, took evidence on the treatment of the Hong Kong's Chinese population. One of the witnesses, Alexander Matheson, pointed to inequities, including excessive flogging, unrealistic fines and the cutting of queues. Matheson pointed out that for the Chinese the cutting of the queue was such a terrible punishment that it deterred respectable Chinese businessmen from coming to the colony.[21]

Because of the furor in England about the treatment of the Chinese, imprisonment was substituted for flogging. However, the colonists were vociferously opposed to incarceration as the principal form of punishment. They believed that for the Chinese imprisonment in itself was not punishment and that its use would in fact increase criminality and lawlessness because the "promise" of prison, that is, a guaranteed roof over one's head and regular meals, only acted as an incentive to the criminal masses of south China. For the colonists, a successful criminal justice policy was one which had as few prisons and as few prisoners as possible.

Consequently, in 1847 corporal punishment and deportation were reauthorized,[22] and recourse to public flogging became more pronounced in the ensuing decades. In 1865, after an increase in crime, further legislation was passed, "for the further security of the residents in this Colony from personal violence," prescribing flogging and solitary confinement, in addition to any other sentence, for those convicted of armed robbery and personal violence.[23] This ordinance was subsequently strengthened by substituting the cat-o'-nine-tails for the rattan.

In 1866 a new deportation and branding scheme was introduced by the governor, Sir Richard MacDonnell, with prisoners being released from prison and deported if they agreed to be branded "with a small broad arrow on the lobe of the left ear" to make an undetected return to the colony more difficult.[24] As a consequence, branded criminals who were found in the colony were jailed to complete their sentences and flogged. Such was the enthusiasm for this system of branding, deporting, and flogging that it was applied "also to hundreds of prisoners convicted of being suspicious characters, rogues and vagabonds."[25]

The Colonial Office protested that this form of punishment was illegal, on the grounds that it was "at variance with that part of the Royal Instructions which precludes Governors of this Colony from appending to any ordinance whereby persons not of European race are subjected to penalties or disabilities to which persons of the European race are not subjected."[26] However, the colonists made their feelings clear about which race should be flailed. When, in 1866, a European was sentenced to be publicly flogged, a section of the colonial community organized a petition on the grounds that such a flogging would have a more severe effect upon Europeans than upon natives. They also warned of the "disgrace that would attach to the European community by the public flogging of one of their members in the presence of the Chinese."[27] Although the protest failed, no more Europeans were publicly flogged in the colony. MacDonnell's system was discontinued in May 1870. By this time approximately 500 Chinese had been subjected to the flogging, branding, and deportation measures.

The next governor, Sir Arthur Kennedy, persisted with the colonists' preferred law-and-order measure. As a consequence of a renewed newspaper campaign to reintroduce more severe floggings, a new ordinance[28] consolidated the laws relating to deportation, conditional pardons, and the branding and punishment of offenders. In addition, branding was made more visible by imprinting a ring on the offender's neck.[29]

Victoria Prison

The colonists' determination to keep numbers at a minimum determined the nature of the regime in Victoria Prison.[30] There was no pretence of reform or rehabilitation: How could one reform "the heathen Chinese"? Instead hard labor, meager rations, and flogging were the mainstay of the regime. The only classifications were between European and Chinese prisoners and men and women. Concern was expressed intermittently about the conditions in Victoria Prison. In April 1855, for example, Mr. Hillier, the Chief Magistrate reported:

There are no less than one hundred and three prisoners confined in one room. Their crimes vary from the most trivial misdemeanours to some of the most atrocious nature.... Just before and after hours of work, and during the whole of Sunday they are locked up together in this one room, or are restricted to that and the adjoining yard without separation or supervision.[31]

In the aftermath of the controversial death of a prisoner in 1860,[32] there were moves to ease the overcrowding; Victoria prison was partially reconstructed in 1862 and a new prison opened on Stonecutters' Island, in Hong Kong harbor, in 1864. However, there were bitter complaints from leading colonists about the cost and the detrimental effects the changes would have on the colony's crime rates. Despite Colonial Office objections, the new prison was closed in 1874 and more extreme disciplinary measures were resorted to in order to cut the prison population.

It was widely believed that the stern measures introduced by MacDonnell and Kennedy were directly responsible for the decreases in crime reported in annual police reports from 1872 to 1875. In 1877 the Chief Justice was able to state that in the previous ten years crime in Hong Kong had been brought under control. As an editorial in the *Daily Press* noted when appraising Kennedy's governorship:

In 1872 the public safety was far from well assured. Robberies were rife, and European residents could not walk on the less frequented roads after dusk with security. That has all changed now. Not only do we enjoy immunity from "knocking down" but serious crime of all sorts has been increasingly decreased.[33]

The feelings of increased security were dramatically undermined when it was announced that a new governor would take office in April 1877.

SIR JOHN POPE HENNESSY

Sir John Pope Hennessy, an Irish Catholic nationalist, was one of the most controversial figures in the British colonial service. Much of the controversy centered on his "native-race craze," arising from his pursuance of a policy of racial equality wherever he was governor.[34] Even after he had retired from colonial service, Hennessy continued to promote in a controversial and highly public manner the interests of those subjected to British imperial rule.[35] After Hennessy's death in 1891, the *Melbourne Leader* wrote a piece on "the stormy petrel of the Colonial Office" in which it condemned his reckless enthusiasm for "stirring up the natives":

If a man had a black or a copper-coloured skin, it was a foregone conclusion with Sir John that that man was oppressed by some other man who had a white one. The black man might not of himself be able to discover that he had a grievance against anybody. But Sir John knew better. If he did not find one ready made to his hands he manufactured one, set it before the black man's eyes and told him to look at it, turned it over and explained it, and that so persistently that at last the black man himself believed in it, and wondered how it was that that he had not discovered the enormity before.[36]

Prior to his colonial career, the new governor had taken an active interest in British criminal justice matters. During his time as the first Irish-nationalist

Conservative M.P. (1859–1865) there was renewed discussion about penal matters. This was the time of the final move toward a prison-centered penal system. The death penalty was used more sparingly, and corporal punishment was considerably curtailed as a judicial penalty for adults. As David Garland has argued, "The generalised restriction of these punishments of the body was paralleled by an increasing reliance upon incarceration as the central mode of sanctioning."[37]

Hennessy would have been familiar with the main debates and proposed reforms of the Lord Carnarvon's committee on the state of prison discipline, which resulted in the 1865 Prison Act.[38] Its stress on the primacy of deterrence and retribution marked a significant shift away from the reformative ideal. Separate confinement, hard labor, discipline, and obedience were to be the foundation stones of this much more punitive penal regime. Because the committee was also concerned about the lack of uniformity in the prison system, it recommended statutory rules and regulations in order to promote equity, efficiency, and economy. Hennessy, a friend of Henry Herbert, Earl of Carnarvon, would have agreed with the committee's ideas concerning separate confinement and the need for strict adherence to statutory rules. But he would have disagreed with the emphasis on punishment rather than reform because he was an enthusiastic advocate of the Irish or progressive model, with its stress on reform and rehabilitation.[39]

As a member of the British parliament Hennessy had argued for the total abolition of flogging during the debates surrounding the second reading of the Whipping Bill in February 1862.[40] Hennessy believed that the prison should be the instrument of punishment and repeatedly made reference to the superiority of the Irish penal system and advanced it as a model for prison reform elsewhere.

Hennessy also championed the interests of Catholic (and almost by definition Irish) prisoners and focused attention on the discriminatory practices that they had to endure. He campaigned successfully for money to be made available to allow for the religious instruction of Catholic convicts.[41] In May 1862 he brought in the Roman Catholic Prisoners' Bill to make it legal for prisoners of this faith to assemble for religious worship within prisons. The Prison Ministers' Act became law in 1862. He also remonstrated with the government over its treatment of Fenian prisoners sentenced in 1865. Hennessy complained that the British government had departed from the internationally recognized policy of treating political prisoners in a manner different from that used with ordinary criminals. He documented how Fenian prisoners were being made to wear standard prison garb and subjected to precisely the same forms of discipline as common English felons.[42] He was particularly angered by the consequences of this criminalization process for one of his fellow countrymen, John Lynch, who did not survive the first six months of separate confinement.[43]

When he entered the colonial service in 1867, Hennessy carried his ideas concerning criminal justice to the colonies under his jurisdiction. He closely monitored the prison regimes and was proud of the fact that while he was governor of Labuan, the West African Settlements, the Windward Islands, and the Bahamas, no floggings took place. To the consternation of the prison authorities everywhere he was in the habit of regularly visiting prisons, talking to prisoners, and actively intervening to end any malpractice that he found. His willingness to intervene in individual cases and to recognize prisoners as human beings stood in stark contrast to the beliefs and practices of the vast majority of other colonial governors and officials.[44]

As governor of Barbados, for example, he informed the Colonial Office that he thought the savagery of the floggings in the island's prison were "cruel and pernicious" and a "grave scandal," which "showed that in Barbados... some of the worst practices of the days of slavery still prevailed."[45] He also ordered the release on tickets-of-leave of thirty-nine prisoners of good conduct who had served more than two-thirds of their sentences. He personally witnessed their release, giving each of them a suit and a sum of money for a fresh start. These actions caused an unprecedented outcry from the plantation owners. However, when Hennessy addressed the Legislature in March 1876 he reiterated that it was his duty to look after the masses who were living in "intense and hopeless poverty," arguing that the solution to crime and disorder lay in providing regular employment, fair wages, lighter taxation for the poor, and better education.

In the aftermath of the Federation Riots,[46] which broke out in April 1876, the planter class blamed Hennessy for the breakdown of law and order, complaining to the Colonial Office that they had witnessed:

the strange and unprecedented spectacle of a large class of the population in a British colony turning out in immense gangs to plunder and riot believing that they had the sanction and were fulfilling the wishes of the representative of the Queen.[47]

Though he did order the suppression of the riots, Hennessy rejected planter demands for the imposition of martial law, summary shootings, and floggings and ensured through the appointment of a Special Commission that an independent judge was appointed to conduct the post-riot trials. Hennessy made sure that there was no repeat of the aftermath of the Morant Bay Rebellion. Given the nature of the relationship between the governor and the plantation owners in Barbados, it is not surprising that the latter demanded his removal. Although the Colonial Office did not accede to the colonists' wishes, a year later he was appointed governor of Hong Kong.

Prior to his taking up the post, he was asked by Lord Carnarvon, who became the Tory Secretary of State for the Colonies in 1874, as a matter of urgency, to deal with the report of a committee that had been appointed in Hong Kong in October 1875 to consider the subject of improving discipline in Victoria Prison. This instruction ensured Hennessy's early scrutiny of the operation of the criminal justice system in Hong Kong. It also ensured, given his background and beliefs and the colonists' views on law and order matters, that a clash between them would occur.

THE HONG KONG PRISON COMMITTEE REPORT

In its final report, the committee reiterated certain taken-for-granted truths about penal policy in Hong Kong. It stated that the primary objective of punishment was deterrence and that every other objective, for example, reform and self-sufficient prisons, should be subordinate to this aim. Reform was rejected because "any knowledge, any attempt to cultivate their higher faculties and to improve their moral condition seems hopeless."[48] Consequently, the committee recommended that "the only recourse is to make the life of . . . Chinese prisoners, especially, as distasteful as it can possibly be made."[49]

Disciplinary procedures of the prison were to be tightened up in two areas: the diet of the prisoners and the punishments to which they should be subjected. The dietary needs of the prisoners were of primary concern, and across-the-board dietary reductions were implemented because

Chinese prisoners on long sentences have been fed on a scale of diet which must be a positive inducement to the majority of them to return to the gaol, so superior is it, both in quantity and quality, to the fare which the free laborer earning honest wages can command.[50]

In addition, it was argued that there was no justification for giving women prisoners the same amount of food as men.

The committee also supported the introduction of the treadwheel and a policy of making the prisoners undertake the tasks they most disliked. It rejected any return to useful labor. Although the issue of the introduction of the silent system was not addressed, it suggested that more solitary cells should be turned into dark cells. The committee did, in a more benevolent vein, recommend the introduction of limitations to the time period that prisoners could be kept in irons and chains and stated that prisoners should be allowed to begin to grow their queues before leaving the prison. It also stated that the superintendent's powers of punishment for breaches of prison discipline should be curbed.

The administration prevaricated in its response to the report. The reductions in diet were implemented, as was the recommendation that prisoners on a penal diet should be made to do hard labor. In addition, Chinese prisoners were made to undertake more arduous tasks. However, there was a refusal to countenance the recommendations that restricted the powers of the prison superintendent or curbed punishments.[51] Because of the prevarication, Hennessy was instructed by Lord Carnarvon to "review the

whole question of Prison Discipline in Hong Kong; and to make such proposals as will place the system upon a sound basis for the future."[52]

Carnarvon also forwarded his amendments to the committee's recommendations. He did not object to any of the proposals concerning prison
labor. However, it was pointed out that the power of the prison superintendent to put prisoners in irons was "wholly illegal" and that the cutting
of queues was at variance with a despatch that had been sent to Hong Kong
in 1876. He also expressed considerable concern about the proposed reductions in diet. Carnarvon stressed to Hennessy that he wanted the introduction of the separate system as it was "the only true basis of prison
discipline, and among Chinese prisoners there are special reasons for its
adoption."[53] The special reasons were that few of the warders knew Chinese
and that an escape attempt and riot in a Singapore prison in 1877 had
indicated to the Colonial Office the dangers of affording "inscrutible" Chinese prisoners the opportunity to combine. The new governor was instructed
to have the surveyor general draw up plans for the conversion of Victoria
Prison to the separate system.

Therefore, Hennessy's mandated task was to implement the recommendations of the prison committee while paying due attention to Carnarvon's
amendments and suggestions. However, in order to get to the heart of the
matter he decided, in his own inimitable way, to conduct his own investigations into the colony's criminal justice system.

PROPOSALS FOR REFORM

During 1877 and 1878 the new governor publicly denounced the "light and
pass" laws as "a monsterous piece of class [race] legislation" and unveiled
the most wide-ranging and controversial penal reforms that the colony had
ever seen, stating that if these proposals "are open to the imputation of
being humane, that is no reason for being ashamed of such measures."[54]

The Aims of Imprisonment

In September 1876 Hennessy's predecessor had warned the Colonial Office
that the police statistics for the year would show an increase in crime and
that the reason was the cheap-fares policy adopted by ferries coming from
mainland China, thus allowing Canton's criminals to swamp Hong Kong.
Hennessy reanalyzed these statistics and found that the crime rate had been
rising steadily since 1874. He declared that the increases in crime were
nothing to do with the cheap-fares policy but were directly attributable to
the manner in which the prison system was administered. He went on to
argue that the significant increase in prison offenses—to 426 in 1874, 1085
in 1875, and 2726 in 1876—was "*prima facie* evidence of prison disor-
ganization." Hennessy concluded by stating:

I venture to assert that such an amount of crime, and such an extraordinary growth of prison offenses as you have recorded in this Colony in preceding years, is without precedent in any part of the British Empire with a population of only 140,000.[55]

He argued that deterrence and reform were the governing principles of sound prison discipline and that Hong Kong had erronously rejected the possibilities of reforming Chinese prisoners:

Where there is such a total absence of reformatory training, and where you avow it is hopeless to improve the moral condition of the Chinese prisoners, and where you have a set of turnkeys who cannot speak their language, you cannot expect a decrease in crime.[56]

He also proclaimed his intention of reintroducing useful labor that, in addition to providing valuable revenue for the prison, would allow the prisoners to earn money that would be given to them on their release from prison, thus equipping them with the means to start a new life. To this end he advertised for a Chinese trade/manufacturing instructor who could train the prisoners in cloth weaving, tailoring, shoemaking, and carpentry. Ever concerned about the possibilities of rehabilitation, he also announced the setting up of a Discharged Prisoners Aid Association, consisting of representatives of the prison, the police, the government, and the Chinese community. This association, which had the objective of rehabilitating prisoners upon their release by providing them with housing and employment, met for the first time on 27 August 1877.[57]

Flogging

Hennessy condemned the flogging laws on the grounds that they were inhumane, ineffective, and in many instances illegal. He pointed out that Ordinance No. 12 of 1865 was supposed to be strictly confined to crimes that by their violence or atrocity disclosed a brutal or intractable nature. However, this principle was not being adhered to, and flogging was not being used as a punishment of last resort. As a consequence, between 1871 and July 1876 there had been 1,149 floggings in Hong Kong, with a population of 140,000, whereas there had been 4,988 floggings in England, with a population of twenty-four million: "There seemed to be an excessive use of the lash in this Colony. As far as I am aware there is no code of laws in any part of Her Majesty's Empire in which the power of flogging is so excessively given to Magistrates and Judges as in Hong Kong."[58] He also criticized the public ritual surrounding floggings in the colony:

the ostentatious marching of the prisoners half naked through the crowded streets and the public exhibition of an English turnkey flogging with a vigorous arm the speedily bleeding body of a Chinaman, tied to the whipping post, is not calculated to do much good to the groups of neglected little children who flock to see it, and to the great majority of whom this spectacle is the only lesson they receive from the civilized Government under which they have been born.[59]

Hennessy's views on flogging were reinforced by his visit to Victoria prison. Shortly after his arrival two criminals were sentenced to, as part of their sentence, three public floggings of twenty-five lashes. Hennessy visited the prison for the first time on 19 May 1877 and reported:

On entering the hospital two attenuated patients, apparently very weak, grovelled at my feet and cried. On sending for an interpretor I found they were the men who had been flogged on the 10th of May. They complained that their flesh had been torn so much that the wounds would not heal and they could not sleep.[60]

On closer inspection it was found that the prisoners had multiple wounds that were still bleeding from the first flogging. Ten days later when Hennessy revisited the prison and "saw blood still flowing from the torn backs of those prisoners," he expressed consternation about the possibility of their being flogged on two more occasions and also began to inquire into why they were so physically weak. He found the cause to lie in the changes to the diet implemented before his arrival. Prisoners were now only on rice and water, chutney having been removed from the Chinese diet. The result was, according to the Colonial Surgeon, a great increase in colic, diarrhea, and dyspepsia.[61] The two prisoners in question had also been subjected to hard labor. As a consequence of his investigations Hennessy suspended the second and third floggings of the two prisoners.

Hennessy also took up the case of Wong A Kwai. During his visit to the prison, this prisoner complained about the severity of the punishment to which he had been subjected. In a subsequent report, the Colonial Surgeon, Dr. Ayres, stated that the prisoner was suffering from an incurable pulmonary disease, that he frequently suffered from hemorrhage of the lungs, and that this was owing to the manner in which he had been flogged:

I have noticed that in all floggings of Chinese by the cat, that they suffer, besides the external injury of the skin, more or less from congestion of the lungs afterwards, and in old cases, where the floggings have been severe, irreparable damage has been done.[62]

Dr. Ayres pointed out that in India flogging was always performed on the breech and that it had none of the injurious effects of the cat. He also argued that the "scars of the cat" effectively branded prisoners, thus making it difficult for them to lead an ordinary life after their release from prison.

As a result Hennessy suspended floggings of the Chinese on the back and substituted flogging with the rattan, as suggested by the colonial surgeon. The governor's views on the pernicious effects of flogging were lent support when another prisoner, Mok A Kwai, died of phthisis on 28 September 1877. He found out that this prisoner had been illegally flogged four times and also subjected to other illegal punishments. This death had such an effect upon the governor that he ordered the release of Wong a kwai because, as a result of his maltreatment in the penal system, he was terminally ill and Hennessy argued that "he should be allowed to die among his friends."[63] In April 1878, Hennessy set up a committee to look into the medical effects of flogging the Chinese.

Branding and Deportation

The governor condemned the branding and deportation ordinance as a "penal enactment of exceptional severity, directed against one race in the colony only, the Chinese, and avowedly based on the allegation that the Chinese population was a very criminal population."[64] He noted, for example, that the petition signed by the Chinese prisoners agreeing to the conditions of this ordinance was in English and that they therefore did not understand its provisions. In addition, the majority of those deported were the elderly and destitute caught begging in the streets, and Hennessy thought it was a scandal that those who had worked all their lives in the colony were forced to beg because no provision had been made for them when they became elderly. He stated to Lord Carnarvon: "It is with pain and reluctance I allow the magistrate to enforce in such cases the law of deportation."[65]

Instead of rubber-stamping the deportation orders, Hennessy personally examined every case and, unless there was overwhelming evidence that the individual was a "person dangerous to the peace and good order" of the colony, he refused to sign the order. The Attorney General was also asked to scrutinize the orders to ascertain whether they were valid or not. If they were not the prisoner was released immediately. Hennessy was able to act on the deportation ordinance when, in July 1877, the Lord Chief Justice noticed that there was an inconsistency in the dating of a set of papers, thus rendering the deportation order illegal. As a consequence, the prisoner was set free and all the deportation orders issued during the previous five years were declared invalid.[66]

Hennessy argued that the ordinance also made a mockery of the two-thirds remission for good behavior rule because it was being applied to prisoners irrespective of sentence, behavior, or the degree of seriousness of the offense. As far as he was concerned, the policy of repeated short sentences on old offenders created and cultivated a criminal class. Under the new regime, prisoners would serve two-thirds of their sentences and their release would be dependent on steady good conduct. The magistrates were also instructed to commit for trial every case of larceny in which there was a previous conviction. Hennessy's objective in having these cases sent to the

Supreme Court was to obtain the infliction of longer terms of sentence than could have been inflicted by the magistrates. He also introduced an amendment to Ordinance No. 4, 1868, so that breaches of prison discipline were punished by an extension to the length of the sentence rather than by flogging.[67]

Prison conditions

Hennessy noticed that European prisoners received better treatment than the Chinese prisoners, particularly with regard to their prison accommodation. Up to seven Chinese prisoners shared a cell, whereas European prisoners had single cells. He also criticized the prison superintendent for abusing his disciplinary powers and claimed that this had resulted in prison indiscipline because the prisoners were aware that they were being unfairly punished. Consequently, he issued orders that the prison regulations should be strictly adhered to, that the police magistrate should take his prison discipline responsibilities more seriously, and that notes should be made for each case of a breach of prison discipline. Two senior European prison officers were appointed by Hennessy to help implement his proposals. On his orders four turnkeys were fired for drunkenness and physically abusing the prisoners. He then took the unprecedented step of hiring two Chinese warders because they spoke Chinese and therefore could communicate effectively with the prisoners. He also believed that they were more likely to be fair and honest.[68]

The governor viewed the introduction of the separate system as the cornerstone of an effective penal regime:

If we have a gaol on the separate system, where the prisoners must do some useful hard work, and where they know there is not the slightest chance of their release before the end of the Judge's sentence except by steady good conduct, if we provide reformatory and industrial training for juvenile criminals, and if we let it be clearly understood that second offenses will be punished with a long sentence, that I think will do more to check the growth of crime than anything else we can devise.[69]

In order to transform the prison to the separate system, five hundred separate cells would be constructed, juveniles removed to industrial and reformatory schools, females relocated in a different establishment (because there was no need for them to be in separate cells), and the mentally ill[70] in an asylum. This necessitated either the radical restructuring of the existing prison or building a new one either on Hong Kong island or on Stonecutters' Island. Hennessy, in an attempt to assuage the financial concerns of the colonists, argued that the total cost of this conversion could be kept down if the Colonial Office accepted his proposal to turn Labuan into a convict colony for Hong Kong's long-term prisoners.

Discriminatory Legal Practices

Hennessy also made it clear that he would use his executive powers as governor to reverse unjust decisions. He commuted the death sentence in the case of Cheung A Shin, who committed a murder in May 1877. This was the first death warrant that Hennessy had to sign, and he refused to do so because he was unhappy about the manner in which the trial had been conducted. He pointed out that in a trial of two Europeans for murder in 1877 the court correctly assigned both counsel and attorney for the defense and allowed ample time for the solicitors to prepare the defense case. Hennessy argued that there were two particular reasons why this practice should be followed as normal practice in Hong Kong. First, Chinese prisoners were unacquainted with the practice and procedure of English courts. Second, the judge and jury did not speak Chinese, placing Chinese prisoners at a considerable disadvantage. The governor pointed out that this procedure had not been adhered to in the trial of Cheung A Shin but that it would be in all future murder trials.[71] Hennessy's critical gaze upon the discriminatory operation of the colony's legal system strengthened his resolve to appoint a Chinese magistrate. This he did in 1880 when Ng Choy, who under his patronage also became the first Chinese member of the Legislative Council, was appointed to the Bench.

THE RESPONSE TO HENNESSY'S PROPOSALS

The Newspapers

Hennessy's criticisms of criminal justice in Hong Kong and his proposed reforms triggered an intense public debate in the colony's English language newspapers, the *China Mail* and *Daily Press*. As far as they were concerned, Governor Kennedy's consolidation measures constituted a "final settlement" of penal matters in the colony, and they mounted a concerted campaign against Hennessy's "unwanted" proposals.

Both newspapers questioned Hennessy's interpretation of what the criminal statistics actually meant. The *China Mail* of 18 September 1877 challenged the governor to make clear whether the statistics took account of changes in the manner in which police returns were prepared and the impact of the many new laws that had been passed in the 1870s under the governorships of MacDonnell and Kennedy. The *Daily Press* of 20 September 1877 argued that an adequate interpretation of the statistics had to take into account the fact that the colony's population was much bigger than in the late 1860s and so, proportionately, was the criminal class, that much of the crime was of a petty nature and that the police were much more efficient than previously. Both argued that, despite Hennessy's attempts to argue otherwise, the colony was, prior to his arrival, a much more secure place than previously; and they warned him not to tamper with the policies that had resulted in this level of improvement.

Therefore, the newspapers were outraged by Hennessy's statements on flogging and the need for prison reform. Both argued that the nature of the Chinese race necessitated harsh measures and that reformation was not possible:

There are poor but honest Chinese, though doubtless they are rarer than among Europeans, owing to their poverty and paganism. The dreary superstition which passes among them for religion exercises no elevating or purifying influence on their minds; it neither imparts joy in life nor sheds a gleam of hope upon the grave. The fear of detection and consequent punishment alone operates as deterrent to evil; to abstain from crime through a sense of duty seldom occurs to them.[72]

The Chinaman is not a man to be caressed. He has never been used to it and does not understand it. Those who are best acquainted with the characteristics of the Chinese criminal class have no manner of doubt that a namby-pamby system of dealing with them would result in their encouragement to even greater acts of rascality.[73]

The *Daily Press* was not opposed to suggestions that flogging should take place in private and be inflicted on the breech rather than the back or that the rattan rather than the cat be used as the instrument of punishment. But it viewed the retention of flogging as essential to the security of the colony. The *China Mail*, by contrast, deemed public flogging with the cat on the back as being the preferred way of dealing with "semi-civilized and noto-riously crafty rascals":

Public whipping with the cat may be brutalizing to cultured foreigners; but are we not now considering the effect it ought to have upon uncultured, unscrupulous and often cruel criminals.[74]

Deterrence would not be achieved if the floggings were carried out in private. Both newspapers warned their readers that if flogging were done away with there would be an unprecedented crime wave.

This support for flogging also determined the newspapers' views on the governor's prison reform program. They argued that any move toward incarceration as the major form of punishment would be interpreted as leniency by the Chinese criminal class:

Instead of maintaining hardened and brutal criminals for long terms of years at the expense of honest and respectable people, we would substitute more frequently than is done at present the lash for imprisonment, believing that the results would not only be advantageous to the community generally, but to the offenders themselves.[75]

Concern was also expressed about the costs to the taxpayer of embarking on an unneccessary building program to implement the separate system. It was argued that this level of "luxury" accommodation combined with the relaxation in punishments would, instead of rendering the prison "a place of dread for evil doers," in fact attract "the two to three millions of scoundrels floating about Canton and the southern provinces of China."[76]

The Crime Wave

The newspapers assiduously reported every incident that they believed demonstrated that law and order was breaking down as a result of Hennessy's policies. Burglars and pickpockets were growing more bold and beggars, coolies, and hawkers were on every pavement. In April 1878 the newspapers' worst fears were confirmed when the 1877 crime statistics were released. Serious crimes had increased in number from 1,485 to 1,966, and minor crimes had increased from 5,061 to 5,422. The report was "the most unsatisfactory of the kind that has ever been presented to the Hong Kong community."[77] The papers held the governor personally responsible and attacked Mr. Creagh, the head of the police, for his complacent attitude towards the figures, that is, for his statement that the majority of crimes were minor and that famine and flood on the mainland and the high price of rice explained the increase. On 24 July 1878, after another spate of "daring" robberies on European households, the China Mail proclaimed, "We are now suffering an interregnum of insecurity and anxiety which can be equalled only by that of 10 years ago."

The breaking point came in September 1878 after an armed gang of between eighty and one hundred Chinese criminals had attacked a goldsmith's shop in central Hong Kong, injuring six police officers and successfully escaping by boat. This was "one of the most daring attacks which had ever taken place in the colony," and the newspapers argued that Britain's honor had been sullied: "The colony has been invaded and plundered... not by a respectable army of Russians, but by half a hundred of wretched, rascally Chinese."[78]

This incident heightened the state of alarm among the colonists. The governor was warned that if stern measures were not taken there would be a stampede of European residents from Hong Kong. The governor responded by setting up an internal investigation into the policing of the colony. However, the newspapers demanded that the Colonial Office set up an independent inquiry into Hennessy's reforms, while the leading colonists called a public meeting to consider "the existing state of insecurity of life and property in the Colony."

The "Community"

The panic over the increases in crime once more revealed the deeper fears of the colonists, that Hennessy's policies would upset the delicate balance of race relations in Hong Kong. Concerns about the increase in crimes against and harassment of the Europeans were joined by fears that the Chinese were increasingly encroaching into the respectable European areas of the city, thus leading to "contagion"[79] and a breakdown in the racial ordering of the colony's residential areas:

It is not desired that the "Heathen Chinese" be prevented from extolling his wares among his own countrymen in the native parts of town, but surely his unintelligible screechings may be suppressed in those portions of the Colony devoted to foreign hongs and residences.[80]

This complaint echoed more general anxieties that China was constantly attempting to encroach upon the British colony. Such fears had heightened since 1867, when the neighboring Chinese authorities set up a customs blockade around the colony in an attempt to combat smuggling.[81] And of course there was the constant concern that the Chinese were awaiting an opportunity to drive the colonists out of Hong Kong, and indeed out of China. As the *China Mail* argued, "Johnnie Chinaman":

like all subjected or inferior races is inclined to bear much insult and possibly injury patiently, but piratical records, if no others, show that only circumstances are required to make "the celestial" as daring and bloodthirsty a rascal as ever cut throats for a living.[82]

The colonists' wider fears found substance in the fact that the commercial balance between the races was visibly changing during this time period. In the late 1870s and early 1880s the colony was becoming a much more complex social formation. Chinese merchants had begun to overtake their European counterparts in terms of wealth and constituted the largest body of ratepayers. The opportunities provided by the free port of Hong Kong was also producing an ever-expanding stratified Chinese middle class made up of landlords, contractors, and compradores.[83]

It was this shift that led Hennessy to conclude, after consultations with leading members of the Chinese community, that it was imperative for the government to recognize the rights of the Chinese in what he realistically, if controversially, described as an Anglo-Chinese colony.[84] Thus, in addition to his proposed penal reforms, Hennessy unveiled proposals for providing more government support for Chinese cultural and welfare bodies, allowing the Chinese to buy property in the main European thoroughfare, opening junior government posts to Chinese candidates, recognizing the Chinese language in government communications, and appointing the first Chinese representative to the Legislative Council. However, the imperative for the colonists was for Government House to hold the line against the ever-encroaching Chinese by prioritizing the rights of the Europeans in this most

British of colonies. The last thing the representative of Her Majesty's government should be doing was effecting a "revolution" in the "mode of governing the native population"[85] by encouraging the Chinese, of any class, to think that they had equal rights to the colonists.[86]

This chasm in understanding about whose interests the Government House should be representing manifested itself during the biggest public meeting ever held in the colony, which took place on 7 October 1878. Much to the consternation of the European colonists, large numbers of the Chinese business community chose to attend to make their feelings known on the crisis in law and order. This was the first time the Chinese had ever attempted to attend a public meeting in the history of the colony. Although it is not clear that the Chinese business class would have had any more sympathy for criminals than their European counterparts, many of the colonists were psychologically incapable of differentiating, in any meaningful sense, between respectable and nonrespectable Chinese. Consequently, the Europeans changed the venue of the meeting and would not allow the discussion to be translated. Unable to participate, the Chinese withdrew in protest. Subsequently, the leading representatives of the European mercantile community passed a series of resolutions stating that the head of the Executive had been found "wanting in that firmness which we expect a Governor to exercise in the repression of crime."[87] Under Hennessy, it was argued, a multitude of criminals had been attracted to Hong Kong because of their belief that the colony was "an El Dorado of riches and a place of unpunished crime." The only way to deter the latter, according to the meeting, was not by restructuring the penal system or building a new prison but by restoring public flogging, branding, and deportation:

The first duty of a foreign minor population placed in the midst of a major and enormously preponderating native population, is not the reformation of the Chinese criminal, but the protection of life and property which is the inherent right of every one of God's creatures.[88]

The colonists complained that their views were not being represented by the present governor and requested that a watch committee, with substantial powers for supervising the policing of the colony, be formed, consisting of the three unofficial members of the Legislative Council and representatives of the merchant community. They also demanded that the home government set up an independent commission to inquire into Hennessy's administration. These resolutions were forwarded to the Colonial Office.

As a result of the meeting, a wider discussion about whose interests should be represented in government policies moved to the forefront of public debate in the colony. In the immediate aftermath, representatives of the Chinese community wrote a letter to the *China Mail* complaining about how they had been treated and stating that the view presented at the meeting was not representative of the Chinese. A handbill was subsequently distributed in Chinese neighborhoods supporting Hennessy's policies, complaining that the Chinese had been treated unfairly at the meeting and that they were being unjustly blamed for the increase in crime in the colony. A petition signed by over 2,000 Chinese business people was forwarded to Queen Victoria on 28 October 1878. This was the largest official Chinese petition ever presented to the British government. It praised the governor for his fairness in dealing with the Chinese and his proposed reform of the penal system. The petitioners also claimed that the increase in crime had been used by the colonists as a pretext to attack the Chinese and Hennessy's governorship. They made it clear that no other governor had garnered so much support among the Chinese community and stated that he must be allowed to remain in Hong Kong.[89]

The *China Mail* argued that Hong Kong could not possibly entertain a situation where the Chinese were allowed equal voice with the Europeans because of the numerical factor:

The majority of Chinese residents in this colony are incapable of judging on the policy of a government conducted on the principles of Western nations, and when the question of the good or bad administration of this, a British colony, is in question, they may very well leave the matter to be decided by the foreign residents.[90]

It was also suggested that Hennessy had attempted to use the Chinese to "pack" the meeting.

At the next Legislative Council meetings in November 1878, William Keswick, the head of Jardine, Matheson and Co., attacked the governor for refusing to recognize Hong Kong's unique position when deciding upon policy reforms:

We should not forget, and I think it is an important matter which should be invariably insisted upon in correspondence with England, that this colony is not as it were part of the territory of Great Britain. It is not an island in Mid-Ocean where the criminal class could be dealt within our own borders but it is an island small enough to be termed a rock, within a stone's throw of Kwangtung, a province which of all others is noted for the turbulence of its inhabitants.[91]

Keswick argued that conditions in Hong Kong prison acted as a positive incentive for the Chinese to come to Hong Kong and engage in criminal acts. Thus he opposed all plans to reform and restructure the prison system.

The moral panic carried through into 1879, because on 17 January there was another raid by a large number of bandits on a Chinese settlement in Kowloon. As E. J. Eitel noted, "The general sense of insecurity was such that a rumour spread among the Chinese and gained credence that preparations were being made by a fleet of pirates to descend upon Hong Kong and to sack the whole town."[92] The panic was fuelled by the publication of the criminal statistics for 1878, which showed a 32.31 percent increase in serious crimes (on top of the 12.86 percent increase of the previous year).

The anger about the crime wave continued to spill over into the more general concern about Hennessy's seeming refusal to respond to the fears and wishes of the colonists. Hennessy stood accused of censoring the information that was reaching the Colonial Office and misrepresenting the Colonial Office's views to the Chinese. As such, the governor was blamed for discovering "that antagonism of conflicting interests, of the existence of which we were in happy unconsciousness, and out of which he seems so eager to attempt the manufacture of political capital."[93]

The colonists' worse fears were confirmed when the Chinese petition was published in English in the *Government Gazette*. They addressed an angry letter to Government House asking why their petition had not been acknowledged:

It is hardly necessary to remind you of the thoroughly representative character of the meeting, including, as it did among its supporters, not only the great majority of the unofficial portion of her majesty's subjects in the colony, but also the leading members of the other foreign communities.[94]

This was compared with the memorial signed by:

a few respectable Chinese and many hundreds of the lower classes of the native population, of whom it may safely be said that they were utterly ignorant of the nature of the document to which they appended their signatures.[95]

Therefore, the colonists looked to the Colonial Office for a favorable response to their petition.

The Colonial Office

Hennessy, from the outset, had kept the Colonial Office informed about the nature of his proposed reforms. However, although he had Colonial Office authorization to implement prison reform, the "rash" manner in which the governor tackled the issue confirmed the worst fears of colonial office officials. Realizing Hennessy's capacity for upsetting the delicate racial status quo in Hong Kong, Sir Robert Herbert, permanent Under Secretary of State for the Colonies, noted:

We must watch all his proceedings very narrowly ... and when we see any tendency to bolt to the right or to the left of established procedure in Hong Kong (which is an intricate one surrounded with special dangers arising from the Chinese character which he does not understand) he should be firmly and as gently as possible led back to it.[96]

Consequently, Lord Carnarvon warned the governor that before implementing any reforms he should take into account the unique circumstances of Hong Kong:

Neither the power of deportation, as the order of banishment is usually called, nor the sentence of flogging for crimes of violence are penalties which in ordinary cases or for criminal offenses are in themselves desirable, but the circumstances of Hong Kong are peculiar and they, as well as the law for carrying lights and papers at night, have been found necessary to secure the general peace of the colony and the security of the inhabitants, who in former years were compelled to wear arms in self-defense, and having regard to what I have said about the peculiar situation of Hong Kong, and to the Chinese character and habits of violence, you will find it necessary to exercise great caution in advising any relaxation of these exceptional but hitherto necessary laws.[97]

Hennessy was subsequently informed that the Colonial Office was not prepared to accept all of his proposals or to sanction alterations to a system that had been generally effective in securing the public peace and personal security. Carnarvon said that, although he wished to abolish all punishments that were brutalizing and injurious to the health of prisoners, because of the Chinese character and the severity of the neighboring Chinese penal system he was not prepared to sanction any reform that might be interpreted as making the colony's criminal justice system more lenient. Hence, he was not prepared to sanction the discontinuance of corporal punishment. Nor was he prepared to accept the proposal for the adoption of rattan as the only instrument of punishment. On the issue of the physical effects of flogging with the cat, Carnarvon stated that it would be the responsibility of the medical inquiry to judge upon the prevalence of pulmonary complaints among prisoners and the physical effects of flogging Chinese prisoners with the cat.

He also refuted the governor's assertion that there was a straightforward link between the nature of the prison regime and the rise in crime. On the high rate of recidivism, he stated, that as far as he was concerned, the prison had not served as a sufficient deterrent and that the governor should concentrate his efforts on reforming the penal regime rather than tampering with the sentencing system. He concluded by reiterating that Hennessy should pay close attention to the advice and suggestions of the community's representatives on the Executive and Legislative Councils.[98] The Colonial Office was well aware that if Hennessy persisted with his proposed reforms he would antagonize and alienate the leading colonial interests in Hong Kong, just as he had in Barbados. As the public meeting all too vividly indicated, this is exactly what happened.

In July 1879 the Colonial Office finally replied to the colonists' resolutions, rejecting their demands for an independent commission of inquiry. The newspapers were furious about the treatment of the colonists, arguing that this was further proof that the Colonial Office could not be trusted. The "feeling of isolation and estrangement" between the European community and Hennessy was now complete. Such was the degree of alienation that the English-language newspapers reported that Chinese criminals had nicknamed him "Number One Good Friend" and printed the rumor that the governor had led his criminal "pets" on another raid on Kowloon "disguised as a Chinese burglar of olden time, his hair tied up in a queue, and his clothes at home."[99] As far as they were concerned Sir John Pope Hennessy had "gone native" and consequently the *China Mail* argued that the time was right for the immediate removal of the governor from the colony and the introduction of representative government.[100]

THE AFTERMATH OF THE PUBLIC MEETING

Hennessy took the Colonial Office vote of confidence as his mandate to proceed with his reforms, and he moved to neutralize his most powerful and vociferous opponent in the Legislative Council. At the Legislative Council meeting of 12 November 1879, when William Keswick once more called for the reintroduction of deportations and floggings, Hennessy retorted, "I shall not break the law myself to punish the meanest of her subjects, nor shall I allow others to do so within the government committed to my care.... I have endeavoured, and I believe successfully, in spite of some little local opposition, to check such abuses. No one shall prevent me from doing so."[101]

The governor charged Keswick with dereliction of duty in relation to his role as a visiting magistrate. According to Hennessy, if Keswick had looked at the prison offense book, as was his duty, he would have noticed that 828 illegal floggings had taken place. The only other explanation was that Keswick had looked at the book, noticed the illegal floggings, and chosen to ignore them. This turned into a personal battle between the governor and Keswick, with the latter denying that he had failed to carry out his duties and Hennessy replying that the prison staff had no recollection of him ever examining the book in question. This argument carried over into 1880, and Hennessy finally wrote to the Colonial Office in August to inform them that, because of work commitments, Keswick had resigned his position as visiting magistrate:

His suggestions have been in the direction of inflicting special and degrading punishments on the Chinese. To some extent due to his influence the branding system, which led to an increase of crime, was kept up for so many years. Apart from his decided views about the Chinese and the treatment of native criminals, there is not a more estimable gentleman in the colony than Mr Keswick.[102]

He also pointed out that fortunately Keswick had only visited the prison infrequently:

With his strong opinion about the Chinese even the very few visits he has made to the gaol for the last thirteen years [16 times between August 1867 and February 1880] have probably done more harm than good.[103]

Fortunately for Hennessy the crime statistics for 1879 and 1880 showed decreases of 8.19 percent and 14.43 percent respectively, and there was no repeat of the sensational criminal escapades that characterized 1878. He was also able to bolster his position when the various committees reported in the course of 1879.

The report of the policing inquiry, which became public in early 1879, fully supported Hennessy's criminal justice policies.[104] It confirmed that crime had been on the increase since 1874 and identified the cause as being the fact that the town was unguarded at night. The committee argued that the police beats needed to be reorganized to make sure that two-thirds of the force was on duty between 10P.M. and 6A.M. It also advocated the general arming of the police and the upgrading of the harbor police. Hennessy implemented these proposals and also transferred responsibility for the prison guards from the head of the police to the superintendent of the prison.[105]

The report of the medical commission into flogging, which was forwarded to the Colonial Office in May 1879, stated that it was difficult to reach a firm conclusion about whether flogging on the back produced phthisis.[106] It also noted that the prevalence of pulmonary disease could be related to the overcrowding and lack of airspace. The recommended airspace was 1,000–1,200 cubic feet per prisoner; however, the allowance in Hong Kong prison was overall only 482–775 cubic feet per prisoner and only 184–221 cubic feet for Chinese prisoners.

This committee was highly critical of the manner in which flogging was carried out. It noted that the rattan in use in the colony (forty-seven inches in length, two inches in circumference) was a more severe instrument than the cat because of its effects on the cellular and muscular tissues (it produced loss of blood by sloughing and therefore delayed the healing process). It therefore recommended that the rattan be reduced in size, weight, and severity. It also recommended that its preferred course of action would be that the rattan should be replaced by a knotless cat. Prisoners under eighteen should be flogged on the breech with a cat with only six tails (as opposed to nine) and those under thirteen should be punished with a birch. In the case of adult prisoners, because they had found no causal connection with phthisis, they recommended that flogging should continue to be on the back. However, they argued for the introduction of a thick canvas to cover and protect the loins and a thick canvas collar to prevent injury to the neck. The use of these coverings was to make sure that the blows only fell "on the muscles covering the shoulderblades and the intermediate spinal space."

The reports allowed Hennessy to implement his reforms. He changed the night-duty system to ensure that the colony was adequately policed during the period of greatest threat. This redeployment necessitated the controversial arming of Chinese officers for the first time. He also asked the Colonial Office to send him officers from the Royal Irish Constabulary to allow him to upgrade the quality of the European officer corps.[107]

Hennessy, while agreeing with most of the recommendations of the medical committee, refused to allow "even with the well intended protections they suggest, of flogging any orientals on the shoulder blades and the intermediate spinal space."[108] He reiterated that punishment on the back had been discontinued in China because of its effects on the lungs[109] and that it was a "degrading punishment" that left lifelong marks. As a consequence he decreed that in future all prisoners be flogged on the breech with the new regulation rattan.

In July 1880 Lord Kimberley, the new Liberal Secretary of State for the Colonies,[110] responded positively to Hennessy's proposals for reforming the penal ordinances. The penal law amendments,[111] laid before the Legislative Council in June 1881, repealed the branding ordinances and all ordinances imposing flogging exclusively on the Chinese and abolished public flogging and flogging the Chinese on the back. It also confirmed that there should be no flogging in Hong Kong except for offenses where it would be sanctioned in England:

The severe penal laws, and the bad system this bill would sweep away, had created and fostered a criminal class. Crime had been manufactured by branding and the lash; whereas a more rational system had now reduced crime.[112]

Ordinance No. 8 1882, on banishment and conditional pardons, was finally forwarded to the Colonial Office in March 1881. Although banishment for five years for crimes against the state was retained, the power of banishment was removed from magistrates and relocated with the governor. In addition this new ordinance eliminated the sections on branding, flogging, and mendicancy. The law that sanctioned the flogging of the Chinese if they did not cooperate with the fire brigade was also repealed. Thus Hennessy succeeded in removing the legislation that formally discriminated against the Chinese. The only part of his reform agenda that was not implemented was the building of a new prison; in this matter the colonists foiled him.

THE NEW PRISON

At the close of 1878 an attempt was made to introduce the separate system on a small scale. Two of the large basement halls of Victoria Prison were divided into separate cells, and the head of the prison, Mr. Tonnochy, in one of his annual reports provides us with a chilling glimpse into the realities of Hennessy's "humane" penal regime:

From the very commencement, as I anticipated, the prisoners disliked the system and tried every means to escape it. In the first month there were several attempts at suicide, but I found they were all feigned and as the prisoners did not get released thereby, but were in addition subjected to rigorous search several times each day to prevent them from secreting articles which might facilitate attempts at suicide, they found it wiser to accept the discipline.[113]

However, in order to convert the whole of the penal regime to the separate system it was necessary either to restructure the existing prison or to build a new one. The debate about the shape, nature, and location of the proposed new gaol continued until the end of Hennessy's governorship; the surveyor general, Mr. Price, took a key role in frustrating the governor's plans. While the latter was in Japan, Price successfully applied to Government House for a postponement on work to the proposed prison on the grounds that his department was overstretched. When Hennessy returned, Price was ordered to proceed with drawing up plans.

In May 1881 Hennessy was able to report to the Colonial Office that he had proposals for different sites. He was highly critical of the sites on Hong Kong island chosen by the surveyor general, noting that one absorbed a corner of the authorized Chinese cemetery. He complained that such insensitivity:

is characteristic of the way in which I found the Survey Department treats the Chinese. It would be difficult to conceive any proceeding of a government department that would be less agreeable to the Chinese community. It would not only be a painful act of desecration but a breech of faith.[114]

Instead, Hennessy opted for Stonecutters' Island. The Colonial Office expressed concern about the cost of the governor's preferred option and called on Price (who was back in England on leave) to submit his professional opinions on the project. Price did so, pointing out that Hennessy's proposal would indeed be costly. But Price, unbeknown to Hennessy, went further than just commenting upon the cost of the different proposals. He also informed the Colonial Office that the public works department program was overburdened and that in any case it should be aware that:

there is a strong consensus of opinion among the better classes in the Colony against a new gaol, or any scheme that will throw upon the rate payers the burden of maintaining in their midst at increased cost, the criminals of a foreign country while there remains the alternative of repatriating them.[115]

The Colonial Office took Price's evaluation seriously and effectively decided that it might not be possible to proceed with the plans for a new prison until a new governor was in post in the colony. Thus the decision was taken to stall Hennessy, and Lord Kimberley wrote to him on 16 August 1881 asking for further details and costings. As a consequence, Hennessy's attempt to implement the separate system in Hong Kong failed.

CONCLUSION

By 1880 the newspapers had to come to terms with the fact that the official crime rate had dropped. Nevertheless, they continued to air their suspicions that Hennessy and his police "lackeys" were manipulating the crime statistics and to berate this "despotic, obstinate governor" for ignoring the wishes of the European community on criminal justice matters. By 1881 and 1882 they were campaigning to ensure that Hennessy's governorship of the colony was not renewed. The *Daily Press* argued that the time was right for the Colonial Office to end Hennessy's colonial career "after the reputation he has made for himself of being always in antagonism with the white communities in every place he has been sent to administer."[116] On the day of his departure, 7 March 1882, this paper made its feelings clear when it stated, "The community will rejoice at his departure; the land will have peace."

Hennessy's actions seem to have received more favorable coverage in Britain, where support was expressed for his reform of the colony's penal system. For example, William Tallack, the Secretary of the Howard Association (an influential penal reform pressure group), stated in 1882:

The news from the colony received from time to time shows that much opposition by some of the colonists has been manifested to the governor's Christian and philanthrophic exertions. But here in Great Britain, there appears to be a general concurrence of public opinion in support of the governor's action, which is regarded as that of a noble hearted and courageous man.[117]

It is clear that Hennessy's determination to reform brutal colonial penal regimes, such as the one he found in Hong Kong, was not motivated only by Christian and philanthrophic considerations. Hennessy had a distinctive and overarching imperial mission. He believed that it was both desirable and possible to obtain, at the very least, the active consent of native populations in order to secure the legitimacy of imperial governance. Hence his determination to make clear that it was the duty of government to "hold the balance evenly between all men" instead of encouraging particular interests. This accounts for his attempts to end formal racial discrimination in the functioning and practices of government departments. The most blatant inequities invariably occurred in the sphere of criminal justice policies. He believed that it was of vital importance that all sections of the community have faith in the fairness of the criminal justice system and that governance was premised on the rule of law rather than the parochial interests of British colonists.[118] He also believed that there was a direct connection between securing the legitimacy of governance and the regulation of crime. In a speech made after he had completed his colonial career he argued that:

whether it be ten thousand miles away or nearer to the heart of the Empire, one general principle holds good—that the machinery for the repression of crime is cheaper and more effective where prudent government has secured on the side of the law the sympathy and support of the people.[119]

Hennessy also reflected on his attempts to reform Hong Kong's penal system and explained why he thought the colonists had opposed his policies: "Those who began to fear the commercial rivalry of the industrious native population did not like them, and . . . denounced the Chinese as a dishonest and violent race that should be ruled with a rod of iron."[120] He argued that as a consequence the colony's law-and-order policies had been obsessively punitive and had contributed to the crime problem. In addition, their arbitrary and discriminatory nature had alienated the vast majority of the Chinese population and undermined the legitimacy not just of the criminal justice system but of British rule.

However, Hennessy's imperial vision had little lasting impact on Hong Kong. After his reforming governorship the colony reverted to a harsh penal regime. A survey of penal matters in the 1880s and 1890s reveals continued reports of overcrowding, increased punishments, flagrant abuse of power, prisoner revolts, escape attempts, deaths from floggings, and prisoner suicides. In addition, all attempts by the Colonial Office to cajole the Hong Kong government into constructing a new prison failed. In April 1886, for example, a commission was appointed to look into the vexed question of insufficient accommodation in the prison. Its report recommended flogging in all cases of petty theft and for released prisoners returning from banishment. Hennessy's attempts to incorporate the Chinese into the criminal justice institutions were also reversed. In 1882 the police returned to the policy of arming only European and Indian officers. The belief that Chinese prison guards were untrustworthy also meant that the authorities quickly reverted to their traditional recruitment practices. The colonists' fear of the Chinese continued to override any other considerations when it came to law-and-order issues, and the governors after Hennessy did not disturb this status quo.

NOTES

The authors wish to thank David Arnold, Joe Sim, and members of the European Centre for Policing Studies at the Open University for their valuable comments and suggestions on an earlier draft of this article.

1. For further biographical information on Hennessy, see James Pope Hennessy, *Verandah* (London, 1964), and Kate Lowe and Eugene McLaughlin, "Sir

John Pope Hennessy and the 'Native Race Craze': Colonial Government in Hong Kong, 1877–1882," *Journal of Imperial and Commonwealth History* 20 (1992).

2. Throughout this article we have used the leading English-language newspapers: the *China Mail* (founded 1845; proprietor and editor during Hennessy's governorship, George Murray Bain); the *Daily Press* (founded 1857; publisher and editor, R. Chatterton Wilcox). Both papers were consistently hostile to Hennessy's governorship. It has not been possible to draw upon Chinese-language newspapers because no runs for these years are known to have survived in Hong Kong. For more information, see Frank H. H. King and P. Clarke, *A Research Guide to Chinacoast Newspapers, 1822–1911* (Cambridge, Mass., 1965).

3. L. H. Gann and Peter Duigan, *The Rulers of British Africa* (London, 1978).

4. Quoted in Jan Nederveen Pieterse, *Empire and Emancipation* (New York, 1989), 223. For other discussions of the connections between race and imperialism see R. A. Huttenback, *Racism and Empire* (Ithaca, 1976); and V.G. Kiernan, *The Lords of Human Kind* (London, 1988).

5. David Arnold, *Police Power and Colonial Rule, Madras 1859–1947* (Delhi, 1986). For a reading of the situation in South Africa, see Clifton C. Crais, *White Supremacy and Black Resistance in Pre-Industrial South Africa* (Cambridge, 1992).

6. For a discussion of the significance of the Morant Bay Rebellion, see Arvel B. Erickson, "Empire or Anarchy: The Jamaica Rebellion of 1865," *Journal of Negro History* 44 (1959): 99–122.

7. For details on the controversy surrounding the First Opium War and the British acquisition of Hong Kong, see David E. Owen, *British Opium Policy in China and India* (New Haven, 1934); John K. Fairbank, *Trade and Diplomacy on the China Coast: The Opening of the Treaty Ports, 1842–1854*; J. Beeching, *The Chinese Opium Wars* (London, 1975); W. O. Walker, *Opium and Foreign Policy* (Chapel Hill, 1991). Hong Kong subsequently became the center of the opium trade. People of all nationalities were attracted to this "imperial station" because of the vast fortunes that could be made by those willing to participate in the lucrative trade of smuggling opium into mainland China. One of the earliest governors, Sir John Davis, reported soon after his arrival in 1844 that "almost every person possessed of capital who is not connected with government employment, is employed in the opium trade." By 1849 three-quarters of the Indian opium crop was handled in Hong Kong, with an average of 40,000 chests worth $16 million lying in store in the colony. By 1870, 83,000 chests of opium worth $48,742,238 were being imported into the colony.

8. For a fuller account of the salient features of the different forms of nineteenth-century British colonial government, see J. W. Cell, *British Colonial Administration in the Mid-nineteenth Century: The Policy Making Process* (New Haven, 1970); B. L. Blakely, *The Colonial Office, 1868–1892* (Durham, N. C., 1972). For a fuller description of Hong Kong's colonial administration and constitution, see George B. Endacott, *Government and People in Hong Kong, 1841–1962* (Hong Kong, 1964).

9. For a description of the Hong Kong merchant houses, see Colin N. Crisswell, *The Taipans, Hong Kong's Merchant Princes* (Hong Kong, 1981); and *The Thistle and the Jade*, ed. Maggie Keswick (London, 1982).

10. For the debate about the exact degree of autonomy enjoyed by colonial governors and the overall relationship between the Colonial Office and its repre-

sentatives, see L. H. Gann and Peter Duigan, *The Rulers of British Africa* and M. Francis, *Governors and Settlers, Images of Authority in the British Colonies* (London, 1992).

11. Blakely, *The Colonial Office*, 67.

12. Endacott, *A History of Hong Kong*, 122.

13. H. W. Lucy, *East by West* (London, 1885), 2: 116.

14. Endacott, *Government and People*, 38.

15. For a description of China's harsh penal regime in this time period, see Isabella L. Bird, *The Golden Chersonese: Travels in Malaya in 1879* (Oxford, 1980), 67–79. For more general overviews of the Chinese penal philosophy, see G. MacCormack, *Traditional Chinese Penal Law* (Edinburgh, 1990); Michael R. Dutton, *Policing and Punishment in China* (Cambridge, 1992).

16. A heavy wooden board worn round the neck as punishment. It originated in China.

17. In 1842 the Chinese were prohibited from being out of doors without a lantern from 8pm until 10pm and from being out at all after 10pm. In 1857 and 1870 laws were passed formalizing the practice of requiring the Chinese to carry passes and/or lanterns: see Elizabeth Sinn, *Power and Charity: The early History of the Tung Wah hospital, Hong Kong* (Hong Kong, 1989), 11, 25, 92–93.

18. Ordinance No. 1, 1845.

19. William P. Morgan, *Triad Societies in Hong Kong* (Hong Kong, 1982), 60.

20. *Hansard*, 3rd ser., LXXXIX (1847), 425.

21. James W. Norton-Kyshe, *The History of the Laws and Courts of Hong Kong from the Earliest Period to 1898* (London, 1898), 1: 133. For an intriguing study of Chinese fears about having their queues cut off, see Phillip A. Kuhn, *Soulstealers: The Chinese Sorcery Scare of 1768* (Cambridge, Mass., 1990).

22. Ordinance No. 6, 1847.

23. Ordinance No. 12, 1865.

24. Ordinance No. 8, 1866.

25. Ernest J. Eitel, *Europe in China* (Hong Kong, 1983), 450.

26. CO 129/189, 266, Hennessy to Colonial Office, 10 Aug. 1880.

27. Norton-Kyshe, *The History of the Laws and Courts*, 2: 90.

28. Ordinance No. 8, 1876.

29. J. D. Frodsham, *The First Chinese Embassy to the West: The Journals of Kuo Sung T'ao, Liu Hsi-Hung and Chang Te-yi* (Oxford, 1974), 180.

30. Victoria Prison, first erected in 1842, stands between present-day Old Bailey Street and Hollywood Road, central Hong Kong.

31. Norton-Kyshe, *The History of the Laws and Courts*, 1: 644.

32. The body of a prisoner was exhumed after rumors spread that he had died in suspicious circumstances. An inquest established that the prisoner had been flogged twice and placed on short rations and in solitary confinement for complaining that he was ill and unable to work.

33. *Daily Press*, 1 March 1877.

34. For a discussion of the controversies engendered by Hennessy's radical beliefs, see Lowe and McLaughlin, "Sir John Pope Hennessy."

35. Sir John Pope Hennessy, "Is Central Africa Worth Having?" *The Nineteenth Century* 28 (1890).

36. Quoted in Norton-Kyshe, *The History of the Laws and Courts*, 2: 354–57.

37. David Garland, *Punishment and Welfare: A History of Penal Strategies* (Aldershot, 1987), 7. For a discussion about the precise meaning of the shift from punishing the body to imprisoning the mind in Western societies, see Michel Foucault, *Discipline and Punish: The Birth of the Prison* (Harmondsworth, 1977); and Michael Ignatieff, *A Just Measure of Pain* (London, 1978).

38. For a discussion of the deliberations of the Carnarvon committee and the deleterious effects of the 1865 Prison Act, see Sir Lionel Fox, *The English Prison and Borstal Systems* (Plymouth, 1952), 14–17; Sean McConville, *A History of English Prison Administration* (London, 1981), 348–58; William J. Forsythe, *The Reform of Prisoners, 1830–1900* (London, 1987), 153–59; Garland, *Punishment and Welfare*, 6–15; Joe Sim, *Medical Power in Prisons* (Milton Keynes, 1990), 41–47.

39. For a summary of the differences between the Irish and English penal systems, see Leon Radzinowicz and Roger Hood, *The Emergence of Penal Policy in Victorian and Edwardian England* (Oxford, 1990), 515–21.

40. *Parliamentary Debates*, CLXV, 745 (1862), 6 Feb.–24 March.

41. *Parliamentary Debates*, CLXVI, 1087 (1862), 25 March–26 May.

42. Sir John Pope Hennessy, "The Treatment of Political Prisoners," in *Transactions of the National Association for the Promotion of Social Science for 1866* (London, 1867).

43. For further discussion of the consequences of criminalization for Irish political prisoners, see Sim, *Medical Power in Prisons*, 45–47.

44. A few other governors were willing to act in a humane manner toward native prisoners, for example, Sir Henry Loch, Governor of Cape Colony, 1889–95, and Sir James Longden, Governor of Sri Lanka, 1878–83. Sir James Stephen was one of the few Secretaries of State for the Colonies who condemned inhumane and racially discriminatory practices in the colonies; see P. Knapland, *James Stephen and the British Colonial System, 1813–1847* (Madison, 1933).

45. B. Hamilton, *Barbados and the Confederation System, 1871–1885* (London, 1956), 72.

46. Much to the consternation of the white planter class, Hennessy unveiled tentative proposals for the effective confederation of the five Windward Islands. Their virulent opposition to his proposals and the decision of black laboring classes to back Hennessy resulted in a heightening of racial tensions. Rioting finally broke out on 18 April 1876 and lasted for a week.

47. Hamilton, *Barbados*, 72.

48. CO 129/177, 1, *Report of the Committee of Inquiry into the Discipline and Dietary of Victoria Gaol*, 28 Feb. 1877.

49. Ibid.

50. Ibid.

51. CO 129/177, 382–3, Gardiner Austin to Carnarvon, 28 March 1877.

52. CO 129/177, 385–6, Carnarvon to Hennessy, 28 May 1877.

53. CO 129/177, 230–1, Carnarvon to Hennessy, 7 March 1877.

54. CO 132/6, Votes and Proceedings of the Legislative Council of Hong Kong, 17 Sept. 1877.

55. Ibid.

56. Ibid.

57. *China Mail*, 6 Sept. 1877; 14 Sept. 1877.

58. *Papers Relating to the Flogging of Prisoners in Hong Kong* (London, 1879), 5.

59. Ibid., 6.

60. Ibid., 5.

61. For details of the controversies surrounding the deaths of prisoners in England in this period, see Sim, *Medical Power in Prisons*, 47–52.

62. Ibid., 9.

63. Ibid., 34–35.

64. CO 129/189, 266, Hennessy to Colonial Office, 10 Aug. 1880.

65. CO 129/177, 442, Hennessy to Carnarvon, 12 July 1877.

66. *China Mail*, 14 Aug. 1877.

67. *China Mail*, 15 Oct. 1878.

68. CO 132/6, Votes and Proceedings Of the Legislative Council of Hong Kong, 17 Sept. 1877.

69. Ibid.

70. On one of his first trips to the prison Hennessy was shocked to find a "lunatic" tethered on a long chain to one of the inner gates and another one languishing in the cells. In December 1881 he finally persuaded the Colonial Office to support the construction of the first asylum for the Chinese population; see CO 129/196, 5 Dec. 1881.

71. CO 131/10, 50, Hennessy to Executive Council, 28 June 1878.

72. *Daily Press*, 17 May 1877.

73. *China Mail*, 22 Aug. 1877.

74. *China Mail*, 10 Sept. 1878.

75. *China Mail*, 9 June 1877.

76. *China Mail*, 19 Oct. 1877.

77. *China Mail*, 8 April 1877.

78. *China Mail*, 25 Sept. 1878.

79. The colonists feared that the "unhygenic" Chinese would carry all manner of diseases into the vulnerable European areas if the administration did not strictly uphold sanitation standards. The first report of public health confirmed many of their suspicions concerning the Chinese; see Osbert Chadwick, *Report on the Sanitary Conditions of Hong Kong* (London, 1882).

80. *China Mail*, 18 July 1878.

81. For a discussion of the impact of this blockade, see Endacott, *A History of Hong Kong*, 189–94.

82. *China Mail*, 22 May 1878.

83. For the sociological shifts that were taking place in this period, see Yen-p'ing Hao, *The Compradore in Nineteenth-century China* (Cambridge, Mass., 1970); Carl T. Smith, *Chinese Christians: Elites, Middlemen and the Church in Hong Kong* (Hong Kong, 1985); Chan Wai Kwan, *The Making of Hong Kong Society* (Oxford, 1992).

84. CO 129/194, 67, Hennessy to Colonial Office, 5 Aug. 1881.

85. *Daily Press*, 5 Nov. 1877.

86. For a more detailed analysis of this debate, see Lowe and McLaughlin, "Sir John Pope Hennessy."

87. *The Insecure Condition of the Colony of Hong Kong: A Report of the Great Public Meeting held at Victoria, Hong Kong, 7 October 1878* (Hong Kong, 1878).

88. Ibid., 12.

89. *China Mail*, 4 Nov. 1878; 7 May 1878; *Daily Press*, 31 Oct. 1878.

90. *China Mail*, 8 Oct. 1878.

91. CO 132/19, 563, Votes and Proceedings of the Legislative Council of Hong Kong, 18 Nov. 1878.

92. Eitel, *Europe in China*, 544–45.

93. *China Mail*, 12 May 1879.

94. CO 129/184, 598, Keswick to Hennessy, 25 May 1879.

95. Ibid.

96. Quoted in Endacott, *Government and People*, 95.

97. CO 129/178, 276–7, Carnarvon to Hennessy, 22 Aug. 1877.

98. *Papers Relating to the Flogging*, 35–40.

99. *China Mail*, 4 Feb. 1879.

100. *China Mail*, 17 July 1879. It should be noted that calls for representative government usually subsided when it was realized that the utilization of even the most restrictive property qualification would still have resulted in the Chinese community having more votes than the colonists.

101. CO 132/20, 665–6, Votes and Procedures of the Legislative Council of Hong Kong, 12 Nov. 1879.

102. CO 129/189, 153, Hennessy to Kimberley, 2 Aug. 1880.

103. Ibid.

104. CO 129/184, 108–117, Report of the Committee on the Police Force and Crime in Hong Kong, 7 Mar. 1879.

105. Norton-Kyshe, *The History of the Laws and Courts*, 2: 295.

106. *Papers Relating to the Flogging*, 45–49.

107. CO 129/189, 608–9, Hennessy to Colonial Office, 20 Sept. 1880.

108. CO 132/20, 674, Votes and Proceedings of the Legislative Council of Hong Kong, 12 Nov. 1879.

109. E. J. Eitel, "Locus Operandi in Flogging," *The China Review* (1878–89), 74–75.

110. The Earl of Kimberley was Secretary of State for the Colonies between April 1880 and Dec. 1882.

111. Ordinance No. 3, 1881.

112. CO 132/21, 512, Votes and Proceedings of the Legislative Council of Hong Kong, 13 June 1881.

113. *Hong Kong Administrative Reports, 1879* (Hong Kong, 1880).

114. CO 129/193, 37, Hennessy to Colonial Office, 5 May 1881.

115. CO 129/196, 374, Price to Kimberley, 30 July 1881.

116. *Daily Press*, 30 Jan. 1882.

117. CO 129/197, 440, Tallack to Bulkeley Johnson, 10 Jan. 1882.

118. For the details of a parallel struggle between the British administration and settlers in India over the representation of native interests in the criminal justice system, see C. Dobbin, "The Ilbert Bill: A Study of Anglo-Indian Opinion in India, 1883," *Historical Studies, Australia and New Zealand* 12 (1965–7): 87–102.

119. Sir John Pope Hennessy, "Repression of Crime," in *Transactions of the National Association for the Promotion of Social Science for 1882* (London, 1883), 220.

120. Sir John Pope Hennessy, "Repression," 214.

The Rise of the Detective in London, 1869–1914

Stefan Petrow
University of Tasmania, Hobart

For over two hundred years the detective has been more reviled than praised, more a figure of suspicion than trust, more likely to be lampooned than respected for the intelligence he exercises in dealing with criminals. From the Bow Street Runners of the mid-eighteenth century onwards, fascination has been mixed with a notion that detective methods, especially spying, offend the English sense of fair play and are an unacceptable interference with individual liberty; they were more suited to autocratic France than liberal England. Apart from wartime, "English opinion" was "generally hostile to spies."[1] Consequently, a detective force was not formed when the Metropolitan Police was established by Home Secretary Robert Peel in 1829. Keenly aware of the great public fear of espionage, Peel seems not to have argued for a detective police: He emphasized prevention, not detection.[2]

Although a small detective force was formed in 1842, was greatly increased in 1869, and became the Criminal Investigation Department (CID) in 1878, prevention remained the keynote of policing to 1914. Prevention held that police should be willing to forgo a conviction if they could stop a crime being committed. Detectives could work in this way. But many believed they were more likely to adopt a problematic strategy of allowing or even encouraging crimes and then arresting, in the hope that conviction would result in a long imprisonment.[3] This strategy meant that secretive methods were employed. Few could be sure how detectives operated. Publicly, it was denied that detectives ever indulged in espionage, used agents provocateurs, or sought information "by underhand or unworthy means."[4] This taintless image, however, jarred with reality the closer we get to 1914. It became increasingly the case that some detective methods verged on the illegal and others were illegal.

It is partly due to this secrecy that historians in the burgeoning field of English police history have tended to neglect the study of detectives and have concentrated on the policing of riots, crowds, and strikes where the naked power of the State was more visible.[5] Studies by Andrew and Porter have demonstrated that the methods used by secret agents and secret police to monitor the activities of foreign spies and political criminals can be recovered by patient delving in the archives.[6] The use of detectives to deal with ordinary criminals has not yet attracted much scholarly interest.[7]

Detective methods raise awkward questions. Was it morally justifiable to catch criminals by resort to lies and tricks, to use informers, or to invade privacy?[8] Was it adequate to regulate relations between detectives and informers by departmental rules and not by acts of Parliament? If a detective perverted the law in an effort to entrap a criminal, did it destroy the difference between himself and the criminal? Between 1869 and 1914 such questions plagued successive Metropolitan Police commissioners and their political masters, the Home Secretaries. Their abiding dilemma was, on the one hand, how to make detectives effective and to give them the widest possible latitude in their encounters with criminals and, on the other hand, how to make detectives accountable to their superiors, to ensure they kept within the law and did not abuse their powers. As lubricious criminals contrived ways of evading detection and exploited social and technological changes—in transport, for example—some argued that tight control had to give way to greater freedom of maneuver. But, as detective numbers increased, it became very difficult to exercise tight control. As detectives became more autonomous, they became more corrupt, "a thoroughly venal private army" by 1922, according to one official police historian.[9] In what follows I will account for the formation and growth of detective police in London, examine how they were controlled, recruited, and trained, and look more closely at methods they employed to monitor the activities of criminals.

The use of detectives began modestly during the 1830s, when some senior officers in the Metropolitan Police recognized that crime could not be prevented solely by using uniformed police and deployed some plainclothes police.[10] In 1842 their advantages were confirmed when Richard Mayne, one of two Metropolitan Police commissioners, felt that more men could be usefully employed to observe "known or suspected criminals" and to detect crime. In June 1842 Mayne persuaded the Home Secretary, Sir James Graham, to employ for a trial period two inspectors and six sergeants on detective work.[11] Numbers remained small until the mid-1860s, when panic over an apparent increase in indictable and violent crime, particularly garotting, created more favourable circumstances for an increase in detectives.[12] In 1867 detective numbers reached fifteen, but in January 1868 Mayne argued for thirteen more.[13] Faced with Mayne's proposals for more detectives and growing public criticism of police effectiveness, on 8, February 1868 Home Secretary Gathorne Hardy appointed a departmental committee to review the administration of the Metropolitan Police.[14]

After assiduously questioning Mayne on the need for more detectives, the committee concluded that the existing detective force was "wholly inadequate to the present requirements of the metropolis."[15] In May the committee recommended that detectives form "a separate division under the control of a special Superintendent and under the immediate command of the head of the police." However, Mayne died in December 1868, before the detective force was reorganized.

In February 1869 a deputation representing metropolitan vestries and district boards met the new Home Secretary, H.A. Bruce, to seek a number of reforms, including the appointment of more detective police because of the "thousands upon thousands of known criminals at large."[16] The new chief commissioner, Edmund Henderson, had been Chairman of the Directors of Convict Prisons and, knowing well the type of prisoners being released, was fully alive to the necessity for more detectives.[17] In May the central force was increased to twenty-six. In July twenty sergeants and 160 constables, taken from the existing uniform strength, were appointed to the divisions. Although Henderson thought detective work was an important police duty, he knew that detectives were regarded with "the greatest suspicion and jealousy by the majority of Englishmen" and were "entirely foreign to the habits and feelings of the Nation."[18] Moreover, detectives were potentially troublesome. They worked "in secret, away from supervision and control, and the greatest care is required in their selection, and in seeing as far as possible that their duty is honestly and faithfully performed."

Divisional and central detectives performed different duties. Divisional detectives were charged with making themselves "well acquainted with all the criminals in their districts—their associates, habits and residences."[19] They used three methods. One method was twice-weekly visits to different prisons to see convicts recently arrested or about to be discharged to their districts. Another was to study divisional registers of thieves, compiled under the Habitual Criminals Act 1869. Finally, when not occupied elsewhere, divisional detectives frequented criminal dens and patrolled the streets. Central detectives, unless directed by the commissioner, were not involved in "preventing or arresting the ordinary cases of crime." They generally worked on important cases, including swindles and fraud, where the stakes were high. The possibility of corruption was realized in April 1877, when five men convicted of fraud and forgery in the "Turf Fraud" case informed the authorities of the complicity of senior central detectives in the crime.[20] Chief Inspectors Palmer and Druscovitch and Inspector Meiklejohn were convicted in November. They had succumbed to bribery, in Meiklejohn's case since 1872, without apparently arousing the suspicion of their superiors.

The case poignantly underlined long-held fears of inadequately supervised and poorly paid detectives becoming debased by intimate contact with criminals. It also raised questions of how many crimes they had allowed to happen and how many innocent people they had arrested. Surprisingly, this massive breach of trust did not lead to demands for the dissolution of the detective force, as many accepted that, to contain the criminal population, it was "a necessary adjunct to every modern police system."[21] The overwhelming cry was for a "more effective system of control" over detectives and an increase in their efficiency. On 13 August, 1877, Home Secretary Richard Assheton Cross responded by appointing a confidential departmental commission to inquire into "the state, discipline and organization of the detective branch."

The commission's report of January 1878 was a striking indictment of the effectiveness of detectives in dealing with criminals. Many of the twenty-two witnesses commented that central and divisional detectives rarely cooperated fully in detecting crime, were extremely jealous of each other, and often refused to share information.[22] Constrained by "limited" numbers, overwork, and the divisional system, divisional detectives could not follow suspected criminals out of their divisions. Both central and divisional detectives were concerned that secrecy was not always possible when conducting an inquiry. In the divisions a lax reporting system enabled uniform officers to become acquainted with the steps being taken to arrest a criminal. At headquarters, clerks and messengers could easily gain similar knowledge, which, "either through gossip or treachery," could be communicated to a suspect. Inspector George Greenham, a central detective, believed that "anybody could become acquainted with the intelligence who cared to purchase it, the detective force being, as it were, under a system of espionage by the thieves."[23]

The commission opined that the major advantage of a detective force was that "through it you obtain such knowledge of the criminal population and their habits as to be able to a great extent to supervise their actions, and thus to render their apprehension so probable as to deter them from crime."[24] However, as such knowledge, virtually absent from the center, was usually confined to a division, it became "almost useless, from the shifting habits" of criminals. Statistics on arrest rates for burglary and housebreaking suggested "the impunity with which the higher classes of crime may be committed in the divisions." For example, the percentage of cases in which arrests were made to cases inquired into by divisional detectives was 17.49 in 1876 and 16.48 in 1877: when divisional and central detectives combined, the percentages were 16.12 in 1876 and 23.68 in 1877. Elsewhere the success rate was much higher, at 80 to 85 percent in Dublin and 60 percent in Birmingham. These percentages seem too high and indicate a certain massaging of the statistics by the Dublin and Birmingham detectives to make the London detectives appear inferior.

The commission's damning final conclusion was that "the present division of detective power" had "utterly failed in leading to a proper detection of crime, or in supervising those who are known to live by it."[25] A precondition for overcoming jealousy and achieving greater efficiency was, the commission recommended, "the abolition of the divisional detective system" and the establishment of "a united and distinct" detective force for "all purposes of organization and control." But the widespread nature of crime in the metropolitan police district required that detectives should be located in each division, where they should act under the direction of the superintendent. The commission "strongly" recommended that the head of the detective branch be an assistant commissioner, "ranking next to the chief commissioner and having charge of the whole force in his absence." These were some of the proposals of a very comprehensive report that showed that detectives were far from infallible. Though serious, the negative findings should not be unduly emphasized. Home Office policy was to strengthen, not weaken, the detective force, by a more coordinated bureaucratic structure, with superintendents taking greater responsibility for detective work. The report was suffused with a firm confidence in the potential of detectives to restrain criminals and to avoid being corrupted by them, once sensible organizational controls were introduced. If the recommendations were implemented, the future of the detective force was assured.

Although Cross told the members of the commission that the reorganization of the detective force was "founded" on their report, the appointment on 6 March, 1878 of Howard Vincent as Director of Criminal Investigation "ignored" one of the main recommendations.[26] As Vincent was not made an assistant commissioner, his powers were not properly defined by statute. It appeared that he was not subordinate to the assistant commissioners and, "although nominally subordinate to," was "practically independent of, the commissioner." He was told unofficially by Cross "to report direct to the Home Office."[27] A less-confident person might have erred on the side of caution and sought authority for his actions. Vincent took the opposite approach by acting independently of the commissioner and the Home Office. Vincent thrust himself before the commission by writing a report praising the Paris detective system, but his appointment was a surprise. Although a lawyer, as the commission had advised, he lacked police experience and at twenty-nine was young for such an important and sensitive post.

I have elsewhere examined Vincent's term as head of the Criminal Investigation Department (CID).[28] Here it is sufficient to note that when Vincent resigned in June 1884 detectives had still not completely proven their worth. To be sure, from 1879 to 1884 arrests by detectives for criminal offences in London increased from 13,128 to 18,344, but their reputation for dealing with other than petty crime was not good.[29] When Vincent was appointed, detectives numbered about 216; when he resigned, they numbered about 294, still a small proportion of the total Metropolitan Police Force.[30] Vincent conceded the impossibility of "exercising continuous and effective disciplinary supervision" over large numbers of detectives "operating over a wide area, who must necessarily by the nature of their duties, be allowed much individual freedom."[31] Therefore, whether Vincent actually purged the CID of corruption is debatable, and relations between detectives and criminals became suspiciously close, as we will see.

James Monro succeeded Vincent on 8 July, 1884. Monro had been a police administrator in India, displaying a flair for detective work.[32] He was the first "trained police official" to be appointed direct to a senior position in the Metropolitan Police. To ensure that Monro did not emulate Vincent's desire for autonomy and to establish that his powers were subordinate to those of the commissioner, an act was passed to give Monro the legal status of assistant commissioner. Monro's relationship with Henderson seems to have been cooperative, but Henderson resigned in March 1886; under his successor, Sir Charles Warren, who was much more autocratic and disliked detective work, a storm brewed.

Monro's plans to gain greater knowledge of criminals were handicapped by lack of men.[33] Despite London's large and increasing population, he complained to Warren in November 1887 that there had been no addition to the strength "worth speaking of" since the CID was established. Consequently, "enquiries are not made in the way in which they should be conducted,... supervision of suspected characters is defective," and "everything is done in a hurry, which is especially injurious to criminal administration." A CID man averaged between ten and eleven hours work daily and "very much longer hours at constantly recurring intervals." In the Metropolitan Police, the percentage of men employed in detective work to those in other duties was 2.42, whereas in Birmingham it was 4.5, Dublin 3.6, Liverpool and Glasgow 3.5, and Manchester 2.7. Thus, "with a specially large and expert criminal population, London has proportionately fewer men employed in the investigation of crime than any of the large towns in the Kingdom." Monro wanted a CID officer located at every police station, "not merely to deal with crime as it occurs but to pick up a knowledge of suspicious characters who may be, or may become, criminals."

None of Monro's efforts to increase the number of detectives and improve their conditions made any headway. Warren preferred to rely more on uniform police than detectives in criminal work. Relations between the two deteriorated, and Monro resigned in August 1888. He was replaced by Robert Anderson, an Anglo-Irish lawyer turned bureaucrat, with some experience in secret service work.[34] The failure to solve the "Jack the Ripper" murders of 1888 confirmed Warren's low opinion of detectives, but his plans to reorganize the detective force were not realized as by 1 December, 1888 he had resigned, alleging excessive Home Office interference.[35]

On December 3, Warren was succeeded by Monro, who had retained the confidence of the Home Office. Monro was the first commissioner to have experience of detective work and sought to buttress the existing organization of detectives. Although not acceding to all his demands, the Home Office sanctioned an increase of twelve sergeants and twenty-eight constables for the divisions, one inspector and two sergeants for headquarters, and the appointment of Melville MacNaghten to the new position of assistant chief constable, CID. After it appeared that the leadership of the CID and the Metropolitan Police had been settled, Monro resigned over differences with the Home Office concerning police administration, especially police pensions, in June 1890.[36]

The next two commissioners were committed to detective work, and it became an increasingly important function of the Metropolitan Police.[37] After a stint as head of the "Political and Secret Department" of the India Office, Edward Bradford served as chief commissioner from 1890 to 1903.[38] His successor Edward Henry gained extensive police experience in India and headed the CID from 1901 to 1903, before serving as chief commissioner from 1903 to 1918. Like Monro, the colonial experiences of Bradford and Henry made them less wedded to the liberal values of English society and the English police tradition of prevention than their predecessors. Faced with an allegedly new and dangerous criminal class, Bradford and, to a greater extent, Henry were willing to condone more secretive methods, if necessary without the approval of the Home Secretaries.

Before 1914 the decentralized organizational structure of the CID remained unchanged, but the outlying districts where—according to police—criminals tended to drift received more attention in two ways. One way was to improve supervision in the eleven outlying districts in 1901 by appointing a deputy to the local detective inspector.[39] Henry thought this change would improve cohesion and efficiency, but it also aimed to prevent the lower-ranked detectives from establishing overly fraternal links with criminals, publicans, and street bookmakers, all willing and able to bribe their way out of arrests.[40] In April 1908 Henry also secured more men for the outer suburbs, with six first-class sergeants and forty-five other detectives to be added to the strength over five years.[41] Some libertarians had always objected in principle—Edward Carpenter had warned, in 1896, that the CID had become "very extensive and powerful" and should be reduced in size—but its numbers were never inordinate. By December 1914 the strength of the CID had reached only 729, or about 3.6 percent of a uniform force of 20,428.

It could be argued that, both politically and for purposes of control, it was inexpedient to have a large detective force. Another more prosaic reason was the dearth since 1868 of trustworthy, intelligent, and capable men suitable for this work.[42] Detectives were typically recruited from the uniform branch and underwent a short probationary period of training with experienced detectives. A few men able to speak foreign languages such as French, Italian, and Greek were recruited from outside the Metropolitan Police.

Witnesses before the 1877 departmental commission complained that the pay and allowances of divisional detectives (sergeants received about £104 per year and constables £83 4s, and both received a £5 plainclothes allowance) were inadequate to attract many uniform police, but this was only part of the explanation.[43] Despite the introduction of, as the departmental commission had recommended, "the most brilliant rate of pay," some "25 to 40 percent in advance of the former standard," Vincent complained in October 1880 that the best men ignored detective appointments. Chief Superintendent Williamson offered a convincing explanation for their reticence. Most policemen disliked "the uncertainty and irregularity" of detective work, which was also

no doubt in many cases very distasteful and repugnant to the better class of men in the service, as their duties constantly bring them into contact with the lowest classes, frequently cause unnecessary drinking and compel them at times to resort to trickery [sic] practices which they dislike.

Moreover, upon moving from the preventive to the detective branch, detectives became cut off from their uniform friends because of the jealousy between the branches, reinforced by the pay increase to detectives.[44] The chance of a detective's becoming a superintendent, to which position most police of ability aspired, was slim. Finally, a lingering "odium" had been attached to detective work since the "Turf Fraud" case of 1877. Some inferred from all this that the kind of men attracted to detective work and prepared to mix with criminals had a different kind of morality, "the morality of the spy," than respectable society: They might be willing to indulge in intrigue, to ditch police conventions and orders, and perhaps be willing to break the law without troubling their conscience too much.[45] In short, there were legitimate doubts that "professional dissemblers" could be trusted.

On the whole, Edward Henry inherited in 1901 a detective force whose personnel were not generally of a high standard. He tried to improve their training by setting up "a small training-school" for detectives in 1902 and by introducing an eight-week "course of instruction," including "practical instruction, illustrated with lantern slides, as well as lectures on criminal law and procedure" in 1913.[46] In 1912 Henry tried to make promotion more rapid by reducing the number of constables and increasing the number of sergeants and increasing the incremental increase in the pay of third-class sergeants.[47] He hoped that these changes would overcome the reluctance of candidates "either in sufficient numbers or of the best kind" to seek admission to the CID.

A well-coordinated administrative structure and proper training were essential prerequisites for an effective detective force, but also crucial were the methods used to monitor the activities of criminals. Underpinning detective work was the accumulation and classification of information on the convictions and methods of criminals and the development of more scientific methods of identification; but here I want to consider the use of informants, impersonation, and agents provocateurs.[48]

Perhaps the most important development was the use of informants, alternatively known as "narks" or, a less derogatory term, "noses."[49] Chief Inspector Littlechild distinguished between an informant and an informer. An informant was "a humble and more or less regular auxiliary of the detective," living in or on the fringes of the criminal subculture. An informer was "a man who himself had been implicated in a crime and turned 'Queen's evidence' " to save himself from prosecution or to reduce his sentence. An informer might also be someone not involved in a crime, who instituted legal proceedings in order to recover "the reward offered by a statute" in betting or disorderly-house cases.[50] In Littlechild's sense an informer was more akin to a witness, who appeared in court, whereas informants remained obscure and never voluntarily appeared in public. CID officers each had their own informants, who were usually not known to their colleagues and were protected from those seeking revenge.

It appears that using informants to monitor "conspiratorial refugees" and political agitators was well established by the mid-1850s, but they were not used as much against ordinary criminals.[51] As the perception of the criminal threat increased, informants were more widely used. By the early 1870s most detectives from the rank of sergeant, especially central detectives, used informants, who were usually paid between one shilling and five shillings depending on the value of the information: Inspector Greenham, a specialist in foreign cases, had up to five informants, whom he met regularly.[52] Chief Commissioner Henderson relied little on paying money to informants because useful information was received "in small cases" but "never" for "large crimes."[53] Money was most often paid to publicans for information, but they expected favors in return: At licensing meetings, for example, police were expected to overlook any offenses they might have committed. Henderson regarded the practice as "nothing more or less than bribery," which should be avoided "wherever it is possible."

Despite Henderson's antipathy, there is evidence that relations between detectives and informants were extended under Howard Vincent. In 1881, in his *Police Code and Manual of Criminal Law*, Vincent stated that detectives "must necessarily have informants and be obliged to meet them when and where they can" but should avoid the public house.[54] Although "refreshment" may be given to an informant, "when possible it is best to give money." An informant should never be "even indirectly invested with any official character or be allowed to act as if actually a police officer." If asked in cross-examination to state from whom his information came, the detective "should decline to answer, unless directed by a Judge." In February 1884 the *Saturday Review* condemned less the principle than the practice of using informants.[55] There now existed an informal understanding between the police and the criminal classes that the minor crimes will not be gone into hotly, when those who commit them can make themselves useful as spies. The person termed the "policeman's nose" is, in London, a minor criminal, who has a certain amount of indulgence extended to him, so long as he does nothing very desperate, and serves the detectives well with hints and suggestions.

The *Saturday Review* did not blame the CID "for acting on the old principle of setting a thief to catch a thief" but complained that it was "applied badly" in London. The thief who acted as the "policeman's nose" was "as a rule, a blockhead," and the typical detective was "seldom a match for a criminal with more than the average intelligence of his class." This might have been so, but the important point is that the use of informants by police was actively encouraged by Vincent and possibly by Home Secretary W.V. Harcourt and became institutionalized.[56] By 1893 informants were relied upon so much that they were "the base of detective duty."[57] Whether the regularity with which they were used justifies calling them agents is doubtful. To the 1900s at least, detectives normally paid informants out of their own limited salaries, which militated against salaried informants.[58] Among the most useful associates of criminals were those servicing the criminal subculture, including publicans, cab men, betting men, managers of common lodging houses, and pawnbrokers.[59]

Not all information was of use. One detective estimated that "a good fifty percent" was "false" or misleading.[60] Wrong information could be deliberately given at short notice to give criminals a freer hand. "To lie like a copper's nark" became a common saying of criminals. Despite the precautions taken by detectives to check information, in 1905 one criminal claimed that detectives relied on narks far too much and that this was "one of the weakest points in the detective system."[61] Narks were "undoubtedly useful at times" but, while accepting money from detectives, they were not averse to accepting money from criminals to keep detectives "off the scent." Using narks was clearly a double-edged weapon that even experienced detectives needed to handle with caution.[62]

Apart from dependence on narks, another danger was that the nark was "very apt to drift into an agent provocateur in his anxiety to secure a conviction."[63] This was especially likely if payment depended on results. The secrecy with which relations between narks and detectives were conducted meant that whether a nark concocted a crime or was forced to concoct a crime by a detective would be difficult to expose. However, this did not always hold. An illuminating example occurred in November 1910 at the County of London Sessions, when two men pleaded guilty to a charge of attempted housebreaking.[64] One of the men, George Davis, who had a number of previous convictions, alleged that the detectives had let a third man escape. This man, Davis said, "had been put forward by the police to tempt them into committing the offence" and was "in the pay" of the police, but Davis refused to identify the man. The next day the third man, Edward Page, surrendered himself to the police and pleaded guilty to attempted housebreaking. As Davis stood by his allegation, the Chairman of the Sessions asked for a Home Office investigation of the charges, which was completed in January 1911.[65] The inquiry concluded that the three men had been wrongly charged and that allegations of police collusion were unfounded. The three men were discharged.

On March 13, in response to a parliamentary question, the Home Secretary Winston Churchill publicly acquitted the police of "improper action."[66] Churchill cut short debate without mentioning that the private inquiry had established that Page was a nark and apparently had attempted to frame the other criminals. This case is significant for a number of reasons. It demonstrates that narks could become agents provocateurs and that, while not formally members of the CID by virtue of regular payment, they were informally members. It shows that the Home Office and the police occluded public discussion of uncomfortable issues concerning the intimate relations between detectives and criminals. Debate was avoided because the Home Office and the chief commissioner knew embarrassingly little of how narks were employed by detectives and found it politically sensible to remain ignorant. Home Office officials mistakenly judged detectives by their own standard, with one claiming that apart from "any question of morality," a detective was too busy "catching real criminals to make it worth his while to manufacture bogus crimes."[67] We could just as easily turn this around and argue that, because they could not catch real criminals, they resorted to manufacturing crime. Finally, the case indicated that police protected useful narks. Chief Inspector Littlechild confessed that he was "often in a position to save" one of his informants "from trouble." While denying that "we connived in crime," he conceded that "in every profession there is a certain amount of 'give and take.' "[68] In short, most Englishmen would agree with the lawyer Edward Abinger, writing in 1911, that to be an informant was "a most contemptible and objectionable calling" but given "the enormous population" of London, it was "almost a necessity to employ such men, if crime is to be detected."

Mixing with criminals and attending prisons, police courts, assizes, and sessions meant that anonymity was generally impossible. Detectives were "often far more widely known (at least by sight) than they themselves are aware of."[69] That criminals knew they were being watched was not necessarily a bad thing if crime prevention was the aim.[70] Criminals might know many detectives, but they could never be sure they knew them all or their informants: Criminals might believe detectives were more omnipresent than they actually were. Contrary to popular belief, derived from fiction, disguises such as wigs or moustaches were not commonly resorted to by detectives, although these were not unknown.[71] The makeup room at headquarters was used less than six times a year. Such devices were obvious to the eye, and criminals were alert to subterfuge.

Usually, depending on the circumstances, detectives would assume a character and dress accordingly. For much of the nineteenth century this procedure was frowned upon as an unwelcome form of state espionage.[72] By 1890, to match the greater cunning of criminals, impersonation by detectives apparently became more acceptable, as the *Spectator* indicated:

No one can doubt that, in order to catch an offender, a detective has a perfect right to assume a character not his own and in that capacity to lay a trap for the capture of the man he wants, even though in so doing he has to enter upon a series of deceptions.[73]

Detectives might wear the attire of a navvy, a sailor, a professional man, a curate, a scavenger, a chimney sweep, a coster, and numerous others.[74] On these occasions it was naturally important for a detective to imitate the speech and manner of the assumed character and to fit in "as closely as possible, chameleon fashion, to the surroundings in which he is going to work."[75]

Some devotees of Paris detectives wanted the CID to be more secretive in its methods. In 1883 the journalist M. L. Meason called for "the establishment of a real detective force...not known to anyone save their immediate chief as belonging in any way to the police."[76] It was unlikely that the Home Office would officially sanction such a proposal or any proposal verging on the illegal. This was made explicit during Vincent's tenure as head of the CID. His drive for success and his enthusiasm for the French system led Vincent to condone, if not encourage, unorthodox methods that pushed the law to its limits.

The clearest example was the well-known Titley case in 1880, when detectives used an agent provocateur to gain the conviction of a chemist who induced abortions.[77] A charge was brought against the detectives for conspiracy. Although severely reprimanded, the detectives were acquitted, as Titley was clearly guilty. On 11 January 1881, while on the one hand stressing the difficulty of getting evidence in some cases and on the other the need to maintain public confidence in the police, Home Secretary Harcourt told the Commons that

the cases in which it is necessary or justifiable for the police to resort to artifice of the description practised in this case must be rare indeed. As a rule, the police ought not to set traps for people; but if there is to be a departure from this rule under extraordinary circumstances the matter is one of such difficulty that the discretion ought not to rest with the police authorities.[78]

Harcourt directed that no similar action should be taken again "without direct communication or authority from the Home Office." As resort to artifice or "any system of espionage" was irreconcilable with the English conception of liberty, Vincent and his successors accepted the fact that the official legal powers of the police would remain much impaired in comparison with most continental forces.[79] But unofficially detectives were less restrained. Robert Anderson once obliquely admitted that at times detectives had to take "some liberties with Blackstone and the 'British Constitution' generally" and that some detective methods were "extra-legal" or, less euphemistically, "utterly unlawful."[80]

For our picture of their methods we have largely depended upon the memoirs of detectives. A telling, if not unique, corrective to these self-congratulatory and sanitized accounts has been supplied by Arthur Harding. Born in 1886, he was brought up in the Nichol in Bethnal Green, a notorious slum cradle for criminals. He progressed from minor larcenist to become, by 1907, according to one detective, "a most slippery and dangerous criminal . . . the leader of a numerous band of thieves, by whom he is feared on account of his various acts of violence." Harding was smart enough to buy secondhand books to teach himself "the finer point of law" and "the art of cross-examining." After one arrest, Harding's room was searched and Stone's *Justice's Manual* was discovered "carefully underlined and noted up."[81]

In a written submission to the 1906 Royal Commission on the Metropolitan Police, Harding claimed that "the police system, and its administration in the H Division in particular, tended to manufacture criminals." Local detectives continually harassed anyone with previous convictions.[82] One, Frederick Wensley, succeeded once and tried on other occasions to secure Harding's conviction for crimes he did not commit.[83] Harding developed a close familiarity with detective types:

The CID chaps at Commercial Street were good policemen. They were brutal but they were proper policemen. At Leman Street—the headquarters of "H" Division the CID [where Wensley was in charge]—they were villains. There was more money about and the police got their cut.[84]

There were, it appears, shifting alliances between detectives and criminals. Some criminals were allowed to operate under certain conditions and at certain times; others were not. Detectives regulated, even protected, certain semicriminal activities such as club and street betting rather than suppressing them.[85] Corruption had become embedded in the detective system, at least in some areas of London, but this had long been predicted and was to a large degree inherent in the work. As Edward Carpenter colorfully observed:

Fancy yourself sitting four or five hours a day for a week or more, in the window-seat of a tavern, in order to command from your point of view a particular street, or house in the street; drinking plentiful beer or spirits to conciliate the landlord;

treating customers, making them more or less drunk, playing a false part, inventing talk and all sorts of stories, worming out secrets—all in order to prove something it is very much to your interest to prove. And fancy living such a life as that, year in and year out.[86]

Although detectives had their uses and were not incorruptible, to Harding and his kind they remained adversaries: "The criminal never forgets that a detective is his mortal enemy, and however friendly he may seem to be, he is always on the watch for a chance to deceive him."[87]

The official perception that criminals became more calculating and professional from the 1890s helps to explain why Home Secretaries and Metropolitan Police commissioners grudgingly acquiesced in or turned a blind eye to detective methods such as spying, using informants, resorting to artifice, and violating privacy.[88] As these methods depended on secrecy, at least two points are open to conjecture. First, we cannot be sure how necessary they were and how successfully they were used. Other developments such as the greater use of fingerprints from 1903 were probably more effective in dealing with criminals and certainly in increasing public confidence in detectives. Second, we do not know how much these practices were used, but there is little reason to doubt that had parliamentary approval been sought, it would have been withheld in all but quite exceptional circumstances. The rise of the London detective illustrates yet again the official view that what the English public does not know will not hurt it and that official secrecy is always the best policy.[89]

NOTES

The author thanks both Dr. Vic Gatrell of Cambridge University for comments on earlier drafts and an anonymous publisher's reader.

1. *Public Opinion*, 26 October 1888, 512.

2. W. L. Melville Lee, *A History of Police in England* (London, 1901), 372.

3. Bernard Porter, *The Origins of the Vigilant State: The London Metropolitan Police Special Branch before the First World War* (London, 1987), 59, 147–48, 183–85.

4. *Encyclopaedia Britannica*, 11th ed., 29 vols. (London, 1910–11), 21:979; George Dilnot, *Scotland Yard: The Methods and Organisation of the Metropolitan Police* (London, 1915), 21; Lee, *Police in England*, 366–67.

5. Porter, *Vigilant State*; Jane Morgan, *Conflict and Order: The Police and Labour Disputes in England and Wales 1900–1939* (Oxford, 1987); Phillip Thurmond Smith, *Policing Victorian London: Political Policing, Public Order and the London Metropolitan Police* (Westport, 1987).

6. Christopher Andrew, *Secret Service: The Making of the British Intelligence Community* (London, 1985); Porter, *Vigilant State*.

7. The latest history of the English police barely mentions detectives; see Clive

Emsley, *The English Police: A Political and Social History* (Hemel Hempstead, 1991).

8. Generally see Gary T. Marx, *Undercover: Police Surveillance in America* (Berkeley, 1988).

9. David Ascoli, *The Queen's Peace: The Origin and Development of the Metropolitan Police 1829–1979* (London, 1979), 210.

10. Emsley, *The English Police*, 27–28.

11. Departmental Committee on the System of Police: Minutes of Evidence (1868), 97. This report was consulted in the library of New Scotland Yard, London.

12. Jennifer Davis, "The London Garotting Panic of 1862: A Moral Panic and the Creation of a Criminal Class in mid-Victorian England" in *Crime and the Law: The Social History of Crime in Western Europe since 1500*, ed. V. A. C. Gatrell, Bruce Lenman, and Geoffrey Parker (London, 1980), 190–213.

13. Departmental Committee on System of Police, 97–9, 82.

14. Ibid., 82–5, 93–5.

15. Ibid., 17–19, 21–2.

16. *The Times*, 4 February 1869, 5; 8 February 1869, 9.

17. Public Record Office (PRO), Metropolitan Police (MEPO) 7/31, Police Order 15 May 1869, 137 and 27 July 1869, 209.

18. *Annual Report of the Metropolitan Police Commissioner 1869*, Parliamentary Papers 36 (1870): 3–4.

19. *Hansard*, 3d ser., 200 (28 March 1870): col. 729; PRO Home Office (HO) 45/9442/66692, Departmental Commission of Inquiry into the Detective Force, v.

20. George Dilnot, ed., *Trial of the Detectives* (London, 1928).

21. *The Times*, 22 November 1877, 9; *Pall Mall Gazette*, 21 November 1877, 1; *Saturday Review*, 24 November 1877, 650, 1 December 1877, 682–3; for a critical view see *Reynolds's Newspaper*, 25 November 1877, 4.

22. PROHO 45/9442/66692 Departmental Commission of Inquiry into the Detective Force, iii, vi, viii.

23. Ibid., ix, questions 1349–51.

24. Ibid., ix–xi.

25. Ibid., xv–xvii, for the conclusions and recommendations.

26. Ibid., letter by Cross, 12 April 1878; Robert Anderson, *The Lighter Side of My Official Life* (London, 1910), 125.

27. PROHO 45/9567/74577A, Metropolitan Police (Departmental) Commission (1879), xvii, question 5058; S. H. Jeyes and P. D. How, *The Life of Sir Howard Vincent* (London, 1912), 60; Bodleian Library, Ms Harcourt, Box 100 fols. 34–5, Vincent to Harcourt, 6 June 1881.

28. For Vincent's work see Stefan Petrow, *Policing Morals: The Metropolitan Police and the Home Office 1870–1914* (Oxford, forthcoming), Part II.

29. Ascoli, *Queen's Peace*, 150n; *Saturday Review*, 9 February 1884, 177–9; Anon., "Our Detective Police," *Chamber's Journal* (1884), 337–39.

30. PROMEPO 7/46, Police Order 14 June 1884, 142, gives 294, but it is unclear how many men were employed in the Special Irish Branch, for which see Porter, *Vigilant State*, 84–85.

31. PROMEPO 2/134, memorandum, by Vincent, 27 October 1880.

32. *The Times*, 30 January 1920, 16; George Dilnot, *Scotland Yard: Its History and Organization 1829–1929* (London, 1929), 258.

33. PROHO 45/10002/A49463, memorandum by Monro, 11 November 1887; PROHO 144/190/A46472B, memorandum by Monro, 15 February 1888.

34. Porter, *Vigilant State*, 87.

35. Jill Pellew, *The Home Office 1848–1914: From Clerks to Bureaucrats* (London, 1982), 47–52.

36. Ascoli, *Queen's Peace*, 169.

37. Porter, *Vigilant State*, 72.

38. For the habitual criminal see Leon Radzinowicz and Roger Hood, *A History of English Criminal Law*, 5 vols. (London, 1986), 5:231–87.

39. PROHO 45/10566/173919, Henry to HO, 23 November 1901.

40. Bribery of police is a major theme of Petrow, *Policing Morals*.

41. PROMEPO 2/1148, HO to Henry, 10 April 1908; Edward Carpenter, "Who Shall Watch the Watchman? A Criticism of Our Police System," *Free Review* 6 (1896): 144–45.

42. Departmental Committee on the System of Police, 280, 282, 285–88, 302, 309–10, 315–18; PROHO 45/9442/66692, Departmental Commission of Inquiry into the Detective Force, vii–viii.

43. PROHO 45/9442/66692, Departmental Commission of Inquiry into the Detective Force, iv; PROMEPO 2/134, memorandum by Vincent, 27 October 1880, report by Williamson, 22 October 1880; Porter, *Vigilant State*, 7.

44. PROHO 45/9567/74577A, Metropolitan Police (Departmental) Commission, xxi.

45. Porter, *Vigilant State*, 63–72, 192.

46. Ascoli, *Queen's Peace*, 184; PROMEPO 2/697, report by Gooding, 15 August 1908; PROMEPO 2/1570, Henry to HO, 16 October 1913; *Annual Report of the Metropolitan Police Commissioner 1913*, Parliamentary Papers 32 (1914–16): 8.

47. PROHO 45/11000/223532, Henry to HO, 13 May, 15 August 1912.

48. For the growth of criminal records see Petrow, *Policing Morals*, ch. 4.

49. Cecil Bishop, *From Information Received: The Reminiscences of Cecil Bishop, late C.I.D., New Scotland Yard* (London, 1932), 39; John George Littlechild, *Reminiscences of Chief Inspector Littlechild*, 2nd. edn. (London, 1894), 95.

50. *Encyclopaedia of the Laws of England*, 13 vols. (London, 1897–1903), 6: 459.

51. Bernard Porter, *The Refugee Question in Mid-Victorian Politics* (Cambridge, 1979), 153; Smith, *Policing Victorian London*, 72–74.

52. PROMEPO 2/134, memorandum by Cross, 21 May 1875; PROHO 45/9442/66692, Departmental Commission of Inquiry into the Detective Force, questions 821–31, 926, 942, 1224.

53. Ibid., questions 3973, 5194, 5458, 5456.

54. Charles Edward Howard Vincent, *Police Code and Manual of Criminal Law* (London, 1881), 104–5, 202.

55. *Saturday Review*, 9 February 1884, 177–79.

56. Harcourt apparently relied on informers for information on the Irish bombers; Porter, *Vigilant State*, 41, 55, 57–59.

57. PROHO 144/249/A54906, memorandum by Swanson, 27 June 1893.

58. Littlechild, *Reminiscences*, 117; Maurice Moser and Charles F. Rideal, *Stories from Scotland Yard as told by Inspector Moser* (London, 1890), 201–6.

59. Moser, *Stories*, 57, 234, 50; Littlechild, *Reminiscences*, 109–10, 117; James

Berrett, *When I Was at Scotland Yard* (London, 1932), 53; Robert A. Fuller, *Recollections of a Detective* (London, 1912), 45, 54.

60. Bishop, *From Information Received*, 41, 127.

61. Edwin William Pugh, *The City of the World: A Book about London and the Londoner* (London, 1912), 273; Anon., "Why Detectives Fail: Some Secrets Revealed by an Ex-convict," *London Magazine* 13 (1904–5): 65.

62. British Library of Political and Economic Science, Booth Collection Group B, 353 (4 July 1898): 225, 229.

63. Littlechild, *Reminiscences*, 96.

64. *The Times*, 9 November 1910, 3, 10 November 1910, 3, 24 November 1910, 3.

65. Ibid., 18 January 1911, 4.

66. *Hansard*, 5th ser., 22 (Commons), (13 March 1911): cols. 1863–4; PROHO 144/1105/200206 is the relevant file on the case.

67. PROHO 144/1105/200206, memorandum by E. B., 12 January 1911.

68. Littlechild, *Reminiscences,* 117; Edward Abinger, "The Police and the Public," *English Review* 8 (1911): 675.

69. Fuller, *Recollections*, 216.

70. Vincent, *Police Code*, 105.

71. PROHO 45/9442/66692, Departmental Commission of Inquiry into the Detective Force, questions 141, 880–83, 2644; Fuller, *Recollections*, 214; Bishop, *From Information Received*, 135; Dilnot, *Scotland Yard: Methods*, 48.

72. Public disapproval of impersonation by police was strikingly expressed during the Popay affair of 1833; see Ascoli, *Queen's Peace*, 104–7.

73. *Spectator*, 30 August 1890, 211–12.

74. Bishop, *From Information Received*, 160; Fuller, *Recollections*, 215; Littlechild, *Reminiscences*, 76–7, 88–9; Tom Divall, *Scoundrels and Scallywags and Some Honest Men* (London, 1929), 100–1.

75. Francis Carlin, *Reminiscences of an Ex-detective* (London, 1927), 221; Divall, *Scoundrels*, 101; Fuller, *Recollections*, 213.

76. Malcolm Laing Meason, "Detective Police," *Nineteenth Century*, 13 (1883): 765, 772–74.

77. PROHO 144/73/A212 provides details of the case.

78. *Hansard*, 3rd ser., 257, (11 January 1881): 443–4; *Daily News*, 12 January 1881, 5.

79. Charles Tempest Clarkson and J. Hall Richardson, *Police!* (London, 1889), 264; Lee, *Police in England*, 366–67; Charles Edward Howard Vincent, "Address," *Transactions of the National Association for the Promotion of Social Science* (1883): 204–5.

80. Robert Anderson, *Criminals and Crime: Some Facts and Suggestions* (London, 1907), 82; Porter, *Vigilant State*, 136–67.

81. Raphael Samuel, *East End Underworld: Chapters in the Life of Arthur Harding* (London, 1981), vii, 190; Chartres Biron, *Without Prejudice: Impressions of Life and Law* (London, 1936), 252–53.

82. *Royal Commission on the Metropolitan Police*, Parliamentary Papers 50 (1908): 300. This submission was not published and was probably destroyed, but see James Timewell, *The Royal Commission on the Metropolitan Police*, 2nd rev.

edn. (London, 1909), 9–11, where it is possibly Harding's submission, under the name of Tresarden, that is discussed.

83. Samuel, *East End*, 192, 200–1, 188–89.

84. Ibid., 200.

85. Petrow, *Policing Morals*, ch. 10.

86. Carpenter, "Who Shall Watch," 144–45.

87. Anon., "Why Detectives Fail," 66.

88. That the perception of a new type of professional criminal was unfounded has been convincingly demonstrated in V. A. C. Gatrell, "Crime, Authority, and the Policeman-state" in *The Cambridge Social History of Britain 1750–1950*, 3 vols., ed. F. M. L. Thompson (Cambridge, 1990), 3: 302–4.

89. David Vincent, "The Origins of Public Secrecy in Britain," *Transactions of the Royal Historical Society*, 6th ser., 1 (1991): 229–48.

"Dime Novel Toughs": Legal Culture and Criminal Law in Red Deer, Alberta, 1907–1920

Jonathan Swainger
University of Northern British Columbia, Prince George

The reappearance of James Oscar Triplett in the small lumber community of Rocky Mountain House, Alberta, on 11 December 1918 failed to bode well for the local citizenry. Triplett, who had been released from the Ponoka Asylum for the insane located in central Alberta, was known to the police as "a dangerous lunatic." Shortly after his arrival, stories circulated quickly that Triplett was roaming around the district wreaking havoc and verbally abusing everyone with whom he came into contact. On 12 December he arrived at the Temple farm in search of Mr. Temple who had gone west on a hunting trip. After making a number of attempts to force his way into the house and then waiving an axe at Lois Mary Temple and her daughter, Triplett left the farm and spent the night with Jacob Strutsman, a former acquaintance.

The time that Strutsman spent in the company of Triplett was horrific. For much of the evening Triplett ran around naked, raved like a madman, urinated on Strutsman's food, and attempted to destroy almost everything in the cabin. At one point in the early morning Triplett unsuccessfully attempted to strangle Strutsman. Triplett set out once again for the Temple farm at daybreak, and Strutsman raced cross-country to warn Lois Mary that Triplet was on the loose. Arriving at the Temple farm before Triplett, Strutsman decided to stay and help Temple with her farm chores and, in the process, keep an eye on things.

Upon Strutsman's arrival, Temple thought she would take the opportunity of checking on her daughter, whom she had left unattended in the house. Turning to walk towards the house, she was stricken with the sight of Triplett standing on the porch only moments away from entering the front door. Temple screamed for Strutsman and ran down the hill in an attempt to protect her child from the madman Triplett. Startled by Temple's scream, Triplett ran for the chicken coop, where he savaged the birds by breaking their necks and throwing the dead chickens into the air. Triplett stormed around the Temple farm threatening to burn the barn and cabin and actually managed to start a small fire on the cabin's roof. At one point, Triplett grabbed a rope that had been tied to a cowbell and attempted to strike Strutsman, who was feverishly trying to bring Triplett under control. Both Temple and Strutsman fired weapons at Triplett a number of times, once with Triplett crumbling to the ground, only to jump to his feet and growl, "You'll never kill me." Finally, Triplett managed to corner Temple and her child in the cabin, to which they had both retreated. At the very moment that Triplett was about to enter, Strutsman emerged from behind the cabin, leveled his rifle at Triplett, slipped, and fired over his head. Mere seconds later, as Triplett's left hand turned the doorknob, Temple fired her rifle through the closed door; her bullet grazed off his left hand, ricocheted upwards, and hit Triplett below the left eye, killing him instantly.

The coroner's inquest held on 18 December before Dr. Henry George of Red Deer, Alberta, determined the case to be one of justifiable homicide, with Lois Mary Temple acting in defense of her honor and life and also the life of her child. In exonerating Temple, however, the jury concluded that a full investigation should be made of the release of Triplett from the insane asylum at Ponoka and that blame should be fixed for permitting a criminally insane man to be at large to terrorize a community where his inclinations were so well known.[1] One wonders how Triplett's release and the events leading to his violent death affected a small community such as Rocky Mountain House. Perhaps more pointedly, in light of the jury's conclusion that further investigation was needed, did the events of mid-December 1918 alter the community's impressions of the legal system responsible for re-leasing James Oscar Triplett? Finally, if the Triplett case and other incidents did give reason to reexamine assumptions, what had central Albertans ex-pected from the administration of justice prior to these events?

The evidence from criminal prosecutions tried before the Supreme Court sitting in Red Deer, Alberta, from 1907 to 1920, documents that the legal system provided central Albertans with a respectable degree of confidence. During these years, the Red Deer district enjoyed a conviction rate of almost 62 percent for those cases in which a verdict was recorded.[2] In comparison, a study of crime in New Zealand reveals that from 1906 to 1920 the conviction rate in four classes of violent offenses was slightly over 57 percent of charges laid.[3] Writing of criminal trials in Alameda county, California, Lawrence Friedman and Robert Percival note that with a conviction rate of 58 percent for the years from 1900 to 1910, defendants had a fighting chance once they appeared in court; those in central Alberta were equally fortunate.[4] A preliminary survey of 1,020 cases heard by central Albertan justices of the peace from 1907 to 1914, however, reveals a higher prob-ability of conviction. In these cases the prosecution was successful in slightly over 78 percent of summary hearings.[5] Therefore, as an indication of what central Albertans came to expect from the administration of criminal justice, these conviction rates suggest that a sense of security, in the form of a reasonable proportion of convictions to cases tried, was an important ingredient of the region's legal culture. However, while illuminating, the figures relate only part of the picture, for they do not reveal how the legal system actually functioned as it achieved these conviction rates.

Sketching how the administration of justice operated in central Alberta depends on a perspective embracing both the legal system and the community it served. The rampage of a "madman," the existence of an organized gang of cattle thieves, or the rape of a young girl by a local farm boy were not matters for local law enforcement officials alone; these were also events of grave concern for central Albertans.[6] The region's legal culture, however, was shaped not only by how these crimes were handled, but also by the district's ethnic profile, economic orientation and, for the lack of a better phrase, a frontier practicality that colored almost every aspect of life in central Alberta before 1920.[7] This practicality did not usually manifest itself in the form of vigilantism witnessed occasionally in the American West, but rather in the perspective that other forms of dispute resolution were available rather than immediately turning to the official system of criminal justice.[8] For some this might have involved turning to local leaders to arbitrate disputes or possibly exacting some measure of community retribution or chastisement without redress to the courts. There were, however, occasions when these unofficial alternatives or the responses they generated crossed the line between frontier independence and taking criminal license, a step almost invariably ending in court.[9]

Thus we can detect two of the strains running through central Alberta's legal culture. First, the legal system provided the community with the assurance that criminals were regularly brought to court and convicted for their activities. The administration of justice, therefore, had a demonstrable veneer of efficiency. On the other hand, it seems evident that, for various reasons, reliance on the official court system was mitigated by unofficial methods of settling disputes. Despite the possibility of success through the legal system, apparently there was a class of conflicts and misunderstandings that fell outside of the system. Quite possibly, the failings of the courts to deal with certain offenses to the satisfaction of certain individuals provided a justification to take the law into their own hands. Although the attorney-general's office undoubtedly devoted considerable energy to reducing those incidents where the legal system apparently failed the community, the daily reality of the administration of justice restricted such efforts. In fact, the actual composition of the administration of justice assured central Albertans and, by extension, the entire province ample opportunity to question how effectively their interests were being protected.

SOURCES AND EVIDENCE

The sources that form the basis of this study are the case files of the 407 trials heard by the Supreme Court sitting at Red Deer, various police investigations, and coroners' inquests conducted in the district from 1907 to 1920. The absence of the somewhat less spectacular cases of public drunkenness, vagrancy, disturbing the peace, and other minor infractions is a reflection of the fact that these cases were not heard in the Supreme Court but were instead disposed of summarily by police magistrates and justices of the peace. Overall, representing what can be considered the most serious charges brought before criminal tribunals in the district, these cases concerned behavior that undoubtedly was perceived as the greatest threat to central Albertan society.

A canvas of these records demonstrates some basic characteristics of recorded criminal activity in central Alberta. In common with the findings of Friedman and Percival for Alameda county, California, theft maintained a dominant position on the Supreme Court docket in Red Deer; consistent with the region's agricultural character, many of these indictments involved agricultural chattel.[10] For the 121 documented verdicts from 1907 to 1920, the Red Deer district achieved a conviction rate of almost 79 percent. Second to theft in occurrence were those indictments falling under the general category of offenses against the person. However, unlike cases of theft, the seventy recorded verdicts included only thirty-nine convictions, almost a 56 percent success rate.[11] A final notable category embraces the commercial offenses of forgery, fraud, and false pretenses. Totaling forty-nine cases, of which forty-one recorded verdicts, these commercial crimes produced a conviction rate of slightly over 56 percent.[12] The combination of these three classes of crimes accounted for over 76 percent of the docket in central Alberta during these years and therefore constitutes the clear majority of the court's business.[13]

While illuminating, these figures were but one factor molding the perceptions of central Albertans toward the administration of justice. The region's legal culture reflected not only conviction rates, but how effectively the legal functionaries and courts responded to the social and political realities of central Alberta. No single ingredient determined the legal culture, but rather a combination of the actual workings of the system and perceptions of how the courts ought to serve the community. It is only through an appreciation of the daily administration of justice that we gain insight into the legal system and the community of which it was a part. The image which emerges is that of a well-staffed Supreme Court served poorly by a broader "supporting" structure periodically hampered by ill-trained individual officials and significant shortages of police. The practical result was that, while central Albertans may have been given cause to question the efficacy of their court system, the circumstances of the day allowed few, if any, alternatives.

POLICING THE RED DEER DISTRICT

One of the greatest challenges confronting the legal system in central Alberta involved policing. The Supreme Court district of Red Deer was an ethnically and economically diverse region running from the prairie expanse of east-central Alberta westward to the foothills and the western slope of the Rocky Mountains. Roughly seventy kilometers wide at its longest point, running north to south and 300 kilometers from west to east, the district was a geographic, demographic, and economic cross-section of all that Alberta was in the first two decades of the twentieth century. This diversity and the corresponding absence of a dominating social vision provided a considerable challenge to the various police forces such as the North West Mounted Police (NWMP), town and city detachments, and the Alberta Provincial Police (APP) after 1917.[14] There is little indication that any real attempt was made to train the police before they started their patrols, besides the drilling that the NWMP recruits received. Apparently when confronted with a crime, common sense and hard work sufficed, while investigatory skills were acquired through on-the-job experience.

At a time when professional policing was emerging in Britain and the United States, the absence of training was consistent with the older notion that the primary function of the police was to act in a social welfare role rather than as crime fighters.[15] Indeed, the peacekeeper and caregiver duties of the NWMP certainly played a predominant role in their relations with pioneers throughout the West prior to World War I.[16] These responsibilities were not, however, limited to the NWMP. The local Red Deer police used their cells as overnight accommodation for transients in the hope that a bed and meal would prevent these individuals from turning to crime for the necessities of life. Unfortunately, such measures did not always produce the desired result. For example, while sleeping in his room at the Arlington Hotel in downtown Red Deer, Bruce Hogarth was awakened by creaking floorboards as an intruder was leaving the room. Hogarth discovered that his wallet had been stolen and notified city constables Arthur Innis and Michael Riedy, who then undertook a search for suspicious characters. When Charles Morris was unable to give a satisfactory account of himself, he was arrested for vagrancy. A search of his possessions produced Hogarth's money and a meal ticket given to the accused by Police Chief Charles Anderson. Although Morris claimed the money was his, he admitted that his search for employment in Red Deer had been unsuccessful. Eventually found guilty, Morris was sentenced to three months hard labor in the Fort Saskatchewan jail.[17]

The peacekeeping responsibilities of the police, while not demanding great investigatory skills, did require a certain visibility and presence. Perhaps predictably in a district the size of central Alberta, there never seemed to be enough police to meet expectations. Unfortunately, the shortage could not be alleviated through cooperation and shared duties between the various forces because relations were often rather tense. When James McNichol JP requested that a mounted policeman be stationed in Blackfalds to enforce the liquor laws and control the railway crews, the response was that Blackfalds did not need a constable because Lacombe and Red Deer were so close.[18] Two years later L. G. Taylor, a JP in Rocky Mountain House, made a similar request that a constable be stationed in the town in January 1912 to quell the drinking and fighting of railway work crews. The NWMP made it clear that the transfer would result in Red Deer being short a constable for the foreseeable future.[19] Ten months after Taylor's application, Secretary-Treasurer A. T. Stephenson of Red Deer asked that an officer be stationed at Red Deer to look after the immediate district. Stephenson stated that, though a constable was located there, his territory was too large, and often he was away for as long as a week. The secretary-treasurer continued:

Our town police consists of four men including the Chief [,] two men doing day duty and two night duty. The force is small enough as it is, but it is enough for our requirements. When the Mounted Police constable is away our police are frequently called upon to look after cases from outside of the Town. This they do cheerfully whenever it is possible for them to do so, but sometimes it is impossible for them to attend to them and in other cases duties are forced on them when they have not time to attend to them.[sic][20]

Though Stephenson was no doubt accurate in portraying the situation, Rod Macleod has argued that town police forces were either too small or incompetent to be of value and that the Mounted Police were forced to do both jobs.[21]

Patrolling the town of Red Deer offered special problems for both the NWMP and the local force. Macleod relates the incident of the founding Gaetz family charging Sergeant Dunning, in command of the Red Deer detachment, on two separate occasions with failing to protect "the respectable portion of the citizenry, by which they meant themselves."[22] The investigations into both reports resulted in the sergeant being exonerated with an assurance by prominent criminal lawyer P. J. Nolan, "that the Gaetz family resented the police because the police insisted on treating them exactly as they did everyone else in the community."[23] It would appear that the Gaetz family expected the police to protect their interests with greater vigor than employed in behalf of other, less important citizens.

"DIME NOVEL TOUGHS"

While the local hierarchy presented special challenges for the police, a more serious concern was the belief that Red Deer was relatively free from crime and that police duties were comprised of strolling around the town. While one chronicler of the Gaetz family suggested that policing the community was easy because it "was too small to make crime pay," such a sentiment did not reflect the reality of police work.[24] The danger was not from daily brawls or gun fights, but rather from the fact that local authorities and the police were so ill-prepared when violence did erupt. One of the best examples can be seen in the course of events involving Police Chiefs George Rothnie and George Bell in 1910 and 1911.

While patrolling the streets of Red Deer on 12, November 1910, Chief Rothnie encountered an intoxicated John Russell, who was wandering around the street acting in a rather obnoxious manner to other pedestrians. According to later depositions, the chief made a number of attempts to convince Russell to go home quietly and sleep it off. Once it became clear that Russell was uninterested, Rothnie attempted to take him into custody. At the very moment that the chief made his move, Russell pulled a revolver from his belt, pointed at Rothnie's face, and declared that he was going to "fix him." Russell squeezed the trigger at least twice, but the gun failed to discharge. Rothnie recovered his composure enough to bring Russell under control and deliver him before a JP for a preliminary hearing; he then handed in his own resignation. According to the *Red Deer Advocate*, Rothnie decided to become Chief of Police in Kamloops, British Columbia, where the chief received $110 per month rather than the $75 he had been paid in Red Deer.[25] Despite pleading not guilty to a complaint of attempting to discharge a loaded revolver with intent to commit murder, the twenty-eight-year-old Russell was found guilty in the Supreme Court on 16 November and was sentenced to three months in the NWMP guardroom in Calgary.[26]

Rothnie's replacement, George Bell, was not as fortunate. Shortly after assuming the duties of chief, Bell stumbled on a robbery shortly before midnight on 1, June 1911. Armed with his police whistle, Bell raced across the street to arrest the robber before he made an escape. Arthur Kelly, who was wearing a leather mask on his face while robbing H. G. Munroe and W. Grant, turned and shot Bell twice. As Bell crumbled to the ground, he continued to blow his police whistle. Munroe took the whistle from the chief and continued to blow it until help arrived for Bell.[27]

As Bell was carried to the Memorial Hospital, where it was expected he would die, city commissioner Stephenson and Constable A. J. Barber of the NWMP organized search parties for the unknown assailant. Though a number of men combed the area around Red Deer, it was not until 9:00 A.M. the following morning that an intrepid group of boy scouts cornered Kelly in a bush on the outskirts of town. He was arrested by Fire Chief Horace

Meeres, who delivered him to a JP for a preliminary hearing. Charged initially with robbery and attempted murder, it was expected that the complaint would be changed to murder because two local doctors had testified, "We do not think it possible for [Bell] to live."[28] Despite these dire predictions and a number of dying declarations from the chief, he managed to survive the attack. Immediately following his preliminary hearing, Kelly was transferred to Calgary in order to protect him from threats of lynching.[29] At his trial on 21 November Kelly was found guilty of attempted murder.[30]

In summarizing the course of events after having received the crime reports, Commissioner R. Burton Deane of the NWMP expressed some concern over what he termed the "indecent haste" with which the case had been rushed. Although Sergeant K. G. Murison had transferred the accused to Calgary in response to the talk of lynching, the action may have been unwarranted. In Deane's opinion, "This boy Kelly is one of the dime novel toughs and a whipping would do him and his class more good than anything."[31] While Deane certainly would not have condoned lynching Kelly, his comments betrayed a certain reticence towards the effectiveness of punishing the boy Kelly. Despite the imprisonment the young man would undergo, Deane seemed to recognize that, however well the justice system functioned, there would always be dime novel toughs, who for one reason or another believed they were too slick to be caught. The persistence of individuals like John Russell and Arthur Kelly made central Alberta, regardless of contrary perceptions, a difficult community to police.

A SLIPPERY FELLOW

When events did warrant an official complaint, the matter was brought before either a justice of the peace (JP) or a police magistrate (PM). Responsible for summary trials in minor cases as well as preliminary hearings for serious charges, appointees were required by provincial statute to be either British by birth or naturalized citizens.[32] The statute did not require nominees to have any legal background, although it did bar them from acting as counsel in criminal proceedings.[33] In practice, few had any previous experience, and most found themselves in office because they were prominent and respectable businessmen or farmers. The fact that JPs were not knowledgeable in the law was recognized by Supreme Court Justice David Lynch Scott in his written judgment for R v. Joseph Mannix. A request for damages against a JP was rejected on the grounds that:

Justices of the Peace are not presumed to be versed in the intricacies of the law and, if unintentional errors in law or procedure which would render their convictions invalid would subject them to payment of the costs of application to quash them, few would be willing to act in that capacity.[34]

The lack of training did not necessarily mean these officials were incompetent. As John Wunder notes in regard to justices in the American Northwest, most attempted to fulfill their duties responsibly.[35]

Shouldering the responsibilities of a JP could be a difficult undertaking, especially because no legal training was required. Common sense undoubtedly sufficed on most occasions, but even the best intentions could flounder on legal technicalities. As a result, most magistrates and justices tended to err on the side of inclusion and send almost everything to trial regardless of whether or not evidence was available to gain a conviction. From the perspective of the attorney general's office, such a policy was ill-advised. A general circular distributed throughout the province on 15 March 1916 addressed the situation:

In going over the accounts of our Agents, I find that in a number of cases the charge is withdrawn in the higher Court for lack of evidence, and in others is dismissed on the complainant's own evidence. I appreciate the difficulty which magistrates have, especially on preliminary hearings, and while it is very desirable that the interests of the Crown should not be neglected, it is equally so that the right of the accused not to be placed on his trial where the evidence does not afford a reasonable doubt of his guilt is one which should be fully protected by the magistrate. Apart from this, the expense to the Province of useless trials is very considerable with no corresponding gain.[36]

JPs and magistrates, pressed by the public to help deliver justice while subjected to the attorney general's concerns over costs and acquittals, were in an awkward position.

The simple fact was that, despite public perceptions and official guidelines, busy justices and magistrates were not equipped to meet all the demands placed at their feet. To require these individuals to be discerning in all matters of law brought before them, constantly accessible for swearing complaints and search warrants, and sitting for preliminary or summary hearings, while also maintaining their own homes and businesses, was a great deal to expect. The situation, however, cut both ways. These officials possessed considerable influence in some communities, and the opportunities to use the magistrate's office for personal ends was considerable. By specifying that appointees held office at the pleasure of the Lieutenant Governor in Council, the provincial statute offered a form of protection from unscrupulous appointees.[37] The key to this protection, however, was the willingness of the Lieutenant Governor and provincial cabinet to take action, and it appears that some hesitancy existed. This was certainly the case in the rather questionable behavior of James Dugald Skinner, one central Albertan justice of the peace.

Skinner first came to the attention of the attorney-general's office in early September 1907, when a series of fires in Lacombe caused considerable concern. An investigation by Joseph C. Fielding of the Pinkerton Detective

Agency revealed that the fire-damaged Russell Block was over-insured by its owner, J. D. Skinner, for $3,000 more than its actual value. After interviewing several people in the community, Fielding concluded that, though absolute proof did not exist, Skinner had been responsible for the fire. A further investigation by C. Driver of the Canadian Investigation Agency came to the same conclusions as the Pinkerton investigator, but Driver was less convinced of Skinner's guilt. The attorney-general's office declined to lay charges.[38] It is rather striking that such an event did not attract any attention when Skinner was granted a commission of the peace in 1914. Four months after the fire, Skinner once again gained notoriety when accused of falsely swearing an oath at a municipal election. Reporting the charge to Attorney-General S. B. Woods on 31, January 1908, Lacombe town councilor George W. Hotson requested that a crown solicitor look after the hearing "as the aforesaid J. D. is of a very slippery nature."[39] Although Corbet L. Durie, agent for the Attorney General at Lacombe, argued the case, the prosecution was unsuccessful.

Skinner managed to maintain a lower profile until he moved to Rocky Mountain House, where he assumed the proprietorship of the *Echo* newspaper in the spring of 1912.[40] As he prepared for his entry into publishing, Skinner became embroiled in a dispute over a printing press that had been seized and placed in storage by J. C. Cloutman.[41] Cloutman stated that he had removed the press to his building on instructions from the Winnipeg firm of Miller and Richards, who evidently held a promissory note on the press. Skinner obtained a legal search warrant for Cloutman's presence; while a local constable and JP were allowed to enter Cloutman's premises to inspect the press, Skinner was not. His response was to kick Cloutman's door twice, with enough force to break the door and its lock. Despite claims that the door was damaged prior to his actions, Skinner was found guilty of willful damage and was obliged to pay a $3 fine and $5 damages.[42] Undaunted, Skinner responded by laying a charge of perjury against Cloutman. Summarizing events for the attorney general's office, presiding justice F. J. Long thought that the second charge was without merit and that Skinner was "actuated by spite."[43] Eighteen months later, on 27 December 1913, Skinner received his commission as justice of the peace in Rocky Mountain House.[44]

Three years after taking over the newspaper, Skinner was again involved in controversy when he was charged with publishing a defamatory libel.[45] Although the entire incident is more reflective of small-town politics, personality conflicts, and poor editorial judgment on Skinner's part, it still begs the question of why he had been granted a legal function in the first place. Perhaps Judge Simmons' comments to Skinner that "in all honesty and decency he ought to resign the Commission of the Peace which he holds" finally alerted the attorney-general's office to Skinner's questionable conduct.[46] Despite the fact that he apparently had some standing as a community leader, Skinner had become a liability, one month after the libel trial concluded, his commission was cancelled.[47] Three months later, he was also replaced as village reeve for Rocky Mountain House.[48]

Skinner's career both before and after he received his commission of the peace raises a number of questions. Although it might be tempting to dismiss his appointment as an aberration, many justices throughout central Alberta found their actions periodically under scrutiny by the attorney-general's office.[49] While Skinner may have been notable for his consistently ill-considered behavior, he certainly was not alone in running afoul of the attorney-general's office. Perhaps the foremost issue, however, concerns how the performance of officials like Skinner colored public perceptions of the administration of justice. Often the first level of the court system encountered by the public, magistrates and justices of the peace occupied an important role for those victimized by crime or accused of a criminal act. These were not inconsequential events. When any magistrate's actions or demeanor failed to demonstrate that the matter would be considered seriously, the entire court system suffered.

THE BAR AND BENCH

The legal profession was the first stage of the administrative structure in which the public was assured of some legal training. The quality and depth of legal knowledge, however, was not guaranteed and revolved around the standards of admission enforced initially by the territorial government and later the law society of the North-West Territories and Alberta.[50] These standards evolved from the situation prior to 1885, when one simply started practicing, to those that surrounded the emergence of a structured legal education at the University of Alberta by 1924.[51] The majority of lawyers who practiced in the Red Deer district from 1907 to 1920 were a product of the transition between former wide-open admission practices and the more selective process. The quality of legal practice that resulted from the unsettled state of admissions thus varied with the knowledge and inclination of the lawyer involved.

Legal practice in the Red Deer district was initially dominated by three men: George Wellington Greene, who arrived in 1891, William Earnest Payne, who joined Greene in 1902, and John Carlyle Moore, who came to the town in August 1904 to help with the land interests of his father, John T. Moore.[52] The picture that emerges is that of men who used legal practice as an avenue to greater rewards. All three had wider business interests that occupied as much if not more time than their legal affairs.[53] The practice of law was not an end in itself, but rather a means to the acquisition of wealth, the bench, or political office. Given these business inclinations, it is less than surprising that none of the three acted as agent for the attorney general in central Alberta.

The responsibilities of acting on the crown's behalf in central Alberta from 1907 to 1920 fell to three men. Corbet L. Durie directed criminal prosecutions from 1907 to 1911, Arthur H. Russell assumed that duty until around 1916, and John Quigg stepped in for the remainder of the decade. Durie appears to have viewed his position as one suited for directing local affairs in accordance with the wishes of the provincial Liberal party and government.[54] Overlooked for a judicial vacancy in the summer of 1910, Durie cited health reasons when he left central Alberta the following September.[55] Although he was expected to resume his duties after a brief rest, he never returned. A. H. Russell filled Durie's place and achieved reasonable success on the crown's behalf.[56] Unfortunately for Russell, his career was marked by a charge and acquittal for counselling perjury in 1922 after resigning as crown prosecutor to devote more attention to his criminal law practice.[57] Like his predecessors, Quigg performed his duties admirably and, in so doing, fit the mold of crown prosecutors who were skilled, if not particularly inspired, lawyers.

The superior courts, which were the final and most important stage of the administration of justice, were blessed not only with stability in membership during this period but also by judges who were both well-read and eclectic in their interests.[58] These traits were reflected in the bench's consistent ability to envision wider implications in its rulings and in the selective creativity of its decisions.[59] For the public at large, this "municipal law" recognized the importance of a region's economic structure, societal beliefs and morals, and its customs in defining the tenets of justice.[60] Thus the significance of the courts was an attribute not only of their role as final arbiter, but of a brand of law that the community deemed was just.

The stability and unity that characterized the Alberta Supreme Court were the result of several factors. All of the judges were born in Canada West or Ontario, and all but Chief Justice Arthur L. Sifton and Justice David L. Scott received their law degrees at the University of Toronto. When Justice William L. Walsh joined the court in 1912, another Toronto and Osgoode Hall graduate was added to the court. All of these men could have stayed in central Canada and had quite lucrative practices, but rather they chose to come west.[61] Their adventuresome character and willingness to experiment are often notable in their judicial decisions.[62] The spirit propelling these young lawyers to come west allowed them to nurture a quintessentially legal culture upon their eventual ascendancy to the bench.

Further, the court was staffed with judges who had sat together on the Supreme Court of the North-West Territories. Of the original members of the Alberta court created in 1907, Chief Justice Sifton and Justices Scott, Horace Harvey, and Charles Stuart had all been on the earlier bench, and Justice Nicholas Beck was appointed shortly after the creation of the court.[63] Indeed, during the first thirteen years of its existence, Chief Justice Sifton was the only member to leave the bench. The core of the original court maintained itself until the early 1920s and worked continually to transform the idea of law from a superimposed body of rules to an integral part of society. Their purpose was to engender a concept of law that was founded upon flexible general principles that chose to focus on the particular circumstances of the society of which it was a part. The challenge was not only to discern an appropriate jurisprudence for central Alberta and the entire province but also to accomplish this end in light of the "supporting" structure of police, magistrates, and crown prosecutors.

THE DUBOIS-HOLT GANG

In an agricultural community such as central Alberta, crimes related to the theft or destruction of livestock were extremely serious. The theft and wounding of livestock accounted for ninety-three cases on the Supreme Court docket in Red Deer from 1907 to 1920. Despite irregular branding practices and the use of open grazing, guilty verdicts were returned in almost 63 percent of the seventy-five recorded verdicts. Marginally above the district's overall conviction rate of 62 percent but considerably lower than the conviction rate of almost 78 percent for all classes of theft, these figures seem to portray an unexceptional pursuit of criminals who victimized a significant segment of the local economy. Given the difficulties of prosecuting livestock thieves like the notorious Dubois-Holt gang, however, a closer examination of the 62 percent conviction rate suggests that it was a considerable achievement.

The methods of the Dubois-Holt gang were deceptively simple. One member of the gang, comprised of Joe Cardinal, Louis Salway, Irven Holt, James Holt, and John Dubois, would steal one or more cows and give them to another member, who would subsequently brand them and claim them as his own. When questioned as to the actual ownership of any animal, each member of the gang would feign ignorance of the transaction.[64] If the animal could be positively identified as one that had been stolen, they would simply argue that the animal had wandered into their herd and had been branded by accident. The irregularity of branding combined with the common practice of grazing cattle wherever land could be found made such explanations plausible, although rather suspicious. Attempting to make their alibis more credible, the gang regularly bought cattle so that they could claim the animal in question was one of many that had been purchased.[65]

When the activities of the Holt gang came to the attention of the NWMP, it fell upon the shoulders of Sergeant Robert W. Ensor to bring "the worst gang that ever operated in Western Canada" to justice.[66] Ensor's determination was incredible. At one point, after rounding up all of the cattle held by the Holts, Ensor roped each of the eighty-five animals personally and clipped the hair around each brand to determine if it covered an older brand of an original owner. As the sergeant reported, "It takes a lot of work to rope and clip eighty-five head of mostly range steers but it is the only way to go after these men. I am prepared to go into Court and describe every animal, so the work is being done in a thorough manner."[67] Given Ensor's zeal, it is perhaps not surprising that in his absence on vacation a year earlier, cattle and horse thefts had become quite frequent in the district he patrolled.[68]

The vigorous efforts of Ensor were needed, as the gang was perceived by many as being "too slick" ever to be caught. Furthermore, it would be difficult to gain a conviction because potential witnesses were afraid to give evidence because of possible retaliation. The sergeant reported, "I am convinced there are lots of people who could give evidence against Dubois but they are afraid of him. Lots of people are in terror of him as they believe if he gets free he will run their cattle off."[69] This sentiment was also shared by the Central Alberta Stockgrowers Association.[70] After months of work by Ensor and with the aid of P. J. Nolan as prosecuting attorney, all but Dubois were found guilty and sentenced to terms of imprisonment ranging from three months to five years.[71] Because Irven Holt had previously been imprisoned in Idaho for horse theft, he was subsequently deported back to the United States.

Despite the high-profile victory over the Dubois-Holt gang and the possibility of further successful prosecutions, not all central Albertans were confident that the legal system was controlling livestock theft. When a three-year-old bay horse belonging to Nels Hanson Kolding of Kevisville disappeared during the first week of June 1918, Kolding, Harold Frederickson, and Theodore Norgaard decided to search a nearby stable owned by Louis Adamson.[72] Not only did they find the bay horse, they also located a two-year-old black mare and a ten-month-old black stallion belonging to Kolding. Rather than reporting their discoveries to authorities, the three men took cover in the bushes to discover who would claim the animals. After a ninety-minute wait, Claude F. House and another man arrived and attempted to catch the horses. When Frederickson jumped out of the bushes and ran towards the stable door, one of the men chasing the horses extinguished his light, and House began firing his revolver. Frederickson and Kolding returned fire and hit House in the chest; he then turned and fled. The man who had accompanied House also fled with two of the horses believed to have been stolen from T. M. Mecklenbourg. House was later arrested by APP Constable Albert Chapman.

Two complaints were initially laid against House on 14 June; he was charged with stealing Kolding's three horses and discharging a revolver at Frederickson with intent to do grievous bodily harm. A preliminary hearing was held by W. G. McArthur on the following day. Evidence of the thefts and gunfight was taken; and despite defense arguments that House was merely looking for horses that had been stolen from him, the accused was committed for trial and released on recognizance of $6,000. Eleven days later, two new complaints were laid against House for discharging a revolver at Kolding with intent to commit murder and for stealing a seven-year-old roan mare belonging to Mecklenbourg.[73] Although defense counsel A. H. Russell thought the new complaints were "brought about vexatiously for the mere purpose of embarrassing" his client, another preliminary hearing was held on 5 July, when the depositions of the original hearing were submitted as evidence and House was again bound over for trial. The trial for attempting to do grievous bodily harm to Frederickson was held on 17 September before Judge Maitland McCarthy; House pleaded not guilty and was acquitted. The acquittal compelled the crown to enter a stay of proceeding in the associated cases.

Kolding, Frederickson, and Norgaard's belief that the horse thieves would not be apprehended unless they took immediate action proved fatal to any prosecution. Although House's claim that he was merely searching for his own stolen horses might appear suspicious, it must be remembered that Kolding and his associates had done exactly the same thing. Given the circumstances, House could have concluded that he was being ambushed by horse thieves. Fortunately for everyone involved, no one was killed despite the exchange of gunfire. Kolding and friends could have cited police cutbacks under the APP as the reason for their actions, although no attempt was made to notify the police until after shots were fired. Although legitimate complaints could be made in specific cases when the legal system fell short of expectations, by taking matters into their own hands Kolding, Frederickson, and Norgaard prevented the system from working. Considerably more troubling was the situation when despite best intentions the legal system rewarded a family's faith in the courts with frustration and disappointment.

"PULL OUR HONORABLE FLAG DOWN"

An early and tragic example of such a failure centers on the case of Henry Weir, who was accused of raping Sarah Anne Hibbert on 15 October 1906. According to a crime report filed by NWMP Constable Albert Johnson, on 2 October 1907 rumors began circulating around the Knee Hill district in November 1906 that Weir had forced himself upon Hibbert. When confronted by her parents, Sarah said nothing and would only sit and cry. It was only when Sarah regained consciousness after giving birth in early July 1907 that she accused "the dirty brute" Henry Weir.[74] As a result, on 6 July Sarah's father Bernard filed a complaint against twenty-one-year-old Henry Weir for having illicit connection with a girl aged fourteen to sixteen, of previously chaste character, contrary to section 211 of the criminal code. Hibbert also filed a complaint for seduction under the promise of marriage under section 212, and a third charge of having carnal knowledge of Sarah Hibbert against her consent, or with her consent as extorted by threats of bodily harm, contrary to section 298 of the Code.[75] The two latter charges were subsequently struck from the complaint.

The initial difficulty with prosecuting Weir was that he had fled to Maida County, North Dakota, where he was living with his sister. According to Hibbert, when he began proceedings to have Weir extradited the Mounted Police said that it would be too expensive to bring Weir back and that it would be wiser simply to wait for him to return on his own accord. For Hibbert such an argument was beyond belief. "If we has [sic] a Canada Government is afraid to defiend [sic] our right for the sake of a few dollars or more then I say pull our Honorable Flag down and say we are not able or Honorable enough to hold it up any longer."[76] Seven weeks later Hibbert had heard nothing of the efforts to get Weir to return but was assured by S. B. Woods, Deputy Attorney General in Edmonton, that the police had the matter well in hand.[77] Woods, however, was less confident than the impression he had given Hibbert and wrote the NWMP Commissioner in Regina on July 20 and requested some indication of how the matter was progressing. Three days later Woods learned "that no such communication has been received in this office from your Department, and I will be obliged if you will send me a copy of the file, which I will attend to immediately."[78] Thus it appears that by the end of September 1907, almost a year after Weir had allegedly forced himself on Hibbert, the accused was no closer to an appearance in court than on the day of the incident.

Finally, at this point the attorney-general's office, in seeking the counsel of Red Deer lawyer J. Carlyle Moore, began to examine the merits of the case against Weir.[79] Moore, who had considered some aspects of the case for his own information, requested a few days to examine closely the issues at hand. Responding on 14 October, Moore began by noting that, though a rape was actually committed, he doubted that sufficient evidence was obtainable to procure a conviction for that offense, "on account of the girl's delay in making a complaint, and the absence of a struggle etc."[80] However, all was not lost. "We could, I feel confident, procure a conviction under section 211 of the Code 1906, and if the offence there described is one for which extradition may be had, I would be very glad if the Department could follow the matter up, as the crime committed is of such a revolting character, and of such vital importance to the community and the Province."[81] Having read Constable Albert Johnson's police report of 2 October and received Moore's advice, Woods then wrote R. Burton Deane, Superintendent NWMP in Calgary, on 17 October and advised that a charge under section 211 should be filed and the proceedings for extradition should be instituted if Weir refused to return voluntarily.[82] As events would reveal, Weir had no intention of returning to Canada.

Given Weir's resistance, the proceedings for extradition were initiated, or at least it appeared that the matter was underway. Unfortunately, Deane believed that Woods had filed the application for extradition with the Canadian Department of Justice, and Woods was of the opposite impression. Therefore, when no official paperwork was received by the American sheriff at Langdon, North Dakota, who was holding Weir, he released the prisoner, who returned to his uncle's farm.[83] The warrant for Weir's extradition was finally issued in early February 1908, and one month later Weir appeared in Red Deer before Joseph Wallace JP, to be bound over on personal recognizance of $2,000, with George Weir and W.J. Baird acting as sureties in $1,000 each.[84] Owing to the poor state of the lockup in Red Deer, Wallace advised Corbet Durie, agent for the attorney general, to proceed with the matter at once. Weir was finally brought to his preliminary hearing on the following day, almost seventeen months after the alleged incident had occurred.

Immediately upon opening the preliminary hearing, Weir's defense counsel, the flamboyant P. J. Nolan, objected to the jurisdiction of the court on the grounds that his client could be tried only on the rape complaint sworn by Deane, and not on the original charge laid by Hibbert. Given the expiration of the statute of limitations on the Hibbert complaint, only Deane's complaint for the charge of rape was read to the accused. Depositions sworn on behalf of the crown on 18 March by Sarah Anne Hibbert and Clement Thomas revealed that Sarah had recently given birth to a child, born as a result of the alleged incident. Both deponents concurred that the accused had been at the house where the incident occurred, and Clement testified to the fact of Hibbert's dress being unbuttoned and the girl looking as if she had been crying after the incident. The accused was bound on his recognizance of $3,000 to appear and answer this complaint, and George Weir and Robert Winn were admitted as sureties in $1,500 each. The trial was held on 21 April in the Supreme Court before Judge Horace Harvey, where Weir pleaded not guilty and was acquitted.

After Weir's dismissal, a second warrant was issued by Joseph Wallace JP on 15 May for his arrest on a charge of seduction laid by Bernard Hibbert. Once again Weir was bound over to appear; when tried for seduction before Judge Stuart of the Supreme Court on 29 October, he was acquitted. Shortly after Judge Stuart wrote Woods and discussed the possibility that the matter might be tried once again, for a third time. The judge suggested that if in the interests of justice, the attorney-general's office decided to proceed with another trial, it would perhaps be best if another judge heard the case. The attorney-general's office made one more attempt to bring in a guilty verdict against Weir, and again the prosecution failed.

Still pushing for yet another attempt in February 1909, Bernard Hibbert suggested that he realized finally why a guilty verdict had not been secured. "Weir and Father is a Masonic and he is an Oddfellow I have been told I would have a hard fight and it has come true. . . . what I want is a juror that is not in any secret Society and do [sic] not know anything of this case and each juror sworn to this."[85] Despite these pleas, the attorney-general's office advised their agent in Red Deer that another attempt to bring Weir before the courts was simply out of the question.

The failed prosecution of Henry Weir demonstrated how forces outside the Red Deer district could adversely affect the local administration of justice. On one other occasion involving the extradition of a fugitive from the United States, the authorities in Canada were simply unable to act decisively.[86] Further difficulties with the Weir case related to the difficulties of marshalling sufficient evidence for a conviction. When the accused absolutely denied any guilt, the victim needed corroborative testimony to gain a conviction. Crimes involving sex rarely, if ever, take place where witnesses are able to substantiate a victim's testimony. Of the twenty-eight sex-related charges in which a verdict was recorded from 1907 through 1920, thirteen gained convictions, nine were dismissed, and six were withdrawn by the agent of the attorney general.[87]

The obstacles to prosecutions in these cases placed the crown attorney in the awkward position of having to pursue complaints with little chance of success. For example, when Alex Johnstone was arrested in late April 1920 for both contributing to and promoting the delinquency of Carrie Reule while seducing her under the promise of marriage, the case presented a difficult challenge. Despite the view of APP Detectives James Scott and W. J. Della Torre, John Quigg suggested to the attorney general's department that a conviction under promise of marriage was unlikely since the sixteen-year-old Ruele went willingly with Johnstone to the Royal Hotel in Innisfail.[88] However, while a conviction was unlikely, Quigg thought that given the notoriety attached to the case, "it would be better to have the matter disposed of in court." He continued:

The girl, no doubt, was an easy mark; but the Status of Chastity only applies to her physical condition, and while mentally or morally the girl may be of loose character the onus is on the Accused of showing that she was physically unchaste.

Although placed on the docket for trial before Judge McCarthy at Red Deer on September 21, 1920, the crown withdrew the case before a judgment was rendered.

While such tactics shifted responsibility to the courts, the same problems of evidence hampered the construction of a case and prevented conviction at the Supreme Court level. The frustration this undoubtedly caused was evident in the comments of Chief Justice Harvey in October 1912, when dismissing a charge of indecent assault against George Cummings:

You are discharged . . . not because I believe you are innocent, the evidence is entirely the other way. What you might say in answer to it [the evidence] I do not know, but you do not go out now because you have been cleared of the charge, but because the evidence has not been sufficient in law to warrant a conviction.[89]

Perhaps what bothered Harvey even more than his belief in Cummings' guilt was the persistence of rumors in the district that the accused had benefitted from his family's business connections and influence.

CONCLUSION

Despite the efforts of the judiciary to engender a regional jurisprudence that was receptive to the needs of both central Alberta and the province at large, institutional weakness in the administration of justice and legal realities limited these efforts. As Lawrence Friedman has noted in regard to criminal law in nineteenth-century America: "It was an aspect of living law that safeguards did not safeguard everybody; it was also an aspect of living law that many more were arrested than convicted, and that in the view of some the law was too soft, rather than too hard."[90] The currency of such a view in late nineteenth-century America and early twentieth-century central Alberta merely affirms that, regardless of what the criminal justice system delivers, it usually falls short of expectations. In that sense, the efforts of the Supreme Court to mold the legal culture to the needs of central Alberta were relatively unappreciated.

However, while the work of the Supreme Court may not have been acknowledged, it was nevertheless generally successful. If the criminal justice system functions to control dangerous behavior, to set out and enforce a moral code, and to keep order, the Alberta Supreme Court was indeed at the top of a reasonably effective legal structure.[91] Specific instances could be cited in which the system apparently failed, but there is no evidence that vigilantism and communal violence were ever really acceptable as a legitimate alternative to the courts. Unlike late nineteenth-century Imperial Russia, horse thieves were not brutalized by bloodthirsty crowds seeking vengeance in the Red Deer district.[92] Indeed, despite the inherent difficulties within the administration of justice in Alberta, the district's conviction rate compares favorably with other jurisdictions in the United States and New Zealand.[93]

Yet when the madman Oscar Triplett was released to wreak havoc on the community of Rocky Mountain House during the Christmas season of 1918, it no doubt caused concern. Events such as the Triplett rampage or Weir rape case were troubling, however, for misplaced reasons. Essentially, too much was expected of the legal system. While the police, magistrates, crown agents and judges endeavored to fulfill the societal expectations of a criminal justice system, there were simply too many contrary factors at play. The police were not trained to investigate crime, lay magistrates interpreted and sometimes misconstrued the law, and crown attorneys were often compelled to reconcile legal distinctions with public opinion. More important, even if all the structural pieces fell into place, the arbitrary nature of crime and the complexities of everyday life insured that criminals would find victims. Given human nature and the limitations of the practical administration of justice, the most to be expected was that, in a majority of cases, the system arrived at what appeared to be the right answer. In this limited sense, central Albertans had little ground for complaint.

NOTES

An earlier version of this paper was presented at "Law for the Elephant, Law for the Beaver: A Transboundary Conference on the Legal History of the West and Northwest of North America," held at the University of Victoria, Victoria, British Columbia, 22 February 1991.

1. Inquest on the body of James Oscar Triplett alias James Oscar, 18 December 1918, Provincial Archives of Alberta [PAA], 67.172, file no. 1192.

2. A total of 331 sentences were recorded in the 407 cases heard in the Supreme Court at Red Deer from 1907 to 1920. Guilty verdicts were returned in 205 of these cases, resulting in a conviction rate of 61 percent of recorded decisions. Of the remaining verdicts, 78 (24 percent) were acquittals and 48 (15 percent) were concluded through a motion of *nolle prosequi*.

3. See Miles Fairburn and Stephen Haslett, "Violent Crime in Old and New Societies: A Case Study Based on New Zealand 1853–1940," *Journal of Social History* 20 (1986): 90–92.

4. Lawrence Friedman and Robert Percival, *The Roots of Justice: Crime and Punishment in Alameda County, California, 1870–1910* (Chapel Hill, 1981), 182.

5. This figure is based on returns filed by eight justices of the peace throughout central Alberta from 1907 to 1914. Although preliminary, these findings correspond with patterns established during this period at Supreme Court trials. The returns are located in the PAA, 69.210. See Frank Whiteside, file 761; F. J. Long, file 1068; N. E. Carruthers, file 181; G. H. Darlow, file 311; W. B. Gray, file 119; Clark King, file 685; J. D. Lauder, file 792; and E. H. Matthias, file 281.

6. Writing of the situation in Calgary, Alberta, from 1907 to 1911, Thorner and Watson note that the inability of the lockup facilities to accommodate all those arrested on relatively minor offenses such as vagrancy and gambling was viewed by contemporaries as "quite serious." See T. Thorner and N. Watson, "Patterns of Prairie Crime: Calgary, 1875–1939," in *Crime and Criminal Justice in Europe and Canada*, ed. Louis A. Knafla (Waterloo, 1981), 226.

7. The question of defining frontier can be perplexing unless a measure of flexibility is employed. Those people living in Red Deer during World War I, for example, probably did not consider themselves on the frontier, although settlers forty miles west of Red Deer probably did. Arguably, the definition of frontier is largely reflective of a state of mind as opposed to a formulaic definition. For some of the problems in searching for such a definition, see John Phillip Reid, "The Layers of Western Legal History," in *Law for the Elephant, Law for the Beaver: Essays in the Legal History of the North American West*, ed. John McLaren, Hamar Foster, and Chet Orloff (Regina, 1992), 26.

8. The depiction of the American West as a wide-open and violent community has come under considered reappraisal. See the divergent viewpoints between Joe B. Frantz, "The Frontier Tradition: An Invitation to Violence," in *The History of*

Violence in America: Historical and Comparative Perspectives, ed. Hugh David Graham and Ted Robert Curr (New York, 1969), 127–54; and Philip D. Jordan, *Frontier Law and Order* (Lincoln, 1970); with Robert R. Dykstra, *The Cattle Towns* (New York, 1968). Also see Gordon Morris Bakken, *Practicing Law in Frontier California* (Lincoln, 1991), 99–113.

9. When J. Bjornsen of Tinastoll accused nine young men of being cowards because they had not enlisted for war duty, they responded by tarring and feathering him. All nine were fined $10 and had to provide Bjornsen with a new suit of clothes. Although the context of the event is not recorded, one wonders if Bjornsen was merely giving voice to the Icelandic community's attempt to shame the young men into enlisting, in view of their lack of action on behalf of Canada. See "Fined for Despicable Assault," *Red Deer Advocate,* 31 May 1918, 1.

10. Friedman and Percival, *Roots of Justice,* 136. In total, 172 cases of theft were brought before the Supreme Court from 1907 to 1920; seventy-nine involved cattle, horses, or sheep. The remainder involved break-and-enter theft, money theft, general theft, and cheque theft.

11. Crimes against the person totaled ninety-one cases during this period; assault, twenty; carnal knowledge, fourteen; and doing grievous bodily harm, ten. The remainder of the offenses such as rape, seduction, attempted rape, attempted murder, murder, and manslaughter each appeared fewer than ten times.

12. There were twenty-three convictions in the forty-one returned verdicts for these commercial crimes.

13. The remainder of the docket during these years was comprised of a wide range of offenses, including arson, obstruction of justice, perjury, and gaming.

14. For the establishment of the APP, see Alberta, "An Act respecting the Police Force of the Province of Alberta" (1917), c. 4.

15. Lynne M. Adrian and Joan E. Crowley, "Hoboes and Homeboys: The Demography of Misdemeanor Convictions in the Allegheny Country Jail, 1892–1923," *Journal of Social History* 25 (1991): 348–49. Also see Clive Emsley, *Crime and Society in England* (London, 1987): 186–94; Eric H. Monkkonen, "From Cop History to Social History: The Significance of the Police in American History," *Journal of Social History* 15 (1982): 581–82; James M. Pitsula, "The Treatment of Tramps in Late Nineteenth-Century Toronto," *Historical Papers* (1980): 116–32; and Nathan Douthit, "August Vollmer, Berkeley's First Chief of Police, and the Emergence of Police Professionalism," in *Police, Prison, and Punishment: Major Historical Interpretations,* ed. Kermit L. Hall (New York, 1987): 225–48.

16. Carl Betke, "Pioneers and Police on the Canadian Prairies, 1885–1914," *Historical Papers* (1980): 9–32. The best history of the NWMP is Roderick C. Macleod, *The North-West Mounted Police and Law Enforcement 1873–1905* (Toronto, 1976).

17. R. v. Morris, Supreme Court Red Deer, PAA 72.220, [SCRD] (1914), file 924.

18. Letter from James McNichol JP to A. Y. Blain, acting Deputy Attorney-General, on 19 September 1910, and letter from Superintendent Cuthbert, commanding "G" division NWMP to Blain on 21 September 1910, PAA 66.166, file no. 498/E.

19. Letter from L. G. Taylor JP to Deputy Attorney General L. F. Clarry on 2

January 1912, and letter from R. Burton Deane, Superintendent "E" division, to NWMP Commissioner on 13 January 1912, PAA 66.166, file no. 498/F.

20. Letter from A. T. Stephenson to Deputy Attorney-General L. F. Clarry on 2 October 1912, PAA 66.166, file no. 498/D.

21. Macleod, *North-West Mounted Police*, 50. A dispute over the costs of maintaining a prisoner soured relations between the NWMP and Red Deer police in 1906. At one point, Superintendent R. Burton Deane, commanding "E" division, pointedly asked in reference to Red Deer Police Chief George Rothnie: "What was the Chief of Police there for? It was a prosecution concerning his own municipality, wherein he had his own cell for taking care of the prisoner (whereas we had none) and it was proper that he should take his case into a Court of law for settlement. . . . it was not right for us to become responsible for expenditure which might or might not be found to have been justifiable." See Police Chief George Rothnie to Attorney-General on 24 October 1906 and Superintendent R. Burton Deane, commanding "E" division NWMP, to the Commissioner, NWMP, Regina on 1 November 1906, PAA 66.166, file no. 498/G.

22. Macleod, *North-West Mounted Police*, quoted at 91–92.

23. Ibid., as cited 92.

24. Linton Leonard Gaetz, *The Family Story* (Calgary, 1978), 2:386.

25. "Narrow Escape" and "Chief Rothnie Resigns," *Red Deer Advocate*, 18 November 1910, 1.

26. R. v. John Russell (SCRD 1910), file no. 341. Russell would return to Red Deer three months later and once again become involved in an attempted murder. On the second occasion, he attempted to stab Sam Lee, a restaurant owner. For this second offense, Russell was sentenced to two years in the Edmonton penitentiary. R. v Russell (SCRD 1911), file no. 358.

27. Crime Report of Sergeant K. G. Murison, NWMP, 3 June 1911; see deposition of H. G. Munroe, in PAA 66.166, file no. 1158.

28. Depositions of Drs. Collison and Gray, ibid.

29. "Feeling runs very high against Kelly and there is talk of lynching him." See Crime Report of Sergeant Murison, 3 June 1911.

30. R. v. Kelly (SCRD 1911), file no. 382.

31. See Deane's comments on margin of Murison's crime report of 3 June 1911.

32. Alberta, "An Act respecting Police Magistrates and Justices of the Peace" (1906), c. 13 s. 4.

33. Ibid., c. 13, s. 1 (4).

34. R v. Joseph Mannix (SCRD, 1917), file no. 1581.

35. John R. Wunder, *Inferior Courts, Superior Justice: A History of the Justices of the Peace on the Northwest Frontier, 1853–1889* (Westport, 1979), 170.

36. General circular, A.G. Browning, attorney general, 15 March 1916, PAA 69.210, G.R.D. Lyon, file 760.

37. "An Act respecting Police Magistrates and Justices of the Peace" (1906), c. 13 s. 1.

38. Investigation of fire at Lacombe, PAA 66.166, file no. 805.

39. Letter from George W. Hotson to Attorney-General Woods on 31 January 1908, PAA 66.166, file no. 580/C.

40. According to a supplement in *The Mountaineer* newspaper commemorating Rocky Mountain House's 75th anniversary, Skinner's ownership of *The Echo* was

"[s]o controversial and despised by some members of the community that a second newspaper was established" on 31 March 1914. *The Mountaineer* Anniversary Supplement, 29 July 1987, 8.

41. Cloutman was a justice of the peace for the community of Gadsby; Justice of the Peace file re: Jullian Curtis Cloutman, PAA 69.210, file 1431.

42. Justice of the Peace file re: F. J. Long, Return dated 3 July 1912, PAA 69.210, file 900.

43. F. J. Long to Deputy Attorney General, 25 April 1912, in ibid.

44. Justice of the Peace file re: J. D. Skinner, commission of the peace issued 27 December 1913, PAA 69.210, file 1509.

45. R. v. James D. Skinner (SCRD, 1915), file no. 1283.

46. See Re: J. D. Skinner, Crime Report filed by Corporal J. G. Hanna, NWMP, 8 February 1916, PAA 72.26, file no. 140/C.

47. Justice of the Peace file re: J. D. Skinner, commission cancelled 20 March 1916, PAA 69.210, file 1509.

48. Skinner had been appointed village reeve in June 1915. *The Mountaineer* Anniversary Supplement, 29 July 1987, 8. Three years later Skinner and Bert Allen JP were involved in the attempted extortion of a local farmer named Arthur Young. Detective Sergeant Brace of the APP described Skinner as a "crook of the first water" and Allen as a crook. See APP crime report re: Complaint of Arthur Young alleged Blackmail, Detective Sergeant Henry Brace, October 1918, PAA 72.26, file 1854.

49. A preliminary review of justice of the peace files for those individuals holding commissions in central Alberta suggests that many appointees were censured at one point during their careers. See generally, PAA 69.210.

50. The evolution of the governance of the legal profession in Alberta has been thoroughly investigated by Peter M. Sibenik in "The Doorkeepers: The Governance of Territorial and Alberta Lawyers, 1885–1928" (Master's thesis, University of Calgary, 1984). Sibenik has expanded on certain aspects of his thesis in "The Black Sheep': The Disciplining of Territorial and Alberta Lawyers, 1885–1928," *Canadian Journal of Law and Society* 3 (1988); and "Doorkeepers: Legal Education in the Territories and Alberta, 1885–1928," *Dalhousie Law Journal* 13 (May 1990).

51. "The Doorkeepers," 86–130.

52. Biographies of Greene can be found in *History of the Province of Alberta*, ed. Archibald Oswald MacRae (Calgary, 1912), 995–96 and in the Red Deer Public Archives [RDPA]; William Earnest Payne biography in *Alberta, Past and Present*, vol. 2, ed. John Blue (Chicago, 1924), 437–38 and in the Red Deer Public Archives (RDPA); Moore's biography is in the RDPA. The only legal records to be found in the RDPA are photocopies of a handful of civil cases from the district. The original records still exist and are stored in the PAA 79.220.

53. See Jonathan S. Swainger, "Ideology, Social Capital, and Entrepreneurship: Lawyers and Business in Red Deer, Alberta, 1900 to 1920," *Beyond the Law: Lawyers and Business in Canada, 1830–1930*, ed. Carol Wilton (Toronto, 1990), 377–402.

54. See the correspondence in PAA 83.210, file 92.

55. J. C. Moore to A. Y. Blain, deputy attorney general, 10 September 1910, PAA 66.166, file 580/A.

56. For biographical notes of A. H. Russell see *Alberta, Past and Present*, 2:23–24.

57. See R. v. Russell, PAA 77.26 file no. 3613; and "A. H. Russell, K. C. Acquitted," *The Red Deer Advocate*, 10 February 1922.

58. Knafla, "From Oral to Written Memory," 54–57; see also Wilbur F. Bowker's "The Honourable Horace Harvey, Chief Justice of Alberta," *The Canadian Bar Review* 31 (1954): 933–81 and 1118–139; "Honorable Horace Harvey," *History of the Province of Alberta*, 646; "Charles Allen Stuart," *History of the Province of Alberta*, 1023–024; "Charles Allen Stuart," *The Macmillan Dictionary of Canadian Biography*, ed. W. Stewart Wallace (Toronto, 1978), 805; "James Duncan Hyndmann," *History of the Province of Alberta*, 647; "Honorable James Duncan Hyndmann," *Alberta, Past and Present*, 2:383–84; "Honorable Nicholas Du Bois Dominic Beck," *Alberta, Past and Present*, 2:69–71; "William Legh Walsh," *Dictionary of Canadian Biography*, ed. Wallace, 871; "Arthur Lewis Sifton," *Dictionary of Canadian Biography*, ed. Wallace, 769; and "David Lynch Scott," *Canadian Dictionary of Biography*, ed. Wallace, 752.

59. Knafla, "From Oral to Written Memory," 60–61.

60. Ibid., 62; and Graham Parker, "Canadian Legal Culture," *Law and Justice in a New Land*, 29.

61. It has been noted by John Guire, in his study of the Rocky Mountain Bench in the United States, that while the derogatory description of some frontier judges as "carpetbaggers" does have some basis in fact, the majority of judges were relatively stable, positive additions to the community. John S. W. Guire, *The Rocky Mountain Bench: The Territorial Supreme Courts of Colorado, Montana, and Wyoming, 1861–1890* (New Haven, 1972), 60–81. Perhaps it is symptomatic of Canadian deference, but there is no indication that any of the judges of the Alberta Supreme Court were ever perceived as carpetbaggers.

62. The idea of experimentation comes from the opinion expressed by the court that they were not bound by previous courts and that the law of England was not necessarily the law in Western Canada. Knafla, "From Oral to Written Memory," as cited, 61.

63. Alberta, "An Act respecting the Supreme Court," (1907), c. 3.

64. These exact methods were also employed by horse thieves in later nineteenth-century Russia. See Christine D. Worobec, "Horse Thieves and Peasant Justice in Post-Emancipation Imperial Russia," *Journal of Social History* 21 (1987): 283.

65. See R. v. Cardinal, Solway, Irven Holt, James Holt and John F. Dubois (SCRD 1909), file nos 170, 216a, 216b, 217, 218, 219, 221, 235, 236; and PAA 66.166, file no. 979.

66. Crime report of Sergeant Robert W. Ensor, 7 April 1909, PAA 66.166, file no. 979 re: John Dubois et al.

67. Ibid.

68. W. B. Gray JP, to the Attorney General, 1 June 1908, and Lestock Forbes JP, to the Attorney General, 1 June 1908, in PAA 66.166, file 498F.

69. Crime Report of Sergeant Robert W. Ensor, 14 April 1909, ibid.

70. Crime report of Sergeant Robert W. Ensor, 30 May 1909, in PAA 66.166, file 979.

71. Frank Whiteside, president of the Central Alberta Stockgrowers Association, wrote Attorney General C. W. Cross suggesting that Nolan should be retained by the government to prevent Dubois and the other using the successful defense attorney. Frank Whiteside to C. W. Cross, 24 March 1909, ibid.

72. The following is based on R. v. Claude F. House (SCRD 1918), file no. 1349.

73. R. v. C. House (SCRD 1918), file no 1352.

74. Crime Report of Constable Alberta Johnson, NWMP, 2 October 1907, PAA 66.166, file 797, extradition of Henry Weir.

75. R. v. Henry Weir (SCRD 1907), file no. S55.

76. Bernard Hibbert to the Deputy Minister of Agriculture, 26 July 1907, PAA 66.166, file 797, extradition of Henry Weir.

77. Bernard Hibbert to Deputy Attorney General, 16 September 1907, and Deputy Attorney General to Hibbert, 20 September 1907, ibid.

78. S. B. Woods to NWMP Commissioner, Regina, 20 September 1907, and Assistant Commissioner to Woods, 23 September 1907, ibid.

79. Moore was the son of John T. Moore, one of the founders of the Saskatchewan Land and Homesteading Company, which first settled the area. See Jonathan Swainger, "Ideology, Social Capital and Entrepreneurship: Lawyers and Business in Red Deer, Alberta, 1900 to 1920," in Beyond the Law, 383–86.

80. J. C. Moore to S. B. Woods, Deputy Attorney General, 14 October 1907, in PAA 66.166, file 797, extradition of Henry Weir.

81. Ibid. Section 211 refers to illicit connection with a girl age 14 to 16, of previously chaste character.

82. S. B. Woods to R. Burton Deane, Superintendent NWMP, Calgary, 17 October 1907, in PAA 66.166, file 797, extradition of Henry Weir. Professor William Baker of the University of Lethbridge is currently involved in an examination of R. Burton Deane's career.

83. See Woods to Deane, 24 October 1907; Deane to Woods, 26 October 1907; Deane to Woods, 9 January 1908; Deputy Minister of Justice to Woods, 20 January 1908; Woods to Deputy Minister of Justice, 27 January 1908; and Deane to Woods, 11 February 1908 in PAA 66.166, file 797, extradition of Henry Weir.

84. R. v. Henry Weir (SCRD 1907), file S55.

85. Bernard Hibbert to S. B. Woods, 8 February 1909, in PAA 66.166, file 797, extradition of Henry Weir.

86. The prosecution for embezzlement of L. C. Fulmer, former secretary-treasurer of Red Deer, was thwarted by the inability of Canadian officials to get him extradited from Washington. See R. v. L. C. Fulmer (SCRD 1908), file no. 140, and PAA 66.166, file no. 984.

87. There were a total of forty-one sex-related complaints during this period. For my purposes, I have used the terminology employed by the JPs and MPs who filed the charges. These offences include rape, attempted rape, seduction, illicit connection, indecent assault, carnal knowledge, and sodomy/gross indecency.

88. Compare crime report of Scott and Della Torre, 30 April 1920, with Quigg letter of 12 May 1920 in Re: Alex Johnstone alias Alex Meyers, PAA 72.26, file 2832/C.

89. Cummings had been accused of assaulting eleven-year-old Ethel Beebe. See "Supreme Court Sittings," Red Deer Advocate, 25 October 1912; and R. v. George Cummings (SCRD, 1912), file no. 705.

90. Lawrence M. Friedman, A History of American Law (New York, 1973), 505.

91. These criteria are Friedman and Percival's in Roots of Justice, 9–15.

92. Worobec, "Horse Thieves and Peasant Justice," 281 and 288–89.

93. See Fairburn and Haslett, "Violent Crime in Old and New Societies"; and Friedman and Percival, Roots of Justice, 182.

Book Review Essay
Policing the Empire

Bernard Porter
University of Newcastle-upon-Tyne

1. David M. Anderson and David Killingray (eds.), *Policing the Empire: Government, Authority and Control, 1830–1940*. Manchester and New York: Manchester University Press, 1991. xii + 260 pp. £35.00.

2. David M. Anderson and David Killingray (eds.), *Policing and Decolonisation: Nationalism, Politics and the Police, 1917–65*. Manchester and New York: Manchester University Press, 1992. xi + 227 pp. £40.00.

It is difficult sometimes to avoid suspicions of hypocrisy about the Victorians, though other reasons have been offered for the disparities between their pretensions and their deeds. One of the biggest disparities arose from their possession of an empire, which for a liberty-loving people seems incongruous, to say the least. Another was their police. Like empires, police forces had always been associated with tyranny—especially French tyranny—in the past. They were incompatible with freedom, as Britain understood it and which, as it took general hold in Britain, was supposed to render both phenomena superfluous. Of course it did not; indeed, it may have had the opposite effect. After all, an aspect of her freedom, free trade, fuelled Britain's enormous commercial expansion in the nineteenth century, which in turn was one of the factors behind the parallel extension of her colonial empire, to embrace customers otherwise reluctant to trade with her. A similar motive, the need to pacify those disaffected by the relentless progress of liberal capitalism at home, lay behind the introduction of regular and formal policing in mainland Britain between 1829 and 1856. "The trouble about a free market economy," wrote Neal Ascherson in 1985, referring to a later stage in that process, "is that it requires so many policemen to make it work" (*Observer*, 26 May 1985). The Victorians would never have admitted that, and they performed mental contortions in order to avoid the inference. Their police were not like other police forces, not, that is, a *gendarmerie*, acting for the state, with all that that implied, but rather a means of social *self*-regulation: visible, reassuring, concerned only with crime and not, for example, with a person's politics; their powers carefully circumscribed and (except in London) locally accountable. Likewise, the empire was not a proper empire, either. It enlarged liberty, rather than diminishing it—freeing its subjects from indigenous tyrannies, exposing them to the opportunities afforded by the world market, and preparing them ultimately for political self-rule. This is what today looks like hypocrisy, though the Victorians themselves saw nothing wrong in it.

In fact, they had a point. The British police and empire were not as tyrannous as some. Both rested on public consent, to some degree. Otherwise they could not have functioned: in the case of the police with such small numbers, relatively, and entirely unarmed (apart from their truncheons); in the case of the empire almost incredibly, in view of the minuscule band of men it was administered by, who could have been overwhelmed quite easily at almost any time if their subjects had shown sufficient will. Of course, other reasons existed for these successes. Simple bluff came into it, to an extent. The British state rarely let on, either to its own working classes or to its colonial subjects, how weak it really was. Indeed, it proved not to be at all weak when it came to isolated rebellions, like Luddism or Chartism at home, or to the Indian mutiny or the Jamaica rebellion, whose firm-handed suppression did a great deal to bolster Britain's *image* of omnipotence. She also used collaborators widely—the middle classes in Britain, chiefs or favored tribal groups abroad—whose function was to do her controlling for her, with less expense and also hopefully less provocation than a more direct rule would have involved. None of this, however, would have been ultimately effective without some degree of at least tacit consent among the classes beneath or outside the collaborating ones. Those classes had to identify with their governors, which meant, in the first instance, the men (and later women) sent to police their activities, who for many were the only tangible manifestation they ever knew of their governors' authority, both at home and abroad.

Hence came Britain's peculiar policing practices, which were fashioned with the need for popular consent in mind and worked famously, most of the time, in Britain itself. Some people felt that practices that worked there could work in the colonies, too, and to the same effect: cementing imperial loyalties, smoothing down potential friction, obviating the need for more repressive measures, and so justifying the British image of the empire as a "consensual" one. It was tried in one or two places. One remarkable example was the Cape Town Police in South Africa, modelled on, and largely recruited from, the London Metropolitan force in the 1850s. It was remembered with respect and even affection later on, when under institutional *apartheid* a very different kind of policing took over. "British Bert he was called," reminisced one old Cape Towner, recalling her local prewar beat "bobby" in an interview with Bill Nasson, whose fascinating chapter in the first of these two volumes deals with the Cape Town force.

Sergeant Thomas was fair, he never beat any person, he had a good name for himself. He used to walk so proud, with a tiny black baton which he kept in his jacket pocket. He was quite a visiting sort of chap, also, dropping in and saying "Morning, no trouble around here today, I hope." Things like that. Then he'd even have a cup of tea. He wasn't all mighty and standoffish like he was European and he was Coloured. Man, in those days, I'm talking about even in the 'thirties and the war, there were *proper* police, they never carried guns. (1, p. 241)

That gives the flavor. Policing like this made all the difference to the public face of imperialism, where it mattered: at the point of contact between ruler and ruled. It made imperialism acceptable, and so easier to impose.

Consequently it was the ideal for many other colonial police forces, from very early times in Hong Kong, New Zealand, Australia, and the West Indies (1, pp. 4, 55, 60, 71) to the last desperate days of British colonialism, when it was hoped that the introduction of "English" or "normal" or "London Metropolitan" methods of policing might be a way of winning disaffected subjects back again. That, for example, was the recommendation made by Sir Arthur Young, Commissioner of the London City Police, to the three colonial forces—the Gold Coast, Malaya, and Kenya—that he was called in to advise in the early 1950s (2, pp. 103, 114–15, 142)—unrealistically, as it turned out. For there were problems. In London (especially Young's own Square Mile) there was a natural basis for a consensual kind of policing; in most colonies there was not. The latter also had recruitment difficulties. Locals were deterred by the poor pay, the stigma that attached to policing in their own communities, and the risk of being shot. The result was that the men who came forward tended to be a low lot: "rank-and-file ex-servicemen, vagabonds and adventurers" in Australia and the other "white" colonies, for example (1, p. 7); illiterates all over Africa (1, p. 117); even "criminals" in India, "whom it was hoped to reform" (1, p. 139). Most of them were strangers, recruited from outside the colonies concerned (1, pp. 7, 86, 116, 122, 128, 153, 171–72). "Where on earth was such a low, rough, almost criminal-looking crew raked together?" asked Emily Hobhouse of the South African Constabulary around 1900 (1, p. 169). This did not help.

Even if police were none of these things, they might be undependable for other reasons. Educated men in particular were distrusted, because they had ideas—sometimes dangerous political ones—of their own (2, pp. 134–35). This could neutralize them in the struggle against nationalism later on, as happened in Cyprus in the later 1950s, for example, where the local police had to be more or less abandoned, so "subverted" were they from without

(2, pp. 195–96, 203–4). One solution to that was to draft in British policemen in order to restore "discipline" and good practice, as was done for example in Cyprus, but usually that met with little success. Bobbies did not transplant well. Fundamental policing principles—and even sometimes basic decencies—withered in these alien soils. The British policeman's worst side came out: racial prejudice, intolerance, and violence, leading sometimes to atrocities, which were obviously counterproductive in the battle for the local peoples' "hearts and minds" (2, pp. 206, 210). This was probably inevitable. "Normal" policing was impossible in an abnormal situation, which is what the colonial relationship inevitably produced. That was the cardinal problem, as even the best-intentioned British imperialists soon discovered, to their disappointment and their cost.

Fortunately for them, at least in the medium term, they had alternatives to fall back upon. In some colonies local indigenous rulers were happy to patrol their own patches, with what was called in Kenya, for example, a "Tribal Police" (2, p. 129). The same kind of thing existed in the Gold Coast and the Sudan (1, pp. 114, 160). That was the lazy way out for the British; it also gave them very little *control*, which vitiated one of the self-evident purposes of colonial policing. Hence arose their frequent recourse to another, quite different pattern of police practice: the Irish one, first developed in the 1820s to cope with what was effectively, as Richard Hawkins points out (1, p. 25), a quasicolonial situation on Britain's own doorstep, which differed from the English pattern in some quite crucial ways. The Irish (later Royal Irish) Constabulary (RIC) was armed, housed in "barracks," and deliberately cut off from its community roots by a rule that officers never patrolled their own areas. It was also under the control of Dublin Castle, the seat of British government in that island, all of which gave it some of the appearance of an army of occupation (1, chap. 2, passim). Such officers were ideal for other occupied countries too, not quite as provocative as red- or khaki-clad soldiers, but performing a similar role. Hence the ubiquity of the RIC "model" of policing all over the empire, from Sind in India to Otago in New Zealand (1, pp. 21, 60), and from Kenya to Canada (1, pp. 94, 184). It was deployed in overwhelming preference to the London Metropolitan model, which—except apparently in Cape Town—was more often a pious aspiration than a genuine example to be followed.

That, at any rate, is what the editors of these volumes call the "conventional wisdom." They have a problem with it. Their introductory chapter to *Policing the Empire* is largely taken up with trying to demolish it, on the grounds that the "Irish model" was never rigidly applied anywhere outside the thirty-two counties, but was adapted to local conditions, often quite "strikingly" (1, pp. 3–5). They have a point, but not a very significant one. Of course the Irish plan was never followed slavishly. The British empire did not work like that. It was probably the most flexible, pragmatic, unplanned, often excruciatingly illogical empire known to history, which is partly why it survived as long as it did. Occasionally the Colonial Office would try to impose a pattern of a kind—as in the 1840s, when it became so enamored by the example of the Metropolitan police—but usually vainly, as local exigencies made nonsense of its high-flown ideas.

Usually those local exigencies held sway. But they were not the only factors. Local colonial officials did not respond to each locality in isolation, entirely indigenously, unaffected by their own or others' experiences elsewhere. They did look to outside examples. In the realm of policing, the RIC was a favorite model, not so much for ideological reasons (ideology, as we have seen, tended to point elsewhere), but because it seemed to work. It worked partly because it was outstandingly adaptable to different colonial situations, far more so than its less robust London rival. Adaptability was part of the model. (Even in Ireland there were variations from place to place.) The RIC infests the pages of these two volumes, both as a prototype for the creation of new colonial forces and as the major source of outside recruits. There are scores of examples, far too many to list. In 1907 the RIC was actually put in charge of a new training course for colonial police officers from all over, based in Dublin (1, p. 184). That was not by chance. Of course, the trainees will not have gone from there to try to police Lagos (or wherever) exactly as Limerick, but in most cases the essentials of the RIC system—central control, barracks, guns—remained the same. This may be a conventional wisdom that does not need to be revised substantially.

On the other hand, the editors of these volumes are right to stress the enormous range of policing methods and philosophies to be found in British colonies in the nineteenth and twentieth centuries, corresponding to the kaleidoscopic nature of the empire itself. Each colony had different law-and-order problems, different kinds of imperial presence, different structures of power, and different interest groups. There were sharp variations even within colonies: in Kenya, for example, the police—whatever they might claim—generally acted in the economic interests of the white settlers, enforcing labor regulations and so on (1, chap. 11). An exception was made in the coastal town of Mombasa, a refuge for labor-contract breakers, who were generally left alone by local police chiefs, who had a different perception of their main policing priorities (1, p. 223).

Likewise, the forms of policing differed widely from place to place. Cape Town represented one extreme. In the middle stood the forces that were modelled, however loosely, on the RIC. At the other extreme were forces that differed little from army militias and were dignified with the name of "police" only in order to reassure the locals. An example of this was the early Canadian North-West Mounted Police, seen by its founder in 1869 as essentially a kind of cavalry, "instructed in rifle exercises" and "in the use of artillery," yet "not... *expressly* military, but... *styled* Police" (my emphases) to avoid provoking the wild men of the Northwest Territories more than was necessary (1, p. 93). The Irish "Black and Tans" were a similar case: redcoats hiding behind blue uniforms (figuratively speaking, of course). That was a far cry from the dear old London "Met."

Despite this seeming chaos, however, there were also connecting threads, common basic models, as we have seen, and links between colonies. Colonial policemen learned not only from the mother country and from their own local experiences but also from other colonial examples, sometimes nearby and sometimes very far away. The Southern Rhodesian police, for example (omitted from this account—a serious gap), acted as an influential source of ideas and personnel for colonies to the north. When Otago in New Zealand wanted advice on how to police the goldseekers who began coming in there in the 1860s, the first place it looked to was Victoria, across the Tasman Sea. The NWMP picked up tips from India (1, p. 94). Afterwards, it passed some of its knowledge and experience on to the South African Constabulary (1, p. 169).

Much later on, when Britain was struggling to retain at least some traces of her empire after World War II, an unprecedented degree of interchange took place among the colonies, partly through the agency of a new Inspectorate General of Colonial Police set up in 1938 (2, pp. 5–6) and partly through personnel moving from one colony to another—often by necessity, as colonies fell one by one to the nationalists—transferring their skills as they went. One example is R. G. B. Spicer, who straddles both these volumes. He was plucked from the Ceylon Police to become head first of the Kenya Force in 1925 and then of the Palestine Police in 1931 (1, pp. 189, 192, 227; 2, p. 65). Literally hundreds of others made similar moves at lower levels. It is this kind of thing, together with the RIC model and also the fact that it is difficult to find examples of similar cross-fertilization between British and foreign police forces (none is mentioned in these two works), that gives a sort of coherence to the history of policing in the British empire.

It only remains now for someone to sit down to write that history. The last attempt was Sir Charles Jeffries's *The Colonial Police*, published in 1952, which badly needs updating. These volumes have made a start. They represent the first synoptic view of British imperial policing since Jeffries's time. They have their flaws, mainly arising from their origin as a series of conference papers. Conferences are rarely entirely satisfactory as sources for books. Contributions tend to be of variable quality and inconsistent in their approaches and to overlap and leave gaps. In this case the editors have gone to great lengths to correct such flaws, by omitting what presumably were the least relevant contributions and commissioning others to fill some of the holes. In general they have been successful. The end-product is far more useful than most such compilations, like a series of exploratory bore-holes into the subject, drilled selectively but fairly rationally and to a good revealing depth.

Of course, there are still omissions—including, it has to be said, *most* of the colonies of the British empire. Another omission is Britain herself, which in a really comprehensive history of colonial policing would need to be covered in some detail simply because of the influences continually acting both ways between the colonies and her. (The impact on Britain of policing methods acquired in Ireland and the empire is touched on by the editors at the end of their introduction to the first volume, but not pursued.) One subject area that is treated rather patchily is political policing and espionage, partly no doubt because the sources are so elusive. Richard Rathbone's account of Special Branch reports on Ghanaian politicians in the 1950s (2, chap. 5) whets the appetite for more of the same from elsewhere, if it still survives. A more general problem is one of definition. "All agents of colonialism and all elements of the colonial administration," writes David Anderson in his chapter on early twentieth-century Kenya, "were, to some extent, involved in policing" (1, p. 183). That could open the door wide. John McCracken, writing on Malawi, where there was no proper formal police force until 1920, exploits this to take the broadest possible view, quite validly (2, chap. 8); but most of his fellow contributors, including Anderson himself, do not. As a general rule of thumb, they call a man a policeman if he called himself one. That is narrower, but is it narrow enough? Should the quasi-militias—the NWMP and the Irish Auxiliaries— be included? Where exactly is the line to be drawn between *police* and *soldiery*? This will have to be sorted out eventually.

None of this, however, should be taken to detract from the value of these volumes, which are full of fascinating information, stimulating ideas, and even the seeds of a generalization or two. Police historians should read them for the breadth of perspective they provide; imperial historians, for their insights into British colonial rule at what Anderson calls, quite rightly, its "cutting edge" (1, p. 198). They also tell an interesting story in its own right, albeit one of ultimate failure. In none of Britain's dependent colonies did the police succeed in their main aim, which was to supplant naked force as the means of keeping colonial peoples loyal. In 1905 a young District Commissioner in Ashanti looked forward to the day, as he wrote to his mother, "when soldiers and Maxims can be done away with and the country ruled with police" (1, p. 115). That day never came. The reason was probably that empire and policing in the young DC's sense of the word were incompatible. There was a basic contradiction there. That is what the Victorians never really understood.

Book Review Essay
Miscarriages of Justice? The Phoenix Park Murders, 1882

John McEldowney
University of Warwick

Jarlath Waldron, *Maamstrasna: The Murder and the Mystery*. Dublin: Edmund Burke Publisher, 1992. 335 pp.

Agrarian violence in the nineteenth century was endemic in Ireland. Secret agrarian societies had almost a continuous existence both before and after the Act of Union 1800. Ireland was rarely governed by the ordinary law alone. The use of strong powers and extraordinary legislation in an attempt to control violence and obtain law and order was a regular occurrence. In 1881 the House of Lords Select Committee on Irish Jury laws recommended the abolition of jury trial for certain specified crimes and for limited periods. Although this recommendation was never implemented, stronger coercive legislation was passed in an attempt to curtail violent crime.

On 6 May 1882, the Phoenix Park murders in Dublin resulted in the deaths of Thomas Burke, the Irish undersecretary at Dublin Castle, and Frederick Cavendish, nephew of Gladstone, the British Prime Minister, and newly installed Chief Secretary to Ireland. Irish violence had reached a new peak. At the time Edward Hamilton, one of Gladstone's private secretaries, wrote in his diary:

It is impossible at present to judge of the effect of the awful catastrophe and its consequences upon the Government. I am inclined to think it will be the death knell of it.[1]

The government, which had been considering for some time the possibility of taking stronger measures, considered with renewed vigor the possibility of abandoning jury trial and introducing a special commission to try serious agrarian offenses. Such events were at the height of the land war, and attempts to ameliorate Irish problems had been largely unsuccessful in preventing further violence. The government was poised on the brink of considering some form of Home Rule for Ireland, and the preparation of the first Home Rule Bill came in 1886.

Jarlath Waldron's book is about the murders on 18 August 1882 of four adults and two young boys, all members of the Joyce family, who lived in Maamstrasna at New Ross, County Wexford. The murders were described as a terrible atrocity, carried out at a time of great violence and unrest in Ireland. Landlords in the area were daily threatened and intimidated, some were murdered, and the catalogue of crimes pointed to the fears that law and order might collapse entirely.

Waldron traces the investigation, arrest, and trial of the chief suspects in the crime. The investigation was carried out by George Bolton, the Crown solicitor for Tipperary. Ireland had, in advance of England and Wales, a system of Crown prosecution whereby responsibility rested on appointed and paid official lawyers to undertake the prosecution of offenses on behalf of the state. Bolton's task was a difficult one, given fear and intimidation and great distrust in the system of criminal justice and its enforcement by the police. In the case of the Maamstrasna murders, eyewitnesses came forward and offered evidence as to the identity of the murderers. Ten men were accused of murder, and the main evidence came from three witnesses who were cousins to four of the accused.

Waldron examines in great detail the collecting of the evidence, its preparation for trial, and the trial itself. As is common with books that set out to prove that miscarriages of justice might have taken place, the text is strongly argued and admirably supported with a wide range of evidence. In the case of the Maamstrasna trials, the procedures introduced under the Prevention of Crimes Act 1882 were adopted, which allowed the trial to be held outside the area where the incident occurred. In this case, the trial took place in Dublin before special jurors, that is, jurors normally used in civil cases who held a higher property qualification than ordinary common or petty jurors.

The case attracted a great deal of publicity, and the prosecution decided to proceed first with the prosecution of one of the defendants, Patrick Joyce, before proceeding with the other nine. Undoubtedly this was a clever prosecution tactic for what was to follow. After a conviction in the first trial, it was considered easier to proceed with the trials of the other defendants. The Crown was led by Attorney General Johnson, assisted by James Murphy, Q.C., and Peter O'Brien, Q.C. The defense counsel was George Orme Malley, Q.C. All were regarded as shrewd, clever lawyers who were very able and had a good mastery of the law. The trial judge was Mr. Justice Barry.

As the trial of Patrick Joyce proceeded, it appeared that the prosecution were intent in coming to an arrangement with the other accused. This process of plea bargaining had a sophisticated technique—obtaining from one or more of the accused the necessary information to convict the others. Throughout the trial of Patrick Joyce, the Crown received important information from the other defendants. In effect three individuals, including Patrick Joyce, were named as the actual perpetrators of the murders and the main planners of the crimes. The source of this information was one of the defendants called Philibin. Another defendant named Tom Casey was also persuaded to give evidence on behalf of the Crown. In return both "traversers," as they were called, were given immunity and a *nolle prosequi* entered on their behalf.

The case therefore raises important issues regarding the use of informers or active perpetrators of crime who are offered immunity by the Crown to give evidence against the other defendants. The trial judge warned the jury on relying on the uncorroborated evidence obtained from such a source: "You cannot act upon the testimony of an informer unless he is corroborated in some material point... by independent witnesses." Nevertheless, the conviction of the first defendant led immediately to the trial of the second defendant, Pat Casey. Much the same evidence was heard as had been introduced in the first trial, and the outcome was a finding that Casey was guilty. The third trial, that of Myles Joyce, took place immediately after, and it too resulted in a conviction. Five remaining defendants were persuaded to plead guilty. Although convicted they had, after some delay, the death penalty commuted at the request of Lord Spencer, the Lord Lieutenant of Ireland. The first three prisoners convicted were duly executed, despite protesting their innocence.

Waldron's main thesis is that the defendants were unjustly convicted. This conclusion is based on a number of arguments, and some of the evidence in the book appears to justify at least unease about the convictions. However, one of the shortcomings in Waldron's account is that more is implied than is expressly stated in the text. One of the difficulties in reading the text is that, although a chronological approach is followed, it is impossible without a very close reading of the text to analyze the exact nature of the case in favor of the conclusion that there may have been miscarriages of justice. Waldron fails to provide an objective summary of his main findings, which leads to a major shortcoming in the work: It fails to provide a dispassionate and balanced view of the exact nature of the miscarriage. Waldron fails to understand the nature of the trial process and the roles of the prosecution and the judge.

The Maamstrasna case raises the issue of uncorroborated evidence. The prosecution in the first three trials relied on mostly circumstantial evidence, but the success of the prosecution case depended on the fact that two of the defendants gave evidence against the accused in return for immunity. This is the crucial issue in the case. Later on, after the executions and the sentencing of the other defendants, the two approvers withdrew their evidence. There is also fairly clear evidence that the approvers were persuaded originally under intense pressure to give evidence against the defendants. The result was to increase the pressure on the defendants to plead guilty.

In recent years in Northern Ireland, obtaining prosecutions through the use of informers or "supergrasses" was common. Eventually, this led to the attorney-general informing the House of Commons in 1983 in a written statement that:

In both jurisdictions (England, Wales, and Northern Ireland) where an accomplice gives evidence for the prosecution it is the duty of the judge to warn the jury that, although it may convict on is evidence, it is dangerous to do so unless it is corroborated. This is an old rule, well recognised and rigidly applied and it now has the force of a rule of law.[2]

In 1983, in a series of cases decided by the Court of Appeal in Northern Ireland, the Court quashed the convictions of defendants convicted only on the evidence, largely uncorroborated, of supergrasses. In 1986, following the outcome of these cases, the attorney-general[3] informed Parliament that any further prosecution cases were unlikely.

In the Maamstrasna case, as no full appeal court existed for criminal cases in Ireland, the mechanisms for reviewing the case at the time were ineffective. Reconstructing the facts of the case is made difficult by the passage of time. There is no clear motive for the killings, although the author accepts the government's view that the murders were conceived as a punishment killing for information given. Waldron points the accusing finger at a number of suspects other than the defendants. Although two of the defendants, Pat Joyce and Pat Casey (both executed), were likely to have been present at the crime, they may not have been involved in the killings.

The author does make out a convincing case that the defendants were not accorded a fair trial. The reasons advanced for the unfairness depend on whether the reader believes that the English authorities were "served by evil officials" (p. 314) or that the intelligence and judgment of Lord Spencer were was "decidedly flawed" (p. 313). At the same time, the author accepts that active secret societies existed in Ireland, that fear and intimidation were widespread, and that killings and lawlessness were common.

The more likely reason for the unfair trials is not dependent on these factors alone. Waldron's book reveals some of the fundamental weaknesses in the presentation of a criminal trial in Ireland, weaknesses that have endured largely unremedied to the present day in England and Wales and in Northern Ireland.[4] The lack of corroborating evidence, the difficulty of making out any appeal on the basis of guilty pleas obtained through pressure, and persuasion all contributed to unfairness in the trial. However, this account overlooks the pre-trial stage, when the police focused their attention on various witnesses and informants. Waldron's description (p. 31) is poignant and to the point. Describing how George Bolton, the Crown Solicitor for Tipperary, conducted his interviews, Waldron writes:

His technique was special. Always accompanied by eight or more of the tallest, beefiest R.I.C. men [the Royal Irish Constabulary, the police force in Ireland until 1922] he could select, he would stalk into the cabin of a suspect, eject everybody, commandeer a chair (if there were such), on which he would sit in majestic state, the representative of the Queen arrived in a remote village. One by one he would interview the household, beginning with the youngest. His very presence was forbidding and frightening. His silences were menacing, but when he spoke, he spoke with a shattering voice. The natives, while understanding not a word he was saying, waited fearfully outside for their turn to enter. Whether innocent or guilty of any misdemeanour, they trembled like trees before a gale.

Newspaper reports caused great public excitement and necessitated the removal of the trial to Dublin before special jurors. The use of special jurors, normally reserved for civil cases and with a higher property qualification, also contributed to the hopeless position of the defendants when it came to a fair trial. Although Waldron mentions the defense counsel, he gives little analysis of their failures. Defense lawyers did not visit the scene of the murders. At the start of the trials all defendants pleaded not guilty, but gradually, as the evidence of the approvers was admitted and the conviction of the first defendants obtained, five of the accused changed their pleas to guilty. The willingness of the defense lawyers to go along with this plea bargain made finding the truth even more difficult.

Taken together, the entire trial process achieved an outcome that was inevitable once the trials had begun. The failures of justice are more deeply rooted than Waldron's account indicates. As McConville has noted in some recent research,[5] the trial threatens the whole basis of the ideology of the prosecution and the police case, namely, that of consensus truth. Doubts or unresolved pieces of evidence are devalued in an effort to ensure the conviction of the defendant. Because the outcome of trials are uncertain, the only way to ensure success is to seek "private determinations legitimated by public displays of unity." This is particularly true in cases where there is a guilty plea, a point particularly pertinent to Waldron's analysis: "The plea of guilty ... ensures that the accused is a party, an agreed not an aggrieved party, to her own downfall and because it is the only way of ensuring that result."[6]

Waldron's book falls between two historical traditions. The first is history based on anecdotal evidence, presented in the form of a narrative, a welltried and tested formula derived from newspapers and contemporary writing on Irish trials. Often sensationalist and maybe slightly exaggerated, such accounts are nonetheless important and valuable histories of the period because they capture the public sentiment and the emotion of the period. However, they do not purport to be objective or even well reasoned, because in Irish history often they represent a nationalist tradition and provide confirmation, to an audience that needs little convincing, of the oppression by the English in Ireland.

The second tradition is a more analytical history than the first. Contemporary accounts are used alongside official records, letters, and miscellaneous sources provided by a rich collection of materials from record offices, public libraries, and books of the period. The second formula avoids value judgement, does not subscribe to a overtly nationalist view of history, and attempts to let the reader consider the evidence.

Waldron's account has elements of both traditions and therefore suffers the weakness of both. His account cannot be dismissed as being over-emotional and nationalistic, because he makes use of a variety of reliable sources, in detail that makes his story of the murders compelling reading. Nor can his account be entirely objectively verified or considered as reliable history, because so much is left unresolved and the loose ends do not add up to his conjectures. The largest gap is his failure to consider in any detail the deficiencies in the defense case. His emotional judgement interferes with his professional judgment, and his value statements alert the reader to problems of verification and objectivity.

Despite these reservations, the book deserves to be read by lawyer and historian alike. This is one of the most useful and detailed accounts of the trial and conviction of defendants in Ireland during the nineteenth century. It is the greatest irony that the author's analysis of reasons for the possible miscarriage of justice explains more about the actual system of criminal justice than those who were attempting to make it work. The book does show that the weaknesses in the system of criminal trials in Ireland in the nineteenth century have a number of similarities to the miscarriages of justice revealed in recent years in England. This is all the more surprising in terms of the contribution of historical scholarship to an understanding of the system of criminal prosecution and conviction. Historical evidence, which Waldron has assembled in this book, has been slow to show the failures in the criminal justice system that writers of the present day have recognised, albeit belatedly. Waldron's analysis leads him to believe in bad faith among officials and the air of conspiratorial malpractice in the law. The reality is that systemic weaknesses in the procedures and practices in the trial system were most likely to blame. The trial and conviction of the accused in the nineteenth century requires further research and attention. By its nature, it might force us to see the deficiencies in a system of justice that developed historically.

NOTES

1. Dudley W. R. Bahlman, *The Diary of Sir Edward Walter Hamilton* (1880–1885) (Oxford, 1972), 268.

2. 47 HC Deb, 24 October 1983, cols. 3–5.

3. 94 HC Deb, 19 March 1986, cols. 186.

4. There is currently a Royal Commission on Criminal Evidence assessing the

value of the trial system and procedures at present in operation in England and Wales.

5. See M. McConville and Chester Mirsky, "Criminal Defense of the Poor in New York City," *Review of Law and Social Change* 15 (1986–87): 582–964.

6. See McConville, Sanders, and Leng, *The Case for the Prosecution* (London, 1992), 204.

Book Review Essay
Custodes Pacis Orbi Terrae:
The History of Conservators, Keepers, and Justices of the Peace in England and Beyond

Louis A. Knafla
The University of Calgary

Sir Thomas Skyrme, *History of the Justices of the Peace.* Chichester: Barry Rose, 1991. Vol. I, *England to 1689,* xlvi + 303 pp., table of statutes, index; Vol. II, *England 1689–1989,* xxxvi + 424 pp., table of statutes, index; Vol. III, *Territories beyond England,* liv + 331 pp., appendixes, bibliog., index. £75.00.

The office of Justice of the Peace is one of those major keys to the history of law enforcement and legal administration in the common-law world that has seldom received major scholarly examination. Poised between the institutions of central and local courts and administration, the longevity of the JPs together with their complex history, woven into the fabric of each of the English counties, has precluded any general attempt at institutional history beyond the classic works of F. W. Maitland, Charles Beard, Bertha Osborne, and Esther Moir,[1] none of which has been based on sufficient sources to become authoritative. Instead, the major histories have been at the county level,[2] where local record societies have been active in the publication of their JP and Quarter Sessions records over the past century[3] and where a few scholars have contributed useful period studies.[4] The appearance, therefore, of a major multivolume history of the JPs should not go unnoticed.

The author has had a long and distinguished career directly associated with the Justices of the Peace. A practitioner of the London and Western circuits, he was secretary to the Lord Chancellor and from 1948 both a practicing magistrate and Secretary of the Commissions of the Peace for England and Wales for thirty years. He also sat on virtually every important committee dealing with magistrates and their courts in this period and founded and was the inaugural president of the Commonwealth Magistrates' and Judges' Association 1970–1979. The author of *The Changing Image of the Magistracy* (1983), where he assessed the evolution of governmental policies since 1947 as a member of the Royal Commission on Justices of the Peace (1946–1948), he has been working on the history of the JPs almost since that time.

Skyrme's position enabled him to examine unpublished papers not only in the various county archives, but also in the Victoria Tower, the House of Lords, and country houses. In addition to the records of Quarter Sessions, he was also interested in those of ecclesiastical and manor courts, and especially of Petty Sessions. Equally prominent has been his effort to understand the quagmire of official records in the Public Record Office, Chancery Lane. In this respect he shows a keen knowledge of commissions of the peace, assize and gaol delivery rolls, pipe and sessions rolls, crown office docket books, letters close and patent, indentures and estreats, and the state papers, although parliamentary statutes and Acts of the Privy Council are more prominent in his citations.

Three themes emerge from this work, the meaning of an administrative system managed by laymen, the close relationship between Quarter Sessions and Assizes, and the adaptability of the institution of the JP. Throughout the centuries, the author emphasizes the diverse political, social, and economic conditions that led to their origins and development. He sees the JPs as breaking the feudal traditions of the medieval world, representing the emergence of the landed gentry and the urban middle classes and resisting the centralization of royal bureaucracy. He perceives their significance as lying more in the social, economic, and political life of the country than in the administration of justice.

As local governors, the monopoly of the JPs was formed in the sixteenth century, and their undisputed rule in the late seventeenth. Their decline was set in the urban centers of the eighteenth century—especially in London. The amputation of their governmental and peacekeeping functions in the nineteenth century is viewed positively as enabling them to reexpand the judicial functions that had been so important to them in the early modern era. The subsequent rise of their judicial function to the mid-twentieth century was attributed as follows: "The linking of the ordinary citizen with the administration of justice was part of the national heritage deeply ingrained in the way of life of the English people which could not be uprooted" (I: xxii).

The work is organized in a peculiar fashion. The first volume, which covers the history of the JPs to 1689, is chronological through the fifteenth century, then covers the palatine counties, returns to the chronology for 1485 to 1688, and concludes with the cities and boroughs through the twentieth century. Volume II begins with a chronology of "The Age of Independence," 1689–1820, then has a section on stipendiary magistrates, and resumes with the chronology to 1989—the era of 1945 to 1989 being termed "A New Challenge." Volume III contains chapters on the history of the JP in Wales, Ireland, Scotland, the United States, Canada, the West Indies, Australia, New Zealand, and the Isle of Man, concluding with analogous institutions in Africa, Asia, and the Pacific.

A series of appendixes provides sample transcriptions of commissions of the peace 1327–1974 (Appendix I), the number of JPs per county in England and Wales (and sometimes Scotland) at various dates 1361–1990 (II), lists of duties from William Lambarde's *Eirenarcha* (III), examples of orders on largely regulatory matters mainly from the sixteenth through the eighteenth centuries (*IV*), women recommended for the office by county in 1920 (V), and powers of removal compiled from various treatises and handbooks (VI). The third volume has a useful bibliography of manuscript and printed sources, including the major contemporary treatises, printed records, and studies of the JPs, Quarter Sessions, and related matters. The last section of the bibliography contains selected works on the history of the office in Australia, Canada, Ireland, New Zealand, Scotland, the United States, and Wales. The separate indexes for each volume are comprehensive as to surnames, places, institutions, and topics.

Skyrme has made a positive contribution to the history of JPs in a number of different ways. On the technical side, he has provided an excellent account of the statutory legislation, improving on the earlier work of Sidney and Beatrice Webb and Sir William Holdsworth.[5] He has also given considerable and detailed attention to their commissions in virtually every period of their history. Sensitive to the national-local conundrum, he has explained their changing relationships with the judges of eyre and of assize, and the central courts and the crown, as well as the ties of JPs individually to London and the local communities. With regards to law, he emphasizes correctly the centrality of their administrative duties; and from the late seventeenth century, when the records evidence is more visible, he explores more happily their judicial procedures and business. In addition, he always keeps a sharp eye on the problem of corruption and on the use of office for private gain or vengeance. On the nonlegal side, he includes some interesting sections on JPs' wealth and social structure and the extent to which they became involved in the economy.

Perhaps the most important revision that Sir Thomas Skyrme has made to the history of the JP is in the era of county self-government, 1689–1835. Contrary to the Webbs, he sees JPs in a more positive light, particularly the rural and clerical JPs. He documents the rise of humanitarian concerns, the cautious handling of frivolous private prosecutions and guilty verdicts, paternalistic sentencing, and the changing uses of gaols and houses of correction. In addition, he documents ably the growth of administrative and financial responsibilities and of petty sessions as a major judicial venue. Morover, he notes the growing legislative power of JPs, with parliamentary committees circulating bills to them for comment before their enrollment, which served as a prelude to their emergence as national legislators. While

Skyrme discounts the recent historiography that has revived the roles of constables and jurors, he is able to place their faults within the context of the social hierarchy and the political agenda of the Hanoverian state.

Mr. Skyrme is perhaps on new ground with his discussion of several nineteenth and twentieth-century subjects. These include his research and assessment of the major nineteenth-century acts on borough councils (II: 186–219) and the systematization of the summary jurisdiction of the JPs. Equally important is his discussion from the original records of the juvenile courts (II: 254–58, 375–84). He discerns the origins of probation from the United States (II: 262–66) and the early history of female magistrates (II: 232–38). More important is his resuscitation of the JP as a legal officer in the twentieth century, again from the original records, including the re-growth of their criminal jurisdiction, of their work in Quarter Sessions, and of the redevelopment of procedural and substantive law (II: 329–41, 354–75).

The multivolume work suffers, however, from material that at times is extraneous to the central subject. For example, the account of the palatine courts and officials, past to present, is neither very scholarly nor particularly useful (I: 74–106). A similar comment can be made for the chapter on city and borough JPs (I: 256–303), which could be more useful, but is not well organized, and the largest section is on the twentieth century (I: 281–303). Occasionally the work centers on politics instead of the JPs. Too often there is a focus on the monarch and politics instead of on the JPs and their work, and at times it is difficult to see the magistrates in this context as a "national" body (as I: 214). There is an overwhelming amount of detailed information for the post-World War II era on ages, qualifications, numbers and occupations, the composition of the benches, and conditions of office including training and salaries (II: 277–94, 299–327).

The strengths of the work, however, are matched by some major weaknesses, which will be discussed as they occur chronologically within the volumes. For the Middle Ages to the early modern era, there are too many attempts to compare the JP with his modern successor. All too frequently, the work of the JPs is defined by their statutory legislation rather than the records, and the author assumes that the law was enforced (as with the regulation of trade and industry at I: 50–59). A few times, when court records are discussed, they are not cited (I: 62–63). He also assumes that commissions appointed actually sat (I: 177), even though the evidence shows that a commission such as Oyer and Terminer did not generally sit from the sixteenth century. And officials such as lords-lieutenant are given perhaps too much attention, while the key practicing figure of the clerk of the peace is given rather brief notice. Absenteeism is considered as a major deficiency (I: 116–19), but the evidence suggests that the tight structure of many county jurisdictions made the large numbers in the commissions honorary and inconsequential. Finally, the interpretation of the reigns of Edward IV through James I tends to follow the old view of the "despotic Tudors," relying too much perhaps on the romantic writings of André Maurois and Sir Winston Churchill (as I: 107, 212–13).

The coverage of the seventeenth and eighteenth centuries has a considerable amount of social history, but too much of it is taken from the ancient but classic volumes of H. J. Traill, just as some constitutional history is taken from J. R. Tanner. The poor laws are carefully laid out from Elizabeth I through the eighteenth century, but there is too much description and insufficient analysis. The punishments in force in the seventeenth century were severe (I: 174–75), but some of them were seldom used, and slavery is perhaps too harsh a depiction for convicted vagrants. Fraud, extortion, and libel were included in the jurisdiction of the JPs (I: 170–71), but there is little evidence that these crimes were prosecuted. The central courts are seen as exercising control of the JPs in the seventeenth century, which belies some of the monographic studies; and the role and importance of the assizes in the seventeenth and eighteenth centuries is perhaps underestimated. In the end, England is seen on the whole as a more integrated and centrally oriented country than the local history suggests.

Some subjects in the later eighteenth and the nineteenth centuries do not receive as much research as others. These include the history of licensing and its enforcement, the early history of the police before the Metropolitan Police, The Middlesex "trading" justices, and the state of London generally speaking. Revisionist historians will regard Skyrme as being too critical of amateur institutions of peacekeeping prior to 1830 (II: 186–88) and as having a too "Whiggish" view of the nineteenth century and the reforms of the 1830s–1840s (II: 167–70). Some historians will have a similar view of his account of the post-World War II era.

The third volume of this magisterial work is even more uneven. The chapter on Wales focuses on the medieval era down to the Acts of Union of 1536 and 1543, with virtually no substantive discussion afterward, and is based largely on legislation (III: 1–28). The Isle of Man is reduced to a bare summary (III: 205–9). The chapter on Ireland, however, is much more historical and legal and within a similar length covers her administrative and judicial history rather evenly down to the present (III: 29–55). Scotland is equally well researched, and the sixteenth- and seventeenth-century history of its law and justices (III: 57–91) is a considerable improvement on the author's account of neighboring England. Moreover, he draws some nice parallels between the two countries, distinguishing similarities and differences as well as cross-influences.

North and Central America, with Pacifica, has a similar problem. The United States is seen as having a more local model of JP, evolving to the national British one in the eighteenth and nineteenth centuries, and as being more administrative than judicial (III: 93–126). A different interpretation would see both as local in the seventeenth century and evolving more gradually to the national model. Each of the original thirteen colonies is covered individually in a page or two, but the significant specialist literature is unused. Skyrme is better on the history of the JP in the American frontier and on explaining how they became small-town tyrants in the rural West by the early twentieth century.

Canada is less well served (III: 127–57). Two-thirds of the discussion is on the maritime colonies, and especially Nova Scotia, where he was assisted by a local researcher (III: 127–47). There is, however, a good assessment of the introduction of English law and institutions and of JPs, stipendary magistrates, and their courts along with their commissions and fees. But then there is a very quick romp through Quebec and Ontario (III: 150–52). When Skyrme reaches the Canadian West, the discussion falls apart (III: 153–57). There is no institutional, legal, or judicial understanding or context. His conclusion that the Canadian JP was a deliberate copy of the British one does not stand the evidence. Neither will the myth of the "mountie." And one might well question the observation that the role of the JP in Canada today is being enhanced as is being done in Britain.

The chapter on the West Indies begins with Oliver Cromwell's capture of Jamaica in 1655 (III: 159–68). The author discusses the growth of stipendary and resident magistrates. The discussion of the resident magistrates with their wide judicial duties acquired in the twentieth century is particularly useful. He then moves to the Cayman Islands, Belize, British Honduras, and Bermuda. But except for the Caymans (III: 163–66), there is no useful research, detail, overview, or conclusion for the other jurisdictions.

Australia is examined beginning with the first settlement in New South Wales in 1788 (III: 169–92). The role of the JPs as voluntary, state officials equipped with the land, local power, and prestige of eighteenth-century British magistrates is well assessed. But perhaps the judicial side of their work is underestimated. The evolution from JP to stipendary magistrate is chronicled effectively, first from 1825 and then from the Commonwealth of 1901. Skyrme concludes Australia as he does Britain, with a description of their appointments and commissions, training, and status and conditions of employment in the various states and territories at the present time.

Concluding chapters on New Zealand and "Analogous Institutions" are more problematic. New Zealand has a bare-bones summary from the charter of 1840 that simply defines the various legal and judicial institutions at their inception, and then moves to the modern post-World War II era (III: 197–203). The final chapter considers "systems similar to, but distinct from" those of the JP in Africa, Asia, and the Pacific Isles (III: 211–34). Although there are some interesting comments, the chapter comprises primarily animadversions on the systems, which are somewhat disparate and disjointed.

In conclusion, Sir Thomas Skyrme has written a major work that will probably never be duplicated in the present generation. Well annotated, replete with the reference aids of statutes and cases cited, and a comprehensive index, the work on the English side is a significant advance over the previous multivolume studies of the Webbs and Holdsworth. Apart from complaints that specialists could make about any attempt to provide an overview as large as this one, the reader might well argue that the research was more consistent for the various parts of the volumes. Too often subjects are discussed frequently in small time periods instead of in larger segments, especially subjects such as vagrancy, the poor laws, agriculture, roads, bridges, and various court officials. But there are a minimum of typos, the work is clearly written, and the reader is provided with some useful over-arching themes.

The author leaves his readers with an interesting question: the conundrum of the British heritage of part-time, unpaid magistrates who still exercise in the late twentieth century significant criminal jurisdiction (II: 415–24 and III: 234), particularly in contrast to other European or industrialized nation-states. How long can this last in the highly professionalized world of the specialist? The presence of low costs, of the ancient belief in the role of the laity in the administration of justice and in courts being responsive to the local communities and their law-abiding citizens, must surely be squared with justices appointed in secrecy, accepting too much evidence at face value and on general impression, and inconsistent sentencing practices. "The British love of tradition and continuity favors the preservation of a system which has long been established as part of the English and Welsh heritage, and it is now too deeply ingrained in the way of life of the people to be easily uprooted." But that day may come, "if, like other institutions that have perished, it is unable to move with the times, to adapt to evolutionary change and to satisfy the diverse demands of a progressive, democratic society" (II: 424).

NOTES

1. F. W. Maitland, *Justice and Police* (London, 1885); Charles A. Beard, *The Office of Justice of the Peace in England, in its origin and development* (New York, 1904); Bertha Osborne, *Justices of the Peace, 1361–1848* (London, 1960); and Esther Moir, *British Institutions: The Justice of the Peace* (London, 1969). It is now nearly a quarter-century since the last general history.

2. Especially Thomas G. Barnes, *Somerset, 1625–1640: A County's Government during the Personal Rule* (Cambridge Mass., 1961); J. S. Cockburn, *The North Riding Justices, 1690–1750* (Wakefield, 1965); E. G. Dowdell, *A Hundred Years of Quarter Sessions: The Government of Middlesex from 1660 to 1760* (Cambridge, 1932); S. J. B. Endelman, *Patronage and Power: A Social Study of the Justice of the Peace in Late Medieval Essex* (Doctoral dissertation, Brown University, 1977); E. G. Kimball, *Oxfordshire Sessions of the Peace in the Reign of Richard II* (Oxford, 1983); Esther A. L. Moir, *Local Government in Gloucestershire, 1775–1880* (Bristol, 1969); B. H. Putnam, *Kent Keepers of the Peace, 1316–17* (Maidstone, 1933); B. W. Quintrell, *The Government of the County of Essex* (Doctoral dissertation,

University of London, 1965); and W. B. Willcox, *Gloucester, A Study of Local Government, 1590–1640* (New Haven, 1940).

3. Namely, the counties of Durham, Essex, Gloucestershire, Lancaster, Lincolnshire, Middlesex, Oxfordshire, Somerset, Staffordshire, Surrey, Warwickshire, Wiltshire, Worcestershire, and Yorkshire North and West Ridings.

4. Particularly, J. M. Beattie, *Crime and the Courts in England, 1660–1880* (Princeton, 1986); Lionel K. J. Glassey, *Politics and the Appointment of Justices of the Peace, 1675–1720* (Oxford, 1979); John H. Gleason, *The Justices of the Peace in England, 1558 to 1640* (Oxford, 1969); Norma Landau, *The Justices of the Peace, 1689–1760* (Berkeley, 1984); and Bertha H. Putnam, *Early Treatises on Justices of the Peace in the Fifteenth and Sixteenth Centuries* (Oxford, 1924). The works of Sidney and Beatrice Webb should not be omitted for the era of the industrial revolution.

5. Sidney and Beatrice Webb, *English Local Government* (London, 1903–1927; repr. 1963), 11 vols.; and Sir William Holdsworth, *A History of English Law* (London, 1903–1948; repr. 1956), 12 vols.

Bibliography
Criminality and Criminal Justice History in Europe, 1250–1850: A Select Bibliography

Xavier Rousseau
The Catholic University of Louvain

This bibliography has been constructed as a result of a general reflection on the history of crime and criminal justice in Europe since the later Middle Ages. It has been developed further during the course of a joint seminar, *Les états et le pénale: Acculturation juridique et intégration nationale,* organized by the CESDIP in Paris and the University of St. Louis in Brussels. For a detailed analysis of the major issues and the current state of research, the reader should consult the author's "From Medieval Cities to National States (1350–1850): Historiography of Crime and Criminal Justice in Europe," in *Crime History and Histories of Crime: Studies in the Historiography of Crime and Criminal Justice,* edited by Clive Emsley and Louis A. Knafla (Westport, 1994).

The bibliography lists only those texts that address broad issues through archival research. It excludes monographs dealing with specific issues (e.g., witchcraft, theft and violence), with individual cases, or with particular legal developments. It is structured chronologically and thus, occasionally, a little arbitrarily. The texts are listed principally by period and subdivided by country or region.

GENERAL AND METHODOLOGICAL WORKS

Bader, K., "Aufgaben, Methoden und Grenzen einer historischen Kriminologie," in *Schweizerische Zeitschrift für Strafrecht* 71 (1956): 17–31.

Bailey, V., "Reato, giustizia penale e autorita in Inghilterra. Un decennio di studi storici, 1969–1979," *Quaderni Storici* 44 (1979): 581–603.

Bailey, V., "Bibliographical Essay: Crime, Criminal Justice and Authority in England," *Bulletin of the Society for the Study of Labour History* 40 (1980): 36–46.

Billacois, F., "Pour une enquête sur la criminalité dans la France d'Ancien Régime," *Annales.Economies.Sociétés.Civilisations* 22 (1967): 340–49.

Billacois, F., "Criminalistes, pénalistes et historiens," *Annales.E.S.C.* 24 (1969): 911–14.

Bercé, Y.M., and Castan, Y. (eds.), *Les archives du délit, empreintes de société* (Toulouse, 1990).

Castan, N., "Bilan de l'apport de la recherche historique à la connaissance de la criminalité et de la justice pénale," in *La recherche historique sur la criminalité et la justice pénale* (Strasbourg, 1984): 9–30.

Cohen, S., and Scull, A., *Social Control and the State: Historical and Comparative Essays* (Oxford, 2nd ed., 1986).

Coll., "Twelve years of research on the history of crime and criminal justice (1978/ 1990)," *I.A.H.C.C.J. Bulletin* 14 (Paris, 1991).

Coutau-Bégarie, H., *Le phénomène "Nouvelle Histoire": Stratégie et idéologie des nouveaux historiens* (Paris, 2nd ed., 1989).

Deyon, P., *Le temps des prisons, essai sur l'histoire de la délinquance et les origines du système pénitentiaire* (Lille, 1975).

Elton, G., "Introduction: Crime and the Historian," in Cockburn, J. S. (ed.), *Crime in England, 1550–1800* (London, 1977): 1–14.

Faber, S., et al. (ed.), *Tien jaar werkgroep strafrechtsgeschiedenis, 1973–1983* (Leiden and Amsterdam, 1983).

Foucault, M., *Discipline and Punish: The Birth of the Prison* (Harmondsworth, 1979). English translation of the original version *Surveiller et punir. Naissance de la prison* (Paris, 1975).

Franke, H., "The Rise and decline of solitary confinement: Socio-historical Explanations of Long-Term Penal Changes," *British Journal of Criminology* 32:2 (1992): 125–43.

Garnot, B. (ed.), *Histoire et Criminalité de l'Antiquité au XXe siècle. Nouvelles approches. Actes du colloque de Dijon, 2–5 octobre 1991* (Dijon, 1992).

Gatrell, V.-A.-C., Lenman, B., and Parker, G., (eds.), *Crime and the Law: The Social History of Crime in Western Europe since 1500* (London, 1980).

Gégot, J. C., "Storia della criminalità: la ricerche in Francia," *Quaderni Storici* 46 (1981): 192–211.

Geremek, B., "Criminalité, vagabondage, paupérisme: La marginalité à l'aube des temps modernes," *Revue d'Histoire Moderne et Contemporaine* 21 (1974): 337–75.

Geremek, B., *Inutiles au monde. Truands et misérables dans l'Europe moderne (1350–1600)* (Paris, 1980).

Geremek, B., *La potence ou la pitié: L'Europe et les pauvres du Moyen Age à nos jours* (Paris, 1987).

Hoffer, P. C., "Counting Crime in Premodern England and America: A Review Essay," *Historical Methods* 14:4 (1981): 187–193.

Hufton, O., "Crime in Pre-Industrial Europe," *IAHCCJ-Newsletter* 4 (1981): 8–35.

Huussen, A.-H., "Strafrechtspraktijk en criminaliteit in het verleden, een tekening in het grensgebied tussen realistische en sociale geschiedenis," *Groniek* (1976): 23–29.

Killias, M., and Rehbinder, M. (ed.), *Rechtsgeschichte und Rechtssociologie* (Berlin, 1985).

Knafla, L. (ed.), *Crime and Criminal Justice in Europe and Canada* (Waterloo Ont., 1981).

Lévy, R., and Robert Ph., "Le sociologue et l'histoire pénale," *Annales.E.S.C.* 39:2 (1984): 400–22.

Lévy, R., and Rousseaux, X., "Etats, justice pénale et histoire: bilans et perspectives," *Droit et Société* 20–21 (1992): 249–79.

McMullan, J. L., "Crime, Law and Order in Early Modern England," *British Journal of Criminology* 27:3 (1987): 252–74.

Monkonnen, E., "Systematic Criminal Justice History: Some Suggestions," *Journal of Interdisciplinary History* 9 (1979): 451–64.

Monkonnen, E., "The History of Crime and Criminal Justice after Twenty-Five Years," *Criminal Justice History* 5 (1984): 161–69.

Moorman van Kappen, O., "Die sogenannte neue Forschungrichtung zur Kriminalitätsgeschichte in den Niederlanden und Belgien," in *Zeitschrift für neuere Rechtgeschichte* 6 (1984): 153–62.

Nye, R.A., "Crime in Modern Societies: Some Research Strategies for Historians," *Journal of Interdisciplinary History* 11 (1978): 491–507.

O' Brien, P. "Crime and Punishment as Historical Problem," *Journal of Social History* 11 (1978): 508–20.

Parker, G., "Crime and the Early Modern Historian. A Review Article," *Tijdschrift voor Geschiedenis* 94 (1981): 595–601.

Pihlajamäky, H. (ed.), *Theatres of Power: Social Control and Criminality in Historical Perspective* (s.l., 1991).

Powell, E., "Social Research and the Use of Medieval Criminal Records," *Michigan Law Review* 79 (1981): 967–78.

Pugh, R. B., "Some Reflections on a Medieval Criminologist," *Proceedings of the British Academy* 59 (1973): 83–104.

Robert, Ph., and Emsley C. (eds.), *Geschichte und Sociologie des Verbrechens. History and Sociology of Crime. Histoire et sociologie du crime* (Pfaffenweiler, 1991).

Robert, Ph., and Lévy, R., "Histoire et question pénale," *Revue d'Histoire Moderne et Contemporaine* 27 (1985): 481–526.

Robert, Ph., and Lévy, R., "A Changing Penal Economy in French Society : In Search of a Historical View," *Historical Social Research* 37 (1986): 17–39.

Rommer, H., "Historische Kriminologie—zum Forschungsstand in der deutschsprachigen Literatur der letzte zwanzig Jahre," *Zeitschrift für Neuere Rechtsgeschichte* 14 (1992): 227–42.

Rousseaux, X., "Existe-t-il une criminalité d'ancien régime (13e–18e s.)? Réflexions sur l'histoire de la criminalité en Europe," in Garnot, B. (ed.), *Histoire et Criminalité de l'Antiquité au XXe siècle. Nouvelles approches. Actes du colloque de Dijon, 2–5 octobre 1991* (Dijon, 1992): 123–66.

Rousseaux, X., "From Medieval Cities to National States: Historiography on Crime and Criminal Justice In Europe 1350–1850 in Europe," in Emsley C., and Knafla L., (eds.), *Crime History and Histories of Crime: Studies in the Historiography of Crime and Criminal Justice* (Westport, Conn., forthcoming 1994).

Roth, R., "Evaluation of the contribution of historical research to crime policy and the forecasting of trends in crime policy, taking into account the changes in the oscial and economic context," in *Historical Research on Crime and Criminal Research: Reports Presented to the Sixth Criminological Colloquium* (Strasbourg, 1985).

Roth, R., "Histoire pénale, histoire sociale: même débat?" *Déviance et Société* 5 (1981): 187–203.

Rusche, G., and Kirchheimer, O., *Punishment and Social Structure* (New York, 1939).

Sack, F., "Kriminalität, Gesellschaft und Geschichte : Berührungsänste der deutschen Kriminologie," *Kriminologisches Journal* 19:4 (1987): 241–68.

Saurer, E., "Dieci anni di studi austriaci di storia della criminalità e del diritto penale," *Quaderni Storici* 49 (1982): 217–25.

Sbriccoli, M., "Fonti giudiziarie e fonti giuridiche. Riflessioni sulla fase attuale degli studi di storia del crimine e della giustizia criminale," *Studi Storici* 2 (1988): 491–501.

Smaus, G., "Kriminologie und geschichte. Eine Einführung," *Kriminologisches Journal* 19:1 (1987): 3–15.

Schwerhoff, G., "Devianz in der alteuropäischen gesellschaft. Umrisse einer historischen Kriminalitätsforschung," *Zeitschrift für historische Forschung* 19:4 (1992): 385–414.

Soman, A., "Deviance and Criminal Justice in Western Europe, 1300–1800: An Essay in Structure," *Criminal Justice History* 1 (1980): 1–28.

Spierenburg, P., "Criminele geschiedenis. Een literatuuroverzicht," *Tijdschrift voor Sociale Geschiedenis* 23 (1981): 251–64.

Spierenburg, P., Evaluation of the Conditions and Main Problems Relating to the Contribution of Historical Research to the Understanding of Crime and Criminal Justice. Report in *Historical Research on Crime and Criminal Research. Reports Presented to the Sixth Criminological Colloquium* (Strasbourg, 1985), 49–95.

Vanhemelryck, F., "De studie van de criminaliteit in het Ancien Régime, Stand van het onderzoek en methode," *Bijdragen tot de Geschiedenis* 56 (1973): 209–42.

Vanhemelryck, F., "Misdaad en straf. Recent onderzoek naar de geschiedenis der criminaliteit," *Bijdragen en Mededelingen betreffende de geschiedenis der Nederlanden* 93:2 (1978): 177–206.

Weisser, M.-R., *Crime and Punishment in Early Modern Europe* (Brighton, 2nd ed., 1982).

Wirtz, R., "Aspetti della storiografia tedesca sulla criminalità," *Quaderni Storici* 46 (1981): 212–24.

CRIMINAL JUSTICE AND COMMUNAL POWER (1250–1450)

Italy

Allocco, M., "La criminalità in Savigliano attraverso i conti della castellania dal 1428 al 1438," *Bolletino della Società per gli studi storici, archeologici ed artistici della provincia di Cuneo* (1984): 109–36.

Becker, M.-B., "Changing Patterns of Violence and Justice in fourteenth and fifteenth-Century Florence," *Comparative Studies for Society and History* 18 (1976):281–96.

Blanshei, S. R., "Criminal Law and Politics in Medieval Bologna," *Criminal Justice History* 2 (1981): 1–30.

Blanshei, S. R., "Crime and Law Enforcement in Medieval Bologna," *Journal of Social History* 16 (1982): 121–38.

Blanshei, S. R., "Criminal Justice in Medieval Perugia and Bologna," *Law and History Review* 1 (1983): 251–75.

Bonfiglio Dosio, G., "Criminalità ed emarginazione a Brescia nel primo Quattrocento," *Archivio storico italiano* 495:6 (1978): 113–64.

Bowsky, W.-M., "The Medieval Commune and Internal Violence: Police Power and Public Safety in Siena, 1287–1355," *American Historical Review* 73 (1967): 1–17.

Bruckner, G. A., "The Florentine Popolo Minuto and its Political Role, 1340–1450," in Martines, L. (ed.), *Violence and Civil Disorder in Italian Cities, 1200–1500* (Los Angeles, 1972), 155–83.

Chojnacki, S., "Crime, Punishment, and the Trecento Venetian State," in Martines, L. (ed.), *Violence and Civil Disorder in Italian Cities, 1200–1500* (Los Angeles, 1972), 184–228.

Cohn, S. K., Jr., "Criminality and the State in Renaissance Florence, 1344–1466," *Journal of Social History* 14 (1981): 211–33.

Dean, T., and Lowe, K., *Crime and Disorder in Renaissance Italy* (Cambridge, forthcoming 1994).

Dorini, U., *Il diritto penale e la delinquenza in Firenze nel sec. XIV* (Lucca, 1923).

Giuffrida, A., *La giustizia nel medioevo siciliano* (Palermo, 1975).

Gundersheimer, W. H., "Crime and Punishment in Ferrara, 1440–1500," in Martines, L. (ed.), *Violence and Civil Disorder in Italian Cities, 1200–1500* (Los Angeles, 1972), 104–28.

Larner, J., "Order and Disorder in Romagna, 1450–1500," in Martines, L. (ed.), *Violence and Civil Disorder in Italian Cities, 1200–1500* (Los Angeles, 1972), 38–71.

Maire Vigueur, J. C., "Justice et politique dans l'Italie communale de la seconde moitié du XIIIe siècle: l'exemple de Pérouse," *Comptes-rendus de l'Académie des Inscriptions et Belles-Lettres* (1986): 312–28.

Martines, L. (ed.), *Violence and Civil Disorder in Italian Cities, 1200–1500* (Los Angeles, 1972).

Papaleoni, G., "La giustizia penale e la delinquenza nelle Giudicature ulteriori alla fine del medioevo," *Studi trentini di scienze storiche* (1937): 229–71.

Pene Vidari, G. S., "Sulla criminalità e sui banni del Comune di Ivrea nei primi anni della dominazione sabauda (1313–1347)," *Bollettino storico-bibliografico subalpino* 68 (1970): 157–211.

Roqué Ferrer, P., "L'Infrazione della legge a Cagliari dal 1340 al 1380," *Quaderni sardi di storia* (1985): 3–26.

Ruggiero, R., "Law and Punishment in Early Renaissance Venice," *Journal of Criminal Law and Criminology* 64 (1978): 243–56.

Ruggiero, R., *Violence in Early Renaissance Venice* (New Brunswick, 1980). (Italian version, *Patrizi e malfattori. la violenza a Venezia nel primo Rinascimento* (Bologne, 1982).

Schioppa, S. "Le fonti giudiziare per una ricerca sulla criminalità a Perugia nel duecento," in *Ricerche su Perugia tra due e quattrocento* (Perugia, 1981), 59–144.

Verga, E., "Le sentenze criminali del podestà milanese, 1385–1429: appunti per la storia della giustizia punitiva in Milano," *Archivio Storico Lombardo* 28 (1901): 96–142.

Zdekauer, L., "Studi sulla criminalità italiana del Duecento e Trecento," *Bolletino Senese di Storia Patria* 8 (1901): 310–32.

Zorzi, A., "Aspetti e problemi dell'amministrazione della giustizia penale nelle Repubblica fiorentina," *Archivio storico italiano*, 533 (1987): 391–453; 534 (1987): 527–578.

Zorzi, A., "Giustizia e società a Firenze in età comunale: spunti per una prima riflessione," *Ricerche storiche* 18 (1988): 449–95.

Zorzi, A., "Giustizia criminale e criminalita nell'Italia del tardo medioevo: Studi e prospettive di ricerca," *Società e Storia* 46 (1989): 923–65.

Zorzi, A., "Contrôle social, ordre public et répression judiciaire à Florence à l'époque communale: Éléments et problèmes," *Annales E.S.C.* 45:5 (1990): 1169–88.

Zorzi, A., "Aspects de la justice criminelle dans les villes italiennes du bas moyen âge," in *Déviance et Société* 15:4 (1991): 439–54.

Zorzi, A., *La giustizia a Firenze in età comunale (1250–1343). Pratiche sociali, sistemi giudiziari, configurazioni istitutionzali* (Rome, forthcoming).

Iberic Territories

Barraqué, J. P., "Le contrôle des conflits à Saragosse (XIVe-début du XVe siècle)," *Revue Historique* 279 (1973): 41–50.

Duarte, L. M., "Justice et criminalité au Moyen Age et au début de l'Epoque Moderne: les traces, les silences, les problèmes," in Berlinguer, L., and Colao, F. (eds.), *Le politiche criminali nel XVIII secolo* (Milan, 1990): 449–60.

French Area

Benveniste, H., *Stratégies judiciaires et rapports sociaux d'après les plaidoiries devant la chambre criminelle du Parlement de Paris (vers 1345–vers 1454)* (Doctoral dissertation in History, Univ. Paris I, 1986).

Bourin, M., and Chevalier, B., "Le comportement criminel dans les Pays de la Loire moyenne, d'après les lettres de rémission (vers 1380–vers 1450)," *Annales de Bretagne et des pays de l'Ouest* 88 (1981): 245–63.

Carbasse, J. M., *Consulats méridionaux et justice criminelle, XII–XIVe siècles* (Doctoral dissertation in Law, Univ. Montpellier, 1974).

Cheyette, F., "La justice et le pouvoir royal à la fin du Moyen Age français," *Revue historique de droit français et étranger* 40 (1962): 373–94.

Chiffoleau, J., "La violence au quotidien: Avignon au XIVe siècle d'après les registres de la Cour temporelle," *Mélanges de l'Ecole française de Rome. Moyen Age, Temps modernes* 92: 2 (1980): 325–71.

Chiffoleau, J., *Les justices du pape. Délinquance et criminalité dans la région d'A-vignon* (Paris, 1984).

Cohen, E., "Patterns of Crime in Fourteenth-Century Paris," *French Historical Studies* 11:3 (1980): 307–27.

Cohen, E., "Violence control in late medieval France: The Social Transformation of the Asseurement," *Legal History Review* 51 (1983): 111–21.

Coopland, G. W., "Crime and Punishment in Paris, September 6, 1389 to May 18, 1390," in *Studies in Honor of A. S. Atiya* (London, 1972), 64–85.

Gasparri, F., *Crimes et châtiments en Provence au temps du roi René* (Paris, 1989).

Gauvard, C., "La criminalité parisienne à la fin du Moyen Age: Une criminalité ordinaire?" in *Villes, bonnes villes, cités et capitales. Mélanges B. Chevalier* (Tours, 1989), 361–70.

Gauvard, C., *"De grace especial": Crime, Etat et Société en France à la fin du Moyen-Age* (Paris, 2 vols., 1991).

Geremek, B., *Les marginaux parisiens aux XIVe–XVe siècles* (Paris, 1976).

Gonon, M., "Violences au Moyen Age en Forez," in *Actes du 102e congrès des Sociétés Savantes, Limoges, sect. Philo. Hist.* 11 (1979), 223–31.

Gonthier, N., *Délinquance, justice et société en Lyonnais (fin XIIIe siècle-début XVIe siècle)*, 4 vols. (Doctoral dissertation in History, Univ. Lyon III, 1988).

Gonthier, N., "La rémission des crimes à Dijon sous les ducs Valois," *Cahiers d'Histoire* 35:2 (1990): 99–118.

Gonthier, N., *Cris de haine et rites d'unité. La violence dans les villes (XIIIe–XVIe siècle)* (Turnhout, 1992).

Grand, R., "Justice criminelle, procédure et peines dans les villes aux XIIIe et XIVe siècles," *Bibliothèque de l'Ecole des chartes* 102 (1941): 58–97.

Langlois, M., and Lanhers, Y., *Confessions et jugements de criminels au Parlement de Paris (1319–1350)* (Paris, 1971).

Lanhers, Y., "Crimes et criminels au XIVe siècle," *Revue Historique* 240 (1968): 325–38.

Lavoie, R., "Justice, criminalité, et peine de mort en France au Moyen Age: Essai de typologie et de régionalisation," in *le Sentiment de la mort au Moyen Age. Etudes présentées au cinquième colloque de l'Institut d'Etudes Médiévales de l'université de Montréal* (Montreal, 1979).

Lavoie, R., "Les statistiques criminelles et le visage du justicier: Justice royale et justice seigneuriale en Provence au Moyen Age," *Provence historique* 48 (1979): 3–20.

Leclercq, P., "Délits et répression dans un village de Provence (fin XVe–début du XVIe siècle)," *Le Moyen Age* 82 (1976): 539–55.

Lorcin, M. Th., "Les paysans et la justice dans la région Lyonnaise aux XIVe et XVe siècles," *Le Moyen Age* 54 (1968): 269–300.

Malaussena, P. L., "Justice pénale et comportements villageois dans une seigneurie provençale au XIIIe siècle," *Mémoires et Travaux de l'Association méditerranéenne d'Histoire et d'Ethnologie*, sér. 2., 2 (1982): 7–53.

Misraki, J., "Criminalité et pauvreté en France à l'époque de la guerre de Cent Ans," in Mollat, M. (ed.), *Etudes sur l'histoire de la pauvreté* (Paris, 1974) 2: 535–46.

Muchembled, R., Anthropologie de la violence dans la France moderne (XVe–XVIIIe siècle), *Revue de Synthèse* 108 (1987): 31–55.

Netherlands

Berents, D. A., *Misdaad in de middeleeuwen: Een onderzoek naar de criminaliteit in het laat-middeleeuwse Utrecht* (Utrecht, 1976).

Berents, D. A., *Het werk van de vos. Samenleving en criminaliteit in de late middeleeuwen* (Zutphen, 1988).

Cullus, Ph., "La délinquance dans les villes du comté de Hainaut à la fin du moyen âge," in *Autour de la ville en Hainaut. Mélanges d'archéologie et d'histoire urbaines offerts à Jean Dugnoille et à René Sansen* (Athens, 1986): 255–75.

Diederiks, H. A., and Roodenburg, H. W., *Misdaad, zoen en straf. Aspekten van de middeleeuwse strafrechtsgeschiedenis in de Nederlanden* (Hilversum, 1991).

Goris, J. A., "Zeden en criminaliteit te Antwerpen in de tweede helft der XIVe eeuw, naar de rekeningen der schouten van 1358 tot 1387," *Revue belge de Philologie et d'Histoire 5* (1926): 871–86.

Kallendorf, C., *Crime and Society in Medieval Flanders: The Oudburg of Ghent 1302–1401* (Doctoral dissertation, Duke Univ. 1981).

Mestayer, M., "La procédure criminelle à Douai à la fin du 14e siècle," *Acta Falconis* 87:7 (1987): 111–20.

Nicholas, D. M., "Crime and Punishment in Fourteenth Century Ghent," *Revue belge de Philologie et d'Histoire* 48:2 (1970): 289–334; 48:4 (1970): 1141–76.

Stabel, P., "Misdaad en misdadiger in een kleine vlaamse stad gedurende de late middeleeuwen (Eeeklo 14de–15de eeuw)," *Appeltjes van het Meetjesland* (1989): 155–66.

Van der Heyden, J., "Misdrijf in Antwerpen. Een onderzoek naar de criminaliteit in de periode 1404–1429," *Acta Falconis* 83:3 (1983): 23.

Van Heerwaarden, J., *The Effects of Social Circumstances of the Administration of Justice: The Example of Enforced Pilgrimages in Certain Towns of the Nederlands (XIVth–XVth centuries)* (Rotterdam, 1978).

Van Heerwaarden, J., *Opgelegde bedevaarten: Een studie over de praktijk van opleggen van bedevaarten (met name in de stedelijke rechtspraak) in de Nederlanden gedurende de late middeleeuwen (ca 1300–1550)* (Assen/Amsterdam, 1978).

Vanhemelryck, F., "Het Brabantse strafrecht en zijn toepassing in de praktijk voornamelijk. te Brussel in de XVe eeuw," *Legal History Review* 34 (1966): 375–401.

Vanhemelryck, F., "Misdaad en straf in de meierij van Rode in de XVe en XVIe eeuw," *Eigen Schoon en de Brabander*, 57:7/8/9. (1975): 233–254; 57:10/11/12 (1975): 399–422.

Vanhemelryck, F., *De criminaliteit in de ammanie van Brussel van de late middeleeuwen tot het einde van het Ancien Régime (1404–1789)* (Brussels, 1981).

British Islands

Bellamy, J. G., "Justice under the Yorkist Kings," *American Journal of Legal History* 9 (1965): 135–55.

Bellamy, J., *Crime and Public Order in England in the Late Middle Ages* (London, 1973).

Given, J.-B., *Society and Homicide in Thirteenth-Century England* (Stanford, 1977).

Hanawalt, B.-A., *Crime and Conflict in English Communities, 1300–1348* (Cambridge, Mass. and London, 1979).

Maddern, P.C., *Violence, Crime and Public Disorder in East Anglia, 1422–1442* (Oxford, 1992).

Post, J. B., "The Justice of Criminal Justice in Late-Fourteenth-Century England," *Criminal Justice History* 7 (1986): 33–49.

Helvetic Cities

Burghartz, S., "Disziplinierung oder Konfliktregelung? Zur Funktion städtischer Gerichte im Spätmittelalter: Das Zürcher Ratsgericht," *Zeitschrift für Historische Forschung* 16 (1989): 385–407.

Burghartz, S., *Ehre und Gut: Delinquenz in Zürich Ende des 14. Jahrhundert* (Zürich, 1990).

Simon-Muscheid, K., "Gewalt und Ehre im spätmittelalterlichen Handwerk am beispiel Basels," *Zeitschrift für Historische Forschung* 18:4 (1991): 1–31.

Germanic Areas

Buchholz, W., "Anfänge der Sozialdisziplinierung im Mittelalter. Die Reichsstadt Nürnberg als Beispiel," *Zeitschrift der Savigny-Stiftung für Rechtsgeschichte*, G. Abt 108 (1991): 117–93.

Buff, A., "Verbrechen und Verbrecher zu Augsburg in der zweiten Hälfte des 14. Jahrhunderts," *Zeitschrift des Historischen Vereins für Schwaben und Neuburg* 4 (1878: 160–231).

Demandt, K. E., "Recht und Gesellschaft. Rechts-, sozial- und sittengeschichtliche Studien zur strafrechtlichen Praxis in einer hessischen Stadt des 15 Jh.," *Zeitschrift des Vereins für hessische Geschichte und Landeskunde* 83 (1972): 9–56.

Marbach, J., *Strafrechtspflege in den hessischen Städten an der Werra am Ausgang des Mittelalters* (Munich, 1980).

Schüssler, M., "Statistische Untersuchung des Verbrechen in Nürnberg im Zeitraum von 1285 bis 1400," *Zeitschrift für Historische Forschung* 18:2 (1991): 129–47.

CRIMINAL JUSTICE AND MONARCHIC POWERS (1450–1650)

Italy

Allegra, L., "Oltre le fonti criminali: Chieri nel '500," *Quaderni Storici* 49 (1982): 265–73.

Berlinguer, L., and Colao, F. (ed.), *Crimine, giustizia e società veneta in età moderna* (Milan, 1979).

Cozzi, G. (ed.), *Stato, società e giustizia nella Repubblica Veneta (sec. XV–XVIII)* (Rome, 2 vols., 1980 & 1985).

Di Simplicio, O., "La criminalità a Siena (1561–1808). Problemi di ricerca," *Quaderni Storici* 49 (1982): 242–64.

Ghiara, C., "Le fonti criminali genovesi: Sondaggi seriali o culturali?" *Quaderni Storici* 44 (1979): 603–14.

Hook, J. A., "Justice, Authority and the Creation of the Ancien Régime in Italy," *Transactions of the Royal Historical Society* 34 (1984): 71–89.

Parisini, A., "Pratiche extragiudiziali di amministrazione della Giustizia: La 'liberazione dalla morte' a Faenza tra '500 e '700," *Quaderni Storici* 67 (1988): 147–68.

Romani, M., "Criminalità e giustizia nel ducato di Mantova alla fine del Cinquecento," *Rivista Storica Italiana* 3:4 (1980): 680–707.

Povolo, C., "Contributi e ricerche in corso sull'amministrazione della giustizia nella republica di Venezia nell'età moderna," *Quaderni Storici* 44 (1979): 614–26.

Trasselli, C., "Du fait divers à l'histoire sociale: Criminalité et moralité en Sicile au début de l'époque moderne," *Annales. E.S.C.* 28 (1973): 226–46.

Zaccarini, D., "Delitti e pene negli Stati estensi nel secolo XVI: Contributo allo studio della delinquenza," *Atti e memorie della Deputazione ferrarese di storia patria* (1928): 3–66.

Iberic World

Carrasco, R., "La violence physique d'après les archives judiciaries: Le cas de Cuenca (1535–1623)," in *Le corps dans la société espagnole des XVIe et XVIIe siècles* (Paris, 1990), 164–71.

Herrera Puga, P., *Sociedad in delincuencia en el siglo de oro* (Madrid, 1974).

Perry, M. E., *Crime and Society in Early Modern Seville* (Hanover, 1980).

Pike, R., "Crime and Criminal in Sixteenth-Century Seville," *Sixteenth-Century Journal* 6 (1975): 3–18.

Pike, R., "Crime and Punishment in 16th Century Spain," *Journal of European Economic History* 5 (1976): 689–704.

Pike, R., *Penal Servitude in Early Modern Spain* (Madison, 1983).

Pike, R., "Penal Practices in Early Modern Spain," *Criminal Justice History* 5 (1984): 45–55.

Thompson, I.-A.-A., "A Map of Crime in Sixteenth-Century Spain," *Economic Historical Review*, 2nd s., 21 (1968): 244–67.

Kingdom of France

Bercé, Y. M., "Aspects de la criminalité au XVIIe siècle," *Revue Historique* 239 (1968): 33–42.

Charnay, A., *Les procès criminels au XVIe siècle dans le ressort de la sénéchaussée de Lyon, Revue du Lyonnais* 2:3 (1980): 129–40.

Davis, N-Z., *Fiction in the Archives: Pardon Tales and Their Tellers in Sixteenth-Century France* (Stanford, 1987).

Dockes, N., "Justice et pouvoir politique à Lyon du XVe au XVIe siècle," in *Mélanges L.Falleti, Annales de la Faculté de Droit et Sciences économiques de Lyon* 2 (1971): 108–29.

Greenshields, M. R., The Economy of Violence in Early Modern France: Criminality in the Haute-Auvergne, 1587–1664 (Doctoral dissertation, Univ. of Sussex, 1986).

Guilleminot, S., *Litiges et criminalité dans le présidial de Caen au XVIIe siècle* (Dissertation in History, University of Caen, 1986).

Guilleminot, S., "La justice d'ancien régime au XVIIe siècle: 11 000 cas dans le Présidial de Caen," *Histoire.Economie.Société* 7 (1988): 187–208.

Hanlon, G., "Les rituels de l'agression en Aquitaine au XVIIe siècle," *Annales.E.S.C.* 40:2 (1985): 244–68.

Lebigre, A., *Les Grands Jours d'Auvergne, désordres et répression au XVIIe siècle* (Paris, 1976).

Lebigre, A., *La justice du Roi: La vie judiciaire dans l'ancienne France* (Paris, 1988).

Plessix-Buisset, Ch., "Criminalité et société rurale en Bretagne au XVIIe siècle: l'exemple de la paroisse de Bothoa," *Mémoires de la Société Hist. Archéol. de Bretagne* 59 (1982): 5–51.

Plessix-Buisset, Ch., *Le criminel devant ses juges en Bretagne aux 16e et 17e siècles* (Paris, Maloine, 1988).

Schnapper, B., "La répression pénale au XVIe siècle, l'exemple du parlement de Bordeaux, 1510–1565," in *Droit pénal et société méridionale. Recueil de mémoires et travaux publiés par la Société d'Histoire du Droit des pays de droit écrit* 8 (1971 [1972]): 1–54.

Schnapper, B., "La justice criminelle rendue par le parlement de Paris sous le règne de François Ier," *Revue d'Histoire du Droit français et étranger* 42 (1974): 252–84.

Soman, A., "Criminal jurisprudence in Ancien Régime France: The Parlement of Paris in the XVIth and XVIIth centuries," in *Crime and Criminal Justice in Europe and Canada*, ed. Knafla, L. (Waterloo, Ont., 1981), 43–76. Expanded French version: "La Justice criminelle aux XVIe–XVIIe siècles: le Parlement de Paris et les sièges subalternes," in *Actes du 107e Congrès national des Sociétés savantes (Brest 1982), Section de Philologie et histoire jusqu'à 1610* (Paris, 2 vols., 1984) 1: 15–52.

Netherlands

Boomgaard, J., "Het Amsterdamse criminaliteitspatroon in de late middeleeuwen," in *Misdaad, zoen en straf. Aspekten van de middeleeuwse strafrechtsgeschiedenis in de Nederlanden*, Diederiks, H. A., and Roodenburg, H. W. (eds.) (Hilversum, 1991), 102–19.

Boomgaard, J., *Misdaad en straf in Amsterdam, Een onderzoek naar de strafrechtspleging van de Amsterdamse schepenbank 1490–1552* (Zwolle, 1992).

Dorban, M., "La criminalité en Gaume d'après les comptes des officiers de justice (1500–1650)," in *La criminalité en Wallonie sous l'Ancien Régime. Trois essais*, d'Arras d'Haudrecy, L., et al. (eds.) (Louvain, 1976), 32–47.

Dupont-Bouchat, M.-S., "La violence et la peur. Des mentalités et des moeurs à

Saint-Hubert au XVIIe siècle," *Saint-Hubert d'Ardenne, Cahiers d'Histoire* 2 (1978): 55–92.

Dupont-Bouchat, M.-S., and Rousseaux, X., "Le prix du sang. Sang et justice à l'époque moderne (1400–1800)," in *Mentalités* 1 (1988): 43–72.

Fouret, C. *L'amour, la violence et le pouvoir: la criminalité à Douai de 1496 à 1520*, Lille, 1984 (Doctoral Diss. in History, Univ. Lille III, 1984).

Fouret, C., Douai au XVIe siècle: une sociabilité de l'agression, *Revue d'histoire moderne et contemporaine* 34 (1987): 3–30.

Le Moal, J., *Recherches sur la criminalité d'après les lettres de rémission de 1590 à 1597* (Lille, 1972).

Maes, L. Th., *Vijf eeuwen stedelijk strafrecht. Bijdrage tot de rechts- en cultuurgeschiedenis der Nederlanden* (Antwerp, 1947).

Monballyu, J., *Het gerecht in de kasselrij Kortrijk (1515–1621)* (Doctoral dissertation in Law, Katholieke Universiteit Leuven, 1976).

Muchembled, R., "Crime et société urbaine. Arras au temps de Charles-Quint (1528–1549)," in *La France d'Ancien Régime. Etudes réunies en l'honneur de Pierre Goubert*, 2 vols. (Toulouse, 1984) 2: 481–90.

Muchembled, R., *La violence au village. Sociabilité et comportements populaires en Artois du XVe au XVIIe siècle* (Turnhout, 1989).

Muchembled, R., *Violence et société. Comportements et mentalités populaires en Artois (1400–1660)*, 3 vols. (Doctoral dissertation in History, Univ. Paris I, 1985).

Muchembled, R., *Le temps des supplices. De l'obéissance sous les Rois absolus. XVe–XVIIIe siècle* (Paris, 1992).

Pineau, M., "Les lettres de rémission lilloises (fin XVe–début XVIe siècle): une source pour l'étude de la criminalité et des mentalités," *Revue du Nord* 55 (1974): 231–39.

Quenée, I., and Morell-Sampol, C., "Crime et société dans la ville et le bailliage de Saint-Omer (1493–1598)," *Bulletin de la Société des Antiquaires de Morinie* 23 (1987), 265–307.

Rousseaux, X., *Taxer ou châtier? L'émergence du pénal. Enquête sur la justice nivelloise (1400–1650)*, 2 vols. (Doctoral Dissertation in History, Université catholique de Louvain, 1990).

British Islands

Bellamy, J.-G., *Criminal Law and Society in Late Medieval and Tudor England* (Gloucester, 1985).

Cockburn, J.-S. (ed.), *Crime in England (1550–1800)* (London, 1977).

Curtis, T., "Explaining Crime in Early Modern England," *Criminal Justice History* 2 (1980): 117–37.

Fletcher, A., and Stevenson, J. (eds.), *Order and Disorder in Early Modern England* (Cambridge, 1985).

Herrup, C. B., *The Common Peace: Participation and the Criminal Law in 17th Century England* (New York, 1987).

Houlbrooke, R., *Church Courts and the People during the English Reformation 1520–1570* (Oxford, 1979).

Ingram, M. J., "Communities and Courts: Law and Disorder in Early Seventeenth

Century Wiltshire," in Cockburn, J. S., (ed.), *Crime in England (1550–1800)* (London, 1977), 110–34.

Ingram, M. J., *Church Courts, Sex and Marriage in England 1570–1640* (Cambridge, 1987).

MacFarlane, A., *Justice and the Mare's Ale: Law and Disorder in 17th Century England* (Oxford, 1981).

Samaha, J., *Law and Order in Historical Perspective: The Case of Elizabethan Essex* (New York and London, 1974).

Samaha, J., *Hanging for Felony: The Rule of Law in Elizabethan Essex* (London, 1978).

Sharpe, J.-A., "Crime and Delinquency in an Essex Parish, 1600–1640," in Cockburn, J. S. (ed.), *Crime in England (1550–1800)* (London, 1977), 90–109.

Sharpe, J.-A., *Crime in Seventeenth-Century England: A County Study* (Cambridge, 1983).

Sharpe, J.-A., *Crime in Early Modern England 1550–1750* (London and New York, 1984).

Sharpe, J.-A., "The History of Crime in Late Medieval and Early Modern England: A Review of the Field," *Social History* 7:2 (1982): 187–203.

Wrighton, K., and Levine, D., *Poverty and Piety in an English Village: Terling, 1525–1700* (New York, 1979).

Scotland

Brown, K. M., *Bloodfeud in Scotland 1573–1625: Violence, Justice and Politics in Early Modern Society* (Edinburgh, 1986).

Lenman, B., and Parker, G., "Crime and Control in Scotland 1500–1800," *History Today* 30:1 (1980): 13–17.

Germanic Areas

Allen, R. M., *Crime and Punishment in Sixteenth-century Reutlingen* (Doctoral dissertation, Univ. of Virginia, 1980).

Boes, M. R., *Crime and Punishment in the City of Frankfurt-Am-main from 1562 to 1569* (Doctoral dissertation, City Univ. of New York, 1989).

Huffschmid, E.-Ph., "Zur Kriminalstatistik des Oldenwalds im XVI und XVII Jahrhundert nach Originalakten des Gr. Hofgerichts zu Mannheim," *Zeitschrift für Deutsche Kulturgeschichte* (1859): 409–34.

Müller, H., " 'Das andere Köln,' Marginalität im späten Mittelalter und in der frühen Neuzeit," *Geschichte in Köln* 18 (1985): 77–80.

Nordhoff-Behne, H., *Gerichtsbarkeit und Strafrechtspflege in der Reichsstadt Schwäbisch-Hall seit dem 15. Jahrundert* (Schwäbisch-Hall, 1971).

Opel, J., "Zur Kriminalstatistik der beiden Städte Zeis und Naumburg, während der Jahre 1549–1664," *Zeitschrift für Deutsche Kulturgeschichte* (1859): 637–51, 774–79.

Schormann, G., "Strafrechtspflege in Braunschweig-Wolfenbüttel 1569–1633," *Braunschweigisches Jahrbuch* 55 (1974): 90–112.

Schwerhoff, G., *Köln im Kreuzverhor. Kriminalität, Herrschaft und Gesellschaft in einer frühneuzeitlichen Stadt* (Bonn and Berlin, 1991).

Van Dülmen, R., *Theatre of Horror: Crime and Punishment in Early Modern Germany* (Cambridge, 1990). Original version, *Theater des Schreckens. Gerichtspraxis und Strafrituale der frühen Neuzeit* (Munich, 1985).

Helvetic Cities

Lescaze, B., "Crimes et criminels à Genève en 1572," in *Pour une histoire qualitative: Etudes offertes à S. Stelling-Michaud* (Geneve, 1975): 45–71.

Monter, E.-W., "Crime and Punishment in Calvin's Geneva, 1562," *Archiv für Reformationsgeschichte* 64 (1973): 281–87.

Monter, E.-W., "The Consistory of Geneva, 1559–1569," *Bibliothèque d'Humanisme et Renaissance, Travaux et documents* 38 (1976): 467–84.

Nordic Countries

Österberg, E., and Lingdström, D., *Crime and Social Control in Medieval and Early Modern Swedish Towns* (Uppsala, 1988).

Ylikangas, H., "Major Fluctuations in Crimes of Violence in Finland: An Historical Analysis," *Scandinavian Journal of History* 1 (1976): 81–103.

CRIMINALITY AND STATE POWERS (1650–1850)

Italian Countries

Berlinguer, L., and F. Colao (eds.), *Criminalità e società in età moderna* (Milan, 1991).

Capra, C., and Ciserani Maria Teresa, "Criminalità e repressione della criminalità in Lombardia nell'età delle riforme: appunti per una ricerca," in Berlinguer, L., and Colao, F., (eds.), *Criminalità e società in età moderna* (Milan, 1991), 1–23.

Donneddu, G., Criminalità e società nella Sardegna del secondo Settecento, in Berlinguer, L., and Colao, F., (eds.), *Criminalità e società in età moderna* (Milan, 1991), 581–632.

Panico, G., "Criminali e peccatori in Principato Citra alla fine del Settecento (1770–1780)," in Berlinguer, L., and Colao, F., (eds.), *Criminalità e società in età moderna* (Milan, 1991), 549–80.

Salvestrini, A., and Cecchini, B.M., "Reati e pene a Firenze prima e dopo la 'Leopoldina.' Per uno studio statistico sulla criminalità fiorentina (1781–1790)," in Berlinguer, L., and Colao, F., (eds.), *Criminalità e società in età moderna* (Milan, 1991), 229–57.

Sardi, L. C., "Analisi statistica sulla criminalità nel 1700 (reati e pene) con riguardo allo stato senese," in Berlinguer, L., and Colao, F., (eds.), *Criminalità e società in età moderna* (Milan, 1991), 327–475.

Zuliani, D., "Reati e pene nel vicariato di Prato prima e dopo la 'Leopoldina' (1781–1790)," in Berlinguer, L., and Colao, F., (eds.), *Criminalità e società in età moderna* (Milan, 1991), 307–25.

Kingdom of France

Abbiateci, A., et al., *Crimes et criminalité en France, 17e–18e siècles* (Paris, 1971).

Blanpain-Varlez, Th., and Bourbon-Young, M., *Recherches sur la délinquance en Flandres, 1714–1750* (Paris, 1973).

Boucheron, V., "La montée du flot des errants de 1760 à 1789 dans la généralité d'Alençon," in *Annales de Normandie* 21 (1971): 55–86.

Bouessel du Bourg, J., *Observations sur la criminalité et le fonctionnement des justices seigneuriales en Bretagne au XVIIIe siècle (1700–1789): l'exemple du duché pairie de Penthièvre* (Doctoral dissertation in Law, Univ. Rennes I, 1984).

Boutelet, B., "Etude par sondage de la criminalité dans le bailliage du Pont-de-l'Arche (XVIIe–XVIIIe siècle). De la violence au vol. En marche vers l'escroquerie," *Annales de Normandie* 12 (1962): 235–62.

Cameron, I., *Crime and Repression in the Auvergne and the Guyenne, 1720–1790* (Cambridge, 1981).

Castan, N., "Caractéristiques criminelles des hautes régions du Languedoc oriental de 1780 à 1790," in *Vivarais et Languedoc, 44e Congrès de la Fédération historique du Languedoc méditerranéen* (Privas, 1972), 229–45.

Castan, N., and Castan, Y., "Une économie de justice à l'âge moderne: composition et dissension. Recours, besoin et sens de la justice devant l'institution judiciaire française au 18e siècle," in *Histoire.Economie.Société* 1:3 (1982): 361–67.

Castan, N., "Délinquance traditionnelle et répression critique à la fin de l'Ancien Régime dans les pays de langue d'oc," *Annales Historiques de la Révolution Française* 228 (1977): 182–203; republished in M. Perrot (ed.), *L'impossible prison, recherches sur le système pénitentiaire au XIXe siècle* (Paris, 1980), 147–64.

Castan, N., and Castan, Y., *Vivre ensemble. Ordre et désordre en Languedoc (XVIIe–XVIIIe siècles)* (Paris, 1981).

Castan, N., *Justice et répression en Languedoc à l'époque des Lumières* (Paris, 1980).

Castan, N., "La criminalité à la fin de l'Ancien Régime dans les pays de Languedoc," *Bulletin d'histoire économique et sociale de la Révolution française* (1970 [1969]): 59–68.

Castan, N., "La justice expéditive," *Annales.E.S.C.* 31 (1976): 331–61.

Castan, N., "Crime and Justice in Languedoc: The Critical Years (1750–1790)," *Criminal Justice History* 1 (1980): 175–84.

Castan, N., *Les criminels en Languedoc. Les exigences d'ordre et les voies du ressentiment dans une société prérévolutionnaire (1750–1790)* (Toulouse, 1977).

Castan, Y., *Honnêteté et relations sociales en Languedoc, 1715–1780* (Paris, 1974).

Champin, M.-M., "Un cas typique de justice bailliagère: la criminalité dans le bailliage d'Alençon de 1715 à 1745," *Annales de Normandie* 22 (1972): 47–84.

Champin, M.-M., "La criminalité dans le bailliage d'Alençon, 1715–1745," *Pays bas-normand* 182 (1986).

Crépillon, P., "Un gibier des prévôts. Mendiants et vagabonds au XVIIIe siècle entre la Vire et la Dives 1720–1789," *Annales de Normandie* 17 (1967): 223–52.

Dautricourt, P., La criminalité et la répression au Parlement des Flandres au XVIIIe siècle (1721–1790) (Doctoral dissertation in Law, Univ. Lille, 1912).

Desfontaines, E., "La délinquance dijonnaise de 1780 à 1790 (d'après les procès criminels de la justice municipale)," *Annales de Bourgogne* 231 (1986): 168–74.

Deyon, P., "Délinquance et répression dans le Nord de la France au XVIIIe siècle," *Bulletin de la Société d'Histoire Moderne* 70 (1972): 10–15.

Dickinson, J.-A., "L'activité judiciaire d'après la procédure civile: le bailliage de Falaise, 1668–1790," *Revue d'Histoire Economique et Sociale* 54:2 (1976): 145–68.

Eleuche-Santini, V., "Violence dans le comté de Nice au XVIIIe siècle," *Provence historique*, 115 (1979): 359–68.

Enser, J., "La criminalité dans le bailliage et siège présidial de Laon au XVIIIe siècle," *Mémoires de la Fédération des Sociétés Historiques et Archéologiques de l'Aisne* 19 (1973): 40–74.

Farge, A., *Délinquance et criminalité: le vol d'aliments à Paris au XVIIIe siècle* (Paris, 1974).

Farge, A., *Vivre dans la rue à Paris au XVIIIe siècle* (Paris, 1979).

Garnot, B., "Délits et châtiments en Anjou au XVIIIe siècle," *Annales de Bretagne et des Pays de l'Ouest* 88 (1981): 283–303.

Garnot, B., "La criminalité en Anjou au XVIIIe siècle," *Revue Historique* 554 (1985): 305–16.

Garnot, B., "Une illusion historiographique: justice et criminalité au XVIIIe siècle," *Revue Historique* 570 (1989): 362–79.

Gégot, J.-C., "Etude par sondage de la criminalité dans le bailliage de Falaise (XVII–XVIIIe siècles). Criminalité diffuse ou société criminelle?" *Annales de Normandie* 16:2 (1966): 103–64.

Guignet, Ph., "L'évolution de la délinquance à Valenciennes au XVIIIe siècle," in *Valenciennes et les Anciens Pays-Bas. Mélanges offerts à Paul Lefrancq (Valenciennes, 1976)*, 111–18.

Hufton, O., "Le paysan et la loi en France au XVIIIe siècle," *Annales.E.S.C.* 38 (1983): 679–701.

Isbled, B., "Le recours à la justice à Saint-Germain-des-prés au milieu du XVIIe siècle," in Bercé, Y-M., and Castan, Y. (eds.), *Les Archives du délit, empreintes de société* (Toulouse, 1990), 65–74.

Lambert, Th., "La criminalité dans le bailliage de Nancy au XVIIIe siècle," *Bulletin de la Société lorraine d'Etudes locales*, n.s. 41 (1971): 1–19; 42 (1971): 1–26.

Laveau, N., "La criminalité à Bordeaux au XVIIIe siècle. Etude par sondages," in *Droit pénal et société méridionale. Recueil de mémoires et travaux publiés par la Société d'Histoire du Droit des pays de droit écrit* 8 (1971 [1972]): 85–144.

Le Roy Ladurie, E., "La décroissance du crime au XVIIIe siècle, bilan d'historiens," *Contrepoint* 9 (1973): 227–33.

Lorgnier, J., *Contribution prévôtale au maintien de l'ordre et de la sécurité publique en Flandres* (Doctoral dissertation in Law, Univ. Lille, 1982).

Lorgnier, J., and Martinage, R., "L'activité judiciaire de la Maréchaussée de Flandres," *Revue du Nord* 61 (1979): 593–608.

Mallen, P., "La criminalité dans le comté de Crussol au XVIIIe siècle," *Bulletin du*

Centre d'Histoire économique et sociale de la Région lyonnaise 4 (1983): 45–63.

Margot, A., "La criminalité dans le bailliage de Mamers, 1695–1750," *Annales de Normandie*, 22:3 (1972): 185–224.

Martin, D., "Approche de la mentalité paysanne dans ses rapports avec la justice seigneuriale: les assises annuelles," in *Histoire et clandestinité du Moyen Age à la Première guerre mondiale* (Albi, 1979), 113–24.

Mer, L.B., "Criminalité et répression en Bretagne. Appréciation statistique (1750–1760)," *Annales de Normandie* 29:4 (1979): 370–71.

Mogensen, N.-W., "Crime and Punishment in Eighteenth-century France: The Example of the Pays d'Auge," *Histoire sociale-Social History* 10 (1977): 337–53.

Muracciole, M.-M., "Quelques aperçus sur la criminalité en Haute-Bretagne dans la deuxième moitié du XVIIIe siècle," *Annales de Bretagne et des Pays de l'Ouest* 88 (1981): 305–26.

Petrovitch, P., "Recherches sur la criminalité à Paris dans la seconde moitié du XVIIIe siècle," in Abbiateci, A., et al., *Crimes et criminalité en France, 17e–18e siècles* (Paris, 1971), 187–261.

Ramin-Pinson, V., *Procès criminels à Rennes au XVIIIe siècle: essai d'analyse judiciaire et sociologique* (Doctoral dissertation in Law, Univ. Rennes I, 1984).

Reinhardt, S.-G., "Crime and Royal Justice in Ancien Régime France: Modes of Analysis," *Journal of Interdisciplinary History* 13 (1983): 437–60.

Reinhardt, S.-G., *Justice in the Sarladais 1770–1790* (Baton Rouge and London, 1991).

Renard, J., La sénéchaussée de Baugé à la fin de l'Ancien Régime (Doctoral dissertation in History, Univ. Rennes II, 1976).

Roche, J., "Pouvoir et délinquances aux limites du Maine et de l'Anjou (1680–1789)," in *Actes du 107e Congrès National des Sociétés Savantes. Brest 1982. Section d'Histoire moderne* (Brest, 1984): 1: 179–88.

Ruff, J.R., *Crime, Justice and Public Order in Old Regime France: The Sénéchaussées of Libourne and Bazas, 1696–1789* (London-Sydney-Dover, N.H., 1984).

Savonnet, B., "Fluctuations économiques et évolution de la criminalité: l'exemple de Dijon à la fin du XVIIe siècle," *Economie du Centre-Est* 79 (1978): 87–107.

Soman, A., "L'infra-justice à Paris d'après les archives notariales," *Histoire. Economie. Société* 3 (1982): 369–76.

Sudre, M., "La criminalité dans la paroisse Saint-Michel de Bordeaux: Étude de l'activité de la Cour des Jurats (1676–1679)," *Revue historique de Bordeaux*, n.ser. 24 (1975): 87–106.

Thevenin, O., "La criminalité dans le ressort du présidial de Vannes, étude comparative des deux périodes: 1730–1745 et 1781–1788," *Bulletin de la Société polymathique du Morbihan* 108 (1981): 45–46.

Ulrich, J., "La répression en Bourgogne au XVIIIe siècle," *Revue d'histoire du droit français et étranger*, 4th ser. 50 (1972): 398–437.

Vié, D., "La criminalité à Bordeaux de 1768 à 1777 d'après les plaintes et informations de la Cour des Jurats," *Positions des Thèses de l'Ecole des Chartes* (1971): 193–99.

Vovelle, M., "Recherches sur la délinquance et la criminalité en Provence au XVIIIe siècle," *Provence historique* 115 (1979): 323–31.

Williams, A., "Patterns of Deviance in Eighteenth-Century Paris," in *Proceedings of the 6th Meeting of the Western Society for French History, San Diego, 1978* (San Diego, 1979), 179–87.

Zysberg, A., Les Fréjusiens et le recours à la justice seigneuriale au milieu du XVIIIe siècle, *Annales du Sud-Est varois* 2 (1977): 1–20.

After the Revolution (1789–1850)

Bouloiseau, M., *Délinquance et répression. Le tribunal correctionnel de Nice (1800– 1814)* (Paris, 1979).

Catez, M., *Evolution de la criminalité et de la répression à la Cour d'Assises du Nord, 1811–1986* (Doctoral dissertation in Law, Univ. Lille II, 1987).

Debauve, M., *La justice révolutionnaire dans le Morbihan de 1790 à 1795* (Doctoral dissertation in Law, Univ. Paris, 1961).

Gay, A., "La délinquance dans le vignoble jurassien au temps du Premier Empire," in Garnot, B. (ed.), *Histoire et Criminalité de l'Antiquité au XXe siècle. Nouvelles approches. Actes du colloque de Dijon, 2–5 octobre 1991*, (Dijon, 1992), 211–22.

Gillis, A.R., "Crime and State Surveillance in Nineteenth-Century France," *American Journal of Sociology* 95:2 (1989): 307–41.

Hommeril, Ph., "La criminalité dans le département du Calvados pendant la Révolution, d'après les jugements du tribunal révolutionnaire," *Annales de Normandie* 39:3 (1989): 285–311.

Martinage, R., *Punir le crime. La répression judiciaire depuis le code pénal* (Lille, 1989).

Perrot, M., "Délinquance et système pénitentiaire en France au XIXe siècle," *Annales. E.S.C.* 30 (1975).

Ros, M., "La criminalité dans les Pyrénées-orientales au XIXe siècle," in Garnot, B. (ed.), *Histoire et Criminalité de l'Antiquité au XXe siècle. Nouvelles approches. Actes du colloque de Dijon, 2–5 octobre 1991* (Dijon, 1992), 231– 40.

Santucci, M., *Délinquance et répression au XIXe siècle. L'exemple de l'Hérault* (Paris, 1986).

Schnapper, B., "L'activité du tribunal criminel de la Vienne (1792–1800)," in *La Révolution et l'ordre juridique privé: rationalité ou scandale?* 2 vols. (Paris, 1988), 2: 623–38.

Wills, A., *Crime and Punishment in Revolutionary Paris* (Westport, Conn., 1981).

Southern Netherlands

Bruneel, C., "Le droit pénal dans les Pays-Bas autrichiens: les hésitations de la pratique (1750–1795)," *Etudes sur le 18e siècle* 13 (1986): 35–66.

Bruneel, C., "Le droit pénal et son application à Bruxelles dans la seconde moitié du XVIIIe siècle," *Cahiers Bruxellois* 14 (1969): 157–78.

d'Arras d'Haudrecy, L., et al., *La criminalité en Wallonie sous l'Ancien Régime. Trois essais* (Louvain, 1976).

d'Arras d'Haudrecy, L., "La déliquance namuroise au XVIIIe siècle," in d'Arras d'Haudrecy et al., *La criminalité en Wallonie...*, 49–173.

Dupont-Bouchat, M. S., "Criminalité et mentalités à Nivelles au XVIIIe siècle," in d'Arras d'Haudrecy et al., *La criminalité en Wallonie...*, 13–31.

Herpin, D., "Een overzicht van de bronnen met de betrekking tot criminaliteit: 's Hertogenbosch en Lier in de achttiende eeuw," *Bijdragen... Geschiedenis der Nederlanden*, 93:2 (1978): 207–23.

Maes, L. T., "De criminaliteit te Antwerpen in de achttiende eeuw," *Bijdragen... Geschiedenis der Nederlanden*, 93:2 (1978): 324–31.

Roets, A-M., "Misdaad en straf te Gent in de 18de eeuw," *Spiegel Historiael* 17 (1982): 528–33.

Roets, A-M., *"Rudessen, dieften ende andere crimen." Misdadigheid te Gent in de 17de en de 18de eeuw. Een Kwantitatieve en kwalitatieve analyse* (Doctoral dissertation in History, Rijksuniversiteit, Gent, 1987).

Rousseaux, X., "Les tribunaux criminels en Brabant sous le Directoire (1795–1800): Acculturation et résistance à la justice républicaine," in Craeybeckx, J., Scheelings, F. G. (ed.), *De Franse Revolutie en Vlaanderen. La Révolution Française et la Flandre* (Brussels, 1990), 277–306.

Rousseaux, X., "Tensions locales et menaces extérieures: Criminalité et répression dans la région nivelloise dans la seconde moitié du XVIIe siècle," in Dupont-Bouchat, M. S., and Rousseaux, X. (eds.), *Crime, justices et pouvoirs: La criminalité en Wallonie sous l'Ancien Régime* (Kortrijk-Heule, forthcoming, 1993).

Rousseaux, X. "Ordre et violence. Criminalité et répression dans une ville brabançonne: Nivelles (1646–1695)," *Revue de droit pénal et de criminologie*, 66–7 (1986): 649–92.

Van den Eerenbeemt, H., *Van mensenjacht en overheidsmacht: Criminogene groepsvorming en afweer in de meierij van 's-Hertogenbosch 1795–1810* (Tilburg, 1970).

Vandenghoer, C., *De rectorale rechbank van de oude leuvense Universiteit (1425–1797)* (Brussels, 1987).

Vanhemelryck, F., "Pauperisme en misdadigheid in Brabant in de 18e eeuw," *Tijdschrift voor Geschiedenis* 88 (1975): 598–612.

Vinck, L.A., "De criminaliteit te Turnhout (1700–1789)," *Taxandria* 50 (1978): 40–83; 51–53 (1979–1981): 55–99.

Northern Netherlands

Diederiks, H. "Patterns of Criminality and Law Enforcement during the Ancien Regime: The Dutch Case," *Criminal Justice History* 1 (1980): 157–74.

Diederiks, H., "Quality and Quantity in Historical Research in Criminality and Criminal Justice: The Case of Leiden in the 17th and 18th centuries," *Historical Social Research* 15:4 (1990): 57–76.

Diederiks, H., "Punishment During the Ancien Regime: The Case of the Eighteenth-Century Dutch Republic," in Knafla, L. A. (ed.), *Crime and Criminal Justice in Europe and Canada* (Waterloo, Ont., 1981), 273–96.

Diederiks, H.-A., and Huussen, A.-H., "Crime and Punishment in the Dutch Republic (XVIII–XIX centuries)," in *La Peine. Punishment, 3d part: Europe since the 18th Century* (Brussels, 1989), 133–59.

Faber, S., "Strafrechtspleging en criminaliteit te Amsterdam in de achttiende eeuw," *Holland* 8 (1976): 108–15.

Faber, S., *Strafrechtspleging en criminaliteit te Amsterdam (1680–1811). De nieuwe menslievenheid* (Arnhem, 1983).

Gerritsma, B., "Pauperisme, kriminaliteit en konjunktuur. Amsterdam 1771/1772," *Tijdschrift voor Sociale Geschiedenis* 24 (1981): 374–91.

Huussen, A. H., "Jurisprudentie en bureaucratie: het Hof van Friesland en zijn criminele rechtspraak in de achttiende eeuw," *Bijdragen ... Geschiedenis der Nederlanden* 93:2 (1978): 241–98.

Noordam, D. J., "Strafrechtspleging en criminaliteit in Delft in de vroeg-moderne tijd," *Tijdschrift voor Sociale geschiedenis* 5, (1989): 209–44.

Roodenburg, H. W., *Onder Censuur. De kerkelijke tucht in de Gereformeerde Gemeente van Amsterdam. 1578–1700* (Hilversum, 1990).

Spierenburg, P., *The Spectacle of Suffering. Executions and the Evolution of Repression: From a Preindustrial Metropolis to the European Experience* (Cambridge, 1984).

Spierenburg, P., "Deviance and Repression in the Netherlands: Historical Evidence and Contemporary Problems," *Historical Social Research* 37 (1986): 4–16.

van den Hoeven, A., *Ten exempel en afschrik. Strafrechtspleging en criminaliteit in Haarlem, 1740–1795* (unpublished thesis, Univ. Amsterdam, 1982).

van Weel, A. J., "De strafrechtspleging in Schiedam (1700–1811)," *Scyedam* 17 (1991): 53–65, 84–95.

British Islands

Bailey, V. (ed.), *Policing and Punishment in Nineteenth-Century Britain* (London, 1981).

Beattie, J.-M., *Crime and the Courts in England, 1660–1800* (Oxford, 1986).

Brewer, J., and Styles, J. (ed.), *The Ungovernable People: The English and Their Law in the 17th and 18th Centuries* (London, 1980).

Conley, C. A., *The Unwritten Law: Criminal Justice in Victorian Kent* (Oxford, 1991).

Emsley, C., *Crime and Society in England 1750–1900* (London and New York, 1987).

Hay, D., Crime, Authority and the Criminal Law: Staffordshire 1750–1800 (Doctoral dissertation, Warwick Univ., 1975).

Hay, D. (ed.), *Albion's fatal tree: Crime and Society in Eighteenth-Century England* (London, 1975).

Hay, D., "Crime and Justice in Eighteenth- and Nineteenth-Century England," *Crime & Justice: An Annual Review of Research* 2 (1980): 45–84.

Hay, D., "The Criminal Prosecution in England and its Historians," *Modern Law Review* 47 (1984): 1–29.

Hay, D., "War, dearth and theft in the 18th century: The record of the English Courts," *Past & Present* 95 (1982): 117–60.

Hay, D., and Snyder, F. (eds.), *Policing and Prosecution in Britain 1750–1850* (Oxford, 1989).

Innes, J., and Styles, J., "The Crime Wave: Recent Writing on Crime and Criminal Justice in Eighteenth-Century England," *Journal of British Studies* 25:4 (1986): 380–435.

Jones, D. J. V., *Crime, Protest, Community and Police in Nineteenth-Century Britain* (London, 1982).

Philips, D., *Crime and Authority in Victorian England: The Black Country 1835– 1860* (London, 1977).

Ramsey, M.-N., "L'évolution du concept de crime. L'étude d'un tournant: l'Angleterre de la fin du XVIIIe siècle," *Déviance et Société* 3 (1979): 131–47.

Rule, J. (ed.), *Outside the Law: Studies in Crime and Order 1650–1850* (Exeter, 1982).

Thompson, E.-P., *Whigs and Hunters: The Origin of the Black Act* (New York, 1975).

Swift, R. E., Crime, Law and Order in Two English Towns during the Early Nineteenth Century: the Experience of Exeter and Wolverhampton 1815–1856 (Doctoral dissertation, Univ. Birmingham, 1981).

Helvetic Cities

Henry, Ph., *Crime, Justice et Société dans la principauté de Neuchâtel au XVIIIe siècle (1707–1806)* (Neuchâtel, 1984).

Porret, M., Le crime et ses "circonstances"...Punir à Genève au XVIIIe siècle: institution, discours, pratiques (Doctoral dissertation in History, Univ. of Genève, 1992).

Germanic Areas

Behringer, W., "Mörder, Diebe, Ehebrecher, Verbrecher und Strafen in Kurbayern vom 16. bis 18. Jh.," in Van Dülmen, R., *Verbrechen, Strafen und soziale Kontrolle* (Frankfort, 1991), 85–132.

Blasius, D., *Bürgerliche Gesellschaft und Kriminalität: Zur Sozialgeschichte Preussens im Vormärz* (Göttingen, 1976).

Blasius, D., *Kriminalität und Alltag, Zur Konfliktgeschichte des Alltagslebens im 19. Jahrhundert* (Göttingen, 1978).

Blasius, D., "Recht und Gerechtigkeit im Umbruch von Von Verfassungs- und Gesellschaftordnung. Zur Situation der Strafrechtspflege in Preussen im 19. Jahrhundert," *Der Staat* 21 (1982): 265–390.

Formella, E., *Rechtsbrucht und Rechtsdurchsetzung im Herzogtum Holstein um die Mitte des 19. Jahrhunderts. Ein Beitrag zum Verhältnis von Kriminalität, Gesellschaft und Staat* (Neumünster, 1985).

Heidenreich, P., *Oldenburgische Kriminalpolitik im 19 Jahrhundert. Strafgesetzgebung und Strafrechtsplege im Spiegel der Strafrechtswissenschaft* (Munich, 1967).

Reif, H. (ed.), *Räuber, Volk und Obrigkeit. Studien zur Geschichte der Kriminalität in Deutschland seit dem 18 Jahrhundert* (Frankfort, 1984).

Reinke, H., "Criminal Justice in the Northwestern Territories of 18th Century Germany," in Berlinguer, L. and Colao, F. (eds.), *Le politiche criminali nel XVIII secolo* (Milan, 1990), 375–85.

Sauer, P., *In Namen des Königs. Strafgesetzgebung und Strafvollzug im Königreich Württemberge von 1806–1871* (Stuttgart, 1984).
Verdenhalven, F., "Die Straffälligkeit in Lippe in der zweiten Hälfte des 18. Jahrhunderts," *Lippische Mitteilungen aus Geschichte und Landeskunde* 43 (1974): 63–144.
Weber, L., "Die aargauische Strafrechtsplege in der ersten Hälfte des 19. Jahrhunderts," in *Aargauisches Strafprozessrecht. Festschrift zum 25jähringen Bestehen des Aargauischen Juristenvereins* (Aargau, 1961), 235–62.

Austrian Empire

Hartl, F., *Das Wiener Kriminalgericht. Strafrechtspflege vom Zeitalter der Aufklärung bis zu österreischischen Revolution* (Graz, 1973).
Panek, J., "Die Halsgerichtsbarkeit der böhmischen Städte und Märkte vom 16. bis zum 18. Jahrhundert," *Mitteilungen des Instituts für Österreichische Geschichtsforschung* 96:1/2 (1988): 95–131.

Nordic Countries

Johansen, J. C. V., "Falster and Elsinore, 1680–1705: A Comparative Study of Rural and Urban Crime," *Social History* 15:1 (1990): 97–109.
Johansen, J. C. V., and Stevnsborg, H., "Hasard ou myopie? Réflexions autour de deux théories de l'histoire du droit," *Annales.E.S.C.* 41:3 (1986): 601–24.
Sundin, J. "Control, Punishment and Reconciliation; A Case Study of Parish Justice in Sweden before 1850," in *Tradition and Transition: Studies in Microdemography and Social Change* (Umea, 1981).
Sundin, J., "Cooperation, Conflict Solution and Social Control: Civil and Ecclesiastical Justice in Preindustrial Sweden," *Historical Social Research* 37 (1986): 50–68.
Sundin, J. "Current Trends in the History of Crime and Criminal Justice: Some Conclusions, with Special Reference to the Swedish Experience," *Historical Social Research* 56 (1990): 184–96.
Von Hofer, H., *Brott och Straff i Sverige: Historik kriminalstatistik 1750–1984: Diagram, tabeller och kommentarer* (Stockholm, 1985).

EUROPEAN INQUISITION COURTS (SPAIN, PORTUGAL, ITALY)

Henningsen, G., Tedeschi J., and Amiel, C. (eds.), *The Inquisition in Early Modern Europe: Studies on Sources and Methods* (Dekalb, 1986).

Portugal

Carvalho dos Santos, M. H. (ed.), *Inquisicao* (Lissabon, 3 vol., 1989).
Saraiva, A. J., *A Inquisiçao portuguesa,* (Lissabon, 2nd ed., 1956).
Veiga Torres, J., "Uma longa guerra social: os ritmos da repressao inquisitorial em Portugal," *Revista de historia economica e social* 1 (1978): 55–68.

Do Carmo Texeira Pinto, M., Luis Ferreira Runa, L. M., "Inquisicao de Evora: dez anos de fucionamento (1541–1550)," *Revista de historia economica e social* 22 (1988): 51–75.

Vasconcelos Vilar, H., "A Inquisiçao do Porto: actuaçao e funcionamento (1541–1542)," *Revista de historia economica e social* 21 (1987): 19–46.

Italy

Monter, E. W., and Tedeschi, J., "Toward a Statistical Profile of the Italian Inquisitions, Sixteenth to Eighteenth Centuries," in Henningsen, G., Tedeschi, J., and Amiel, C., (eds.), *The Inquisition in Early Modern Europe: Studies on Sources and Methods* (Dekalb, 1986), 130–57.

Spain

Contreras, J., and Henningsen, G., "Forty-Four Thousand Cases of the Spanish Inquisition (1540–1700): Analysis of a Historical data bank," in Henningsen, G., Tedeschi, J., and Amiel, C., (eds.), *The Inquisition in Early Modern Europe: Studies on Sources and Methods* (Dekalb, 1986), 100–29.

Contreras, J., *El Santo Oficio de la Inquisicion en Galicia, 1560–1700: Poder, sociedad y cultura* (Madrid, 1982).

Dedieu, J. P., *L'Administration de la Foi: l'Inquisition de Tolède, XVIe–XVIIIe siècles* (Madrid, 1989).

Escamilla-Molins, M., *Crimes et châtiments dans l'Espagne Inquisitoriale* (Paris, 2 vols., 1991).

Garcia Carcel, R., *Origenes de la Inquisicion espanola: El Tribunal de Valencia, 1478–1530* (Barcelone, 1976).

Garcia Carcel, R., *Herejia y sociedad en el siglo XVI. La Inquisicion en Valencia (1530–1609)* (Barcelone, 1980).

Monter, W., "The New Social History and the Spanish Inquisition," *Journal of Social History* 17 (1984): 705–13.

Pérez Villanueva, J. (ed.), *La Inquisicion espanola, Nueva vision. Nuevos horizontes* (Madrid, 1980).

Pérez Villanueva, J., and Escandell Bonet, B. (eds.), *Historia de la Inquisicion de Espana y América* 1 (Madrid, 1984).

Reguera, I., *La Inquisicion espanola en el Pais Vasco. Luteranos, judios, moriscos, brujeria* (San Sebastian, 1984).

Book Reviews

Robert B. Shoemaker, *Prosecution and Punishment: Petty Crime and the Law in London and Rural Middlesex, c. 1660–1725*. Cambridge: Cambridge University Press, 1991. xviii + 351 pp., illus., appendixes, bibliog. $64.50.

The history of crime and prosecution in England has, until now, utilized the records of the assize courts as its primary source; its raw material has thus been drawn overwhelmingly from the prosecution of serious offenses. Shoemaker's study takes a welcome step into the world of petty crime, focusing on the work of lay justices in sessions and hence on the prosecution of misdemeanors. That he has chosen to study Middlesex (a county that included almost the whole of London within its borders) is doubly welcome, since London has hitherto been ill served by historians.

Shoemaker takes us from the change and uncertainty of life after the Restoration to the (comparative) calm of the final years of George I. The former era was a time of tension and insecurity for the whole country; even more so for London, which must have been both an exciting and a dangerous place in which to live. Whether London was as dangerously unstable a place as many contemporaries believed it to be is a moot point, but there was undoubtedly widespread concern about its growth, its disorder, and the poverty and criminal inclinations of its inhabitants.

Misdemeanor prosecutions offer a potentially fascinating perspective on such a society. Far more common than felony prosecutions, they were used in connection with a wide range of aberrant behavior—everything from assault to fraud, prostitution to Sabbath breaking. Because misdemeanors were often rather trivial offenses, plaintiffs and justices enjoyed even greater discretion and flexibility in their choice of prosecution strategies than was available in cases of felony. There was considerable pressure on prosecutors and defendants alike to settle their differences without resorting to trial. Petty crime was in effect seen as a dispute between individuals rather than between an individual and the state. This placed major difficulties in the way of prosecutions for what Shoemaker terms "victimless" crimes, such as vice and regulatory offenses.

The most common prosecution strategy was informal mediation (not just by justices, but also by other well-respected local persons), of a kind that for obvious reasons rarely appears in the records. Mediation was also facilitated by the use of recognizances binding defendants to appear at sessions to answer charges, creating a sort of formal "cooling off" period. Such recognizances were more likely to be discharged than to lead to an indictment.

The use of recognizances as a method of encouraging settlements raises many important questions, not the least of which concern the role (and potential income) of London's notorious trading justices. But in order to use them effectively one needs to be sure that the records are complete. Research into the activities of justices elsewhere, notably Landau's study of Kent, raises the very real possibility that large numbers of agreed recognizances were never certified to the sessions. Shoemaker bases his analysis on a belief that it was normal practice for Middlesex justices to return all recognizances.

Unfortunately, his arguments in this respect are not wholly convincing. He is mistaken in suggesting that the Norris notebook indicates that agreed recognizances were always returned to the sessions; but even if he were not, it would still be difficult to be sure how far it is possible to generalize from the activities of a single highly respectable but relatively inactive individual to those of the few semiprofessional, socially marginal justices who handled the bulk of the county's criminal business. It would be surprising if practices that were commonplace not only in Kent but in other counties had not taken root in Middlesex. Indeed, extracting a fee for mediation by means of a recognizance that was not going to be returned to the sessions would seem to be ideally suited both to urban conditions in general and to the alleged corruption of Middlesex trading justices in particular. It is perhaps unfortunate that Shoemaker did not include an analysis of the interval between the issue of a recognizance and the date of the sessions to which it was returned, as the discovery of a relatively even pattern of distribution would have added to the credibility of his case.

Although Shoemaker characterizes use of the law as being largely instrumental, he is surprisingly naive about the extent of vexatious counter-actions, which he tells us were "relatively rare at quarter sessions." The suggestion that the quarter sessions was somehow immune from vexatious actions, when most research (including Shoemaker's own material elsewhere in the book) suggests that other metropolitan courts were awash with them, is barely credible. It smacks (like his assertion about returned recognizances) of a determination to defend the integrity of his data at the expense of confronting the complexities of real life.

Shoemaker does succeed in giving us a very detailed picture of the prosecution process in a society in which the law was not "the only legitimate arbiter of criminal accusations." It could be used to facilitate informal settlements or to inflict maximum harassment and punishment on opponents. For Shoemaker, therefore, the social significance of the law was neither as a bulwark of social order nor as a service industry; it was merely a set of tools for advancing the interests of those who had access to it. Such a deliberate choice of ideologically neutral imagery should not go unchallenged. Shoemaker demonstrates throughout the book that this particular toolset was markedly more available to men than to women and to the monied rather than to the poor. I think we are entitled to conclude that this was a system that was intended to serve rather than to challenge the existing power structures of society—and that it did its job rather well.

Ruth Paley
London

Peter Linebaugh, *The London Hanged: Crime and Civil Society in the Eighteenth Century.* London: Allen Lane, The Penguin Press, 1991. 512 pp., illus. $44.95.

It is hard to review this book without feeling both admiration and ambivalence. Peter Linebaugh uses language well, extremely well. The book is accessible, readable, and never overtechnical. It's full of stories. Some are fully incorporated into the broader analytical framework. Some are almost freestanding, adding substance by juxtaposition alone. Like the Ordinary's accounts on which it is partly based, the book unfolds as a mixture of narrative and analysis underpinned by deeper ideological assumptions.

Not the least of the book's strengths is the area it focuses on. Although historians always acknowledge its vital role, the capital seems to frighten them. The only substantial work on the social history of eighteenth-century London was written sixty-five years ago.[1] Linebaugh's focus on what he calls "the London working class" is therefore particularly welcome. It locates his work usefully alongside both Peter Earle's book on the London middle class, which ends just after Linebaugh begins, and E. P. Thompson's classic *Making*, which begins roughly when Linebaugh ends and which he explicitly cites as a major inspiration.[2]

Linebaugh's evocative re-creation of the labor process and of the experience of labor covers a variety of trades and laboring contexts: Coopers, sailors, porters, lumpers, butchers, and petty market traders receive attention at various points. The book also contains illuminating chapters on "the waging hand in five trades" (watchmakers, shoemakers, hatters, tailors, and servants) and on silk weaving, as well as a marvellous chapter on the changing nature and organization of work in the shipbuilding trades. In these sections, Linebaugh provides a deep and multidimensional account of the labor process, of the workers' struggles to control the pace and conditions of their labor, of labor relations and negotiations, and of the nature of remuneration, which enables him to contextualize the other key part of his analysis, an exploration of the perks, customary usages, and purloining practices of the London workers. Every trade had its perquisites. Clicking (shoemakers), socking (tobacco porters), and bugging (hatters), like carpenter's chips and tailor's cabbage, are properly located at the heart of communal practices in each trade. No wonder that John Rule in his excellent book *The Experience of Labour in Eighteenth-Century Industry* pays tribute to Linebaugh's work in this area.

The London Hanged has several other strengths. Its wide field of vision, which places London's social and economic history firmly in the context of the Thames' growing role as the "jugular vein of Empire," enables Linebaugh to explore the Afro-American and Irish dimensions of London's history. Linebaugh's sense of process, his exploration of working people's "living struggles" to shape their own destinies, also prevents him from seeing them simply as subjects of exploitation. Excarceration as well as incarceration is explored. The poverty and vulnerability of working people's lives is a constant theme, but so too is the paradoxical nature of London labor —its fluidity and insecurity in contrast to its cooperative nature and its enduring customary practices. Much, if not all, of this important and enlightening work could, however, have been written without reference to the London hanged. The detailed stories of the lives of the condemned may be useful as illustrative material, but they are rarely essential. It is this attempt to link the history of the London trades to the history of the London hanged that pushes the book into more problematic territory.

What was the relationship between the London hanged and the London unhanged? To even attempt a comparison between the 1,242 offenders in the Ordinaries' accounts Linebaugh uses and the London population as a whole implies considerable methodological bravery. Those accused of crimes are not a typical sample of those who commit them. Those indicted for capital crimes are not typical of all indicted offenders. Those who are hanged are not a random sample of those who are sentenced to death. Those about whom ordinaries' accounts have survived are not necessarily representative of those who were hanged. Despite this background, Linebaugh's findings are interesting and thought-provoking. About two-fifths of the London hanged had started an apprenticeship; their occupations, Linebaugh concludes, were similar to those of the London lower orders as a whole. Migration, not surprisingly, played an important role. The proportion of native

Londoners among the hanged (39 percent) was roughly the same as it was in the rest of London's population, and a significant number of the hanged were Irish (14 percent). These findings are broadly confirmed by my own work on the 1790s. Between 1791 and 1794, the place of birth of almost all the Old Bailey accused was recorded; a preliminary sample of 350 offenders suggests that about two-fifths were London-born and over 10 percent were Irish.[3]

When other dimensions of the data are compared, however, the Ordinaries' accounts appear less typical of the London accused. About a quarter of the London accused were women in the 1790s. Only 7 percent of the Ordinaries' accounts involve females. The age structure of the 1790s accused also appears to have been younger than in Linebaugh's sample. The Ordinaries' accounts are an important source and offer a depth of information unavailable even in the 1790s, but the sample derived from them invites extreme caution. Linebaugh may well be correct to conclude that there was no division between the wage-earning part of the population and "the criminal element," but this cannot be satisfactorily established from this source alone. It can be hoped that further work on the 1790s data will enable the relationship between the London hanged and the London indicted to be fully assessed, but the broader relationship between the London hanged and the London working class will be much less easy to unravel.

Linebaugh is right to point out that court records tend to individualize appropriators and remove offenders from the communal and work contexts that may explain or legitimize their actions. By using the life stories of the hanged and reconstructing work experiences and organization in various trades, he helps to redress that balance; but his reliance on the Ordinaries' accounts sometimes distorts his analysis. Women inevitably receive relatively little attention, although there is a brief discussion of women's trades and prostitution. The analysis of highway robbery is particularly problematic. Having discussed the contemporary budget of a family with four children and having argued that highwaymen took to the road from necessity, Linebaugh then describes them as "fathers, husbands, middle-aged" and as having "access to kinship networks often denied to more youthful offenders." Since the 1790s data indicate that more than half those accused of highway robbery were under twenty-five—roughly the average age at marriage—Linebaugh's sample appears to be very untypical, perhaps because older highwaymen with more illustrious criminal careers and with wives and children to mourn their passing made better copy. Linebaugh's analysis fails to properly encompass the single, independent, sometimes violent young footpads who operated in the Metropolis—a group given proper weight in the relevant section of John Beattie's *Crime and the Courts in England 1660–1800*, which Linebaugh does not refer to in this chapter. Linebaugh's interesting account of the transition of the meat trade "from a moral economy to capitalist marketing practices" is not enhanced by his attempts to incorporate it into a chapter on highway robbery using the relatively small number of highwaymen's life stories involving butchers and allied trades.

Whenever it analyzes crime rather than the London trades, this book cries out for the investigation of a broader range of sources. Linebaugh is probably right to avoid the lure of the indictment. On the one occasion he uses indictments systematically they may have led him astray. Finding that the percentage of the London hanged who came from impoverished silkweaving parishes was much greater than the percentage of indictments that came from those parishes and that the opposite was true in central London, he concludes that the authorities were more prone to use hangings to intimidate the textile suburbs than the parishes of central London. However, as indictments usually recorded the place where the crime was committed rather than the abode of the offender, the two sources cannot be usefully compared in this way.

The potential usefulness of other types of source is occasionally hinted at in Linebaugh's analysis, for example, in his brief use of a few 1720s examinations to discuss the attack on socking. He also includes a short analysis of Old Bailey prosecutions against misappropriations by employees, using the printed trial reports of the 1790s. However, one of the most fundamental problems of the book is its failure to examine systematically the records of the courts in which most workplace appropriations were punished. Those forms of employee appropriation that were indictable were rarely regarded as sufficiently grave to be dealt with above the level of the quarter sessions, and only a tiny fraction were ever likely to result in capital indictments at the Old Bailey, let alone in hangings and Ordinaries accounts.

More important, perhaps, many of the forms of pilfering that working people were involved in were not indictable offenses but were triable in the summary courts. Though the book mentions the passing of various summary statutes, it offers no analysis of Bridewell and prison calendars, of summary conviction certificates, or of the few summary court records that are available. It therefore cannot, and does not, address the important and complex issues about the relationship between statutory changes and actual prosecution practices in the summary courts raised by the work of John Styles, Joanna Innes, and others.[4] By simply stating that "an account of the judicial repression of custom is found in the Old Bailey Proceedings" without first locating the few cases that reached the Old Bailey within the hierarchy of courts of which it formed the top layer, Linebaugh makes it difficult to accept his ensuing argument that "the struggles over the material circuits of production of the previous decades became subject to a judicial onslaught in the 1790s." Although he mentions the more extensive use of summary justice in his account of the criminalization of customary takings by silkworkers during the 1790s, he offers no analysis or evidence below the level of the Old Bailey.

At this point, the reader longs for Linebaugh to refer to parallel studies such as Jennifer Davis's work on the widespread nature of workplace appropriation in mid-Victorian London or rural historians' discussions of attacks on various forms of agrarian useright.[5] Are statutory legal changes and formal court prosecutions alone of much use to employers, farmers, and the like in their attempts to control or eradicate forms of appropriation that most of the working community regarded as customary rights? It could be argued that they are not and that it is only by transforming the nature, organization and geography of the workplace or by the creation of informal workplace-based normative orderings and sanctions that this can be achieved. Apart from a brief discussion in his conclusion of the ways skilled artisans acquiesced in the technological recomposition of labor processes in exchange for a system of wage payment, Linebaugh never discusses these issues or relates his findings to the broader literature. Indeed, throughout the book he rarely compares his findings to those of other historians or explores why his conclusions are different from theirs. For example, his conclusion that "If a single individual could be said to have been the planner and theorist of class struggle in the Metropolis it would be Colquhoun," would have been more persuasive if it had been worked out in the context of Ruth Paley's recent argument that Colquhoun had little or no influence and that the publication of his treatise was systematic of his failure to have an impact on government policy.[6]

More centrally, when Linebaugh asserts that "London proletarians, excluded from its hegemony, held the law in contempt," he is ignoring a whole body of literature, including Davis's work on widespread working-class use of the London courts, that indicates that plebeian attitudes to the law were much less monolithic. In a polemic introduction that fits uneasily with the rest of the book, Linebaugh criticizes recent historical work for increasingly transforming the history of crime into the history of administration or of the machinery of justice, which he sees as "denaturing the men and women who fell foul of the law." However, by failing to refer to the fact that the courts were used by the poor as well as against them, he is in danger of doing precisely the same thing for very different reasons. The analysis of malicious prosecutions and of London thief-takers in Douglas Hay and Francis Snyder's *Policing and Prosecution in Britain 1750–1850*[7] could have been usefully incorporated, for example, but is not. Nor does Linebaugh qualify his use of the term "the law" to ensure that readers are aware that a variety of legal frameworks existed within which victims of appropriation might attempt to gain compensation or to impose sanctions on the offender.

For these reasons the student of the criminal law and of crime must approach this book with care. Linebaugh is at his best in his imaginative reconstructions of the experience of labor and in his contextualizations of various types of workplace appropriation. However, the narrowness of his source base and his unwillingness to relate his findings to important parallel work already published by historians such as Beattie, Davis, and Paley make one wonder whether he would not have been better advised to write a book that concentrated on the London unhanged, rather than tying his account of London's working people and their experiences of labor to an analysis of the London hanged.

NOTES

1. M. D. George, *London Life in the Eighteenth Century* (London, 1925).

2. P. Earle, *The Making of the English Middle Class: Business, Society and Family Life in London* (London, 1989); and E. P. Thompson, *The Making of the English Working Class* (London, 1963).

3. Based on Public Record Office, HO 26/1–3.

4. See, for example, the papers given at the 1986 Conference on Custom, Crime and Perquisites, summarized in *Bulletin for the Study of Labour History* 52:1 (1987): 33–45; John Styles, "Embezzlement, Industry and the Law in England 1500–1800," in *Manufacture in Town and County before the Factory*, ed. M. Berg, P. Hudson, and M. Sonenscher (London, 1983); Joanna Innes, "Prisons for the Poor: English Bridewells 1555–1800," in *Labour, Law and Crime: An Historical Perspective*, ed. Francis Snyder and Douglas Hay (London, 1987), 86; and Jennifer Davis, "Law-breaking and Law-Enforcement: The Creation of a Criminal Class in Mid-Victorian London," in *Law, Labour and Crime*.

5. Davis, "Law-breaking and Law-enforcement."

6. Ruth Paley, "An Imperfect, Inadequate and Wretched System? Policing London before Peel," *Criminal Justice History* 10 (1989): 95–130.

7. Douglas Hay and Francis Snyder, ed., *Policing and Prosecution in Britain 1750–1850* (London, 1989).

Peter King
Nene College, Northampton

Frank McLynn, *Crime and Punishment in Eighteenth-Century England.* Oxford: Oxford University Press, 1991. xvi + 392 pp. £7.95.

Over the past two decades, a number of historians have turned serious scholarly attention to the history of crime in eighteenth-century England. A representative but not exhaustive list might include John Beattie, Douglas Hay, Joanna Innes, Peter King, J. H. Langbein, Peter Linebaugh, John Styles, and E. P. Thompson. These and other scholars, focusing on different issues, employing a variety of methodologies, and writing from a range of ideological positions, have produced an impressive and growing corpus of published work on the subject and have engendered a number of lively debates around it. There is, possibly, room for a work of synthesis that would attempt to survey this lively field of historical research and make it accessible to the general reader. Sadly, McLynn's book is not it.

This is not to say that the author is unaware of recent scholarly work. Some of his footnotes reveal an acquaintance with it, as do some of the problems he addresses in the text, while he states his "preference in eighteenth-century historical analysis for the 'empirical Marxism' of E. P. Thompson, Douglas Hay, Peter Linebaugh, and others of that school" (p. 341). One suspects that Marxism, empirical or otherwise, needs all the friends it can get these days, but one also suspects that the book under review does not constitute a major addition to left-wing historiography.

The book's fundamental flaw is that, while the author does have a knowledge of some of the major relevant issues and of some of the recent work in the field, his underlying approach is wonderfully old-fashioned. Not for McLynn that systematic analysis of archives that, while a tedious and demanding process, has contributed so much to our understanding of the eighteenth-century crime: "It would be an elementary error," our author informs us, "to retrieve a profile of minor criminality from court records alone. Literary evidence, carefully used, can be a surer guide" (p. 307). This dazzling insight is followed by a not particularly careful reference to *Tom Jones*. Examination of McLynn's text and footnotes reveals a heavy dependence on a few hackneyed sources: various versions of the *Newgate Calendar*, the correspondence of Horace Walpole, and the works (*Tom Jones* apart) of the Fieldings. The result is the production of an account that often takes the form of disjointed anecdotes, that does not reflect the best modern research, and that, through its privileging of a few sources, gives a very distorted view of the subject under consideration. "In eighteenth-century England," McLynn states, "crime was overwhelmingly a London phenomenon" (p. 1). What he means, of course, is that there are lots of London-based printed sources, dipping into which is a rather less demanding activity than that systematic analysis of archives he later disparages.

The confused and outdated nature of McLynn's approach and conceptual framework are demonstrated most clearly in his treatment of the connections between crime and that largely non-London phenomenon, the Industrial Revolution. This is, obviously, an important subject. But McLynn's treatment of it—skipping from the criminalization of outworkers' embezzlements, the resistance to giving vails to servants among the rich, and the resistance to new forms of labor discipline among the poor—reinforces the sense that we are looking at an undigested ragbag of information and ideas. The connections between the Industrial Revolution and crime were complex and confusing, but McLynn's treatment of the subject does not advance our understanding of it. "The new working classes," we read, "felt the acute stress of regulated assembly line work in the new factories" (p. 301). A nice rhetorical flourish, but we are not told exactly when or where these processes were taking place (or, indeed, what proportion of England's workforce was employed on assembly-line work by 1800). Nor does McLynn linger to demonstrate links between this economic change and patterns of criminality.

Indeed, within three pages we have passed, via the impact of enclosures, to food riots—phenomena that, in that they had been a feature of English life since the 1590s, constitute very unhandy evidence for the emergence of a new economic order in the late eighteenth century.

This, then, is a book whose objectives are unclear and whose treatment of its chosen subject is hopelessly dated and unsophisticated. It has little to offer either scholars working on eighteenth-century English society or the students to whom they may wish to recommend an introductory work on crime in eighteenth-century England.

J. A. Sharpe
University of York

Philippe Robert, ed., *Entre L'Ordre et la Liberté, la Detention Provisoire: Deux Siècles de Débats*. Paris: Editions Harmattan, 1992. 287 pp.

The French Revolution, according to one enthusiastic comparativist, was "primarily a criminal procedure revolution."[1] Such a surprising assertion appears less incongruous in the light of Philippe Robert's excellent collection of essays on French criminal justice history and, in particular, the problems of pretrial custody. The book shows clearly how debates about penal affairs played a crucial political role both in 1789 and thereafter and how they now provide a unique insight into the social and political life of the time. This collection represents a form of penal political history that is almost unknown in England. Recent French work on specific aspects of criminal procedure has successfully combined a long historical perspective (1789–1989 for this collection and also for Royer and Martinage's (1990) companion project on the jury)[2] with a sensitivity to international comparison that is almost completely absent in the English literature. Robert and the GERN group are to be congratulated on coordinating such a wide international range of scholarship. Their work is timely, as the French penal and procedural codes are currently undergoing major revision.

The title of the book, "Between Order and Liberty," suggests a constant dialectic or "duel" (p. 12) between these two elements in French legislative history. Neither concept translates easily. *"L'Ordre Publique"* is a central and much-repeated imperative in French criminal jurisprudence that extends well beyond our corresponding "law and order" to include the support of the legitimacy of the entire social, political, and administrative fabric. As for *"Liberté,"* these debates show vividly how many French jurists have insisted on a political rather than a juridical context for this vital constitutional notion. To many Gaullists, for example, it had no relevance whatsoever to the issue of pretrial detention. It is in these terms and in this way that the evident contradiction between the libertarian ideology declared by successive legislatures from the *Constituante* onward and the repressive and bureaucratic judicial machinery of the French state system was managed. This contradiction has however been exposed most significantly and most persistently in what Robert calls the "zone of chronic instability" (p. 10), the question of the pretrial detention of unconvicted defendants.

The book opens with a fascinating account by Nicole and Yves Castan of the role of detention in the unreformed inquisitorial procedure of the 1690 code, before moving on quickly to consider the radical experimentation of 1789. Roberto Martucci explains the crisis of legality that gave urgency to the deliberations of the *Constituant* between 1789 and 1791. According to him, the question of penal law provided the keystone to the whole reform project of the Assembly (p. 53). The special importance of the Anglo-American presumption of innocence to a revolutionary movement whose most potent symbolism was derived from the destruction of a Royalist prison is well explained. Ironically, the triumphant enactment of the presumption in the Declaration of Human Rights took place at a time when the new municipal authorities were becoming active in rooting out and confining those guilty of the ambiguous crime of *lése-Nation*. In the classic problem of revolutionary politics, a vigorous interpretation of the presumption could (it was thought) empty the prisons of counterrevolutionaries and destabilize the *Constituante* itself. A compromise procedure, enshrined in the *Décret de Beaumetz* of 8–9 October 1789, provided a more moderate alternative allowing arrest subject to warrant and a hearing on the remand issue.

This resolution was to be short-lived and, as Bernard Schnapper explains, it did not survive the Terror. The revisions that were prompted by the successive convulsions of *Thermidor*, *Brumaire*, and the Empire finally led to the historic *Code d'Instruction Pénale* of 1808. Not only did this remarkable Code of Procedure survive in France for 150 years, but it also followed the imperial armies into almost every state in Europe and remains the blueprint for criminal procedure across the continent.

If this collection has a weakness, it is the tendency to focus too sharply on parliamentary debate (sometimes illustrated with bewildering diagrams of voting patterns or amendments), to the exclusion of the world outside the Chamber. Perhaps the chief offenders here are the chapter on the abortive legislation of 1843 and René Levy's work on the imperial reforms of 1865, which unconvincingly resolves the issues into a conflict between judges and advocates in Parliament.

Anglo-American procedure is a constant point of reference in many of the French debates, and Clive Emsley offers a short account of pretrial detention in England and Wales between 1750 and 1900. He notes how the shift to a more rapid summary procedure in the mid-nineteenth century was a far more effective (and cheaper) means of resolving the remand problem than the building of new prisons. However, despite the formal separation of prisoners in 1877, the remand prisoner remained almost "invisible" to the Reformers. Emsley compresses a great deal into a short space, but it is a pity that his period ends when it does. It would have been interesting, for example, to read his views on the collapse of the Victorian bail system in the twentieth century. Equally useful are the excellent comparative chapters by Marie-Sylvie Dupont-Bouchat on Belgium and by Luigi Lacché on Italy.

Robert contributes or collaborates in no less than five essays out of the twelve. Most impressive is his and Jacques Capdeveille's account of the postwar period in France and the imprint left by the Algerian crisis and the events of May 1968 on criminal justice policy. In contrast to some of the other contributors, Robert and Capdeveille ground their account of the legal debates squarely in the social and political events, the scandals and political maneuvering, and the prison unrest and terrorist panics of the period. The essay provides a lively account of the political history of the last forty years in France, written by authors who had obviously lived through and closely observed the events they were describing. It also explains the failure of the Mitterand government, despite a "spiral of legislative hyperinflation," to make real advances in dealing with France's massive remand populations. Ironically, it was the Fourth Republic, in its revised Code of 1959, and the governments of Pompidou and Giscard D'Estaing that succeeded in putting in place real checks on the discretionary power of the examining magistrates to remand in custody at will. The legislation of 1970 created a practical bail system for the first time, and in 1975 pretrial custody was limited to six months for less serious offences committed by first offenders. However, the recent decline of the remand population from its high point of 72,541 in 1983 has little to do with the numerous projects of the Mitterand government, and France still faces a problem of grave dimensions. This collection may help point the way out of the impasse.

NOTES

1. G. O. W. Mueller, "Lessons of Comparative Criminal Procedure," *Am. University Law Rev.* 15 (1966):341–62.

2. R. Martinage and J.-P. Royer, *Les Destinées du Jury Criminal* (Lille, 1990).

Richard Vogler
The Open University, Milton Keynes

Steven G. Reinhardt, *Justice in the Sarladais, 1770–1790.* Baton Rouge and London: Louisiana State University Press, 1991. xxiv + 301 pp., illus. $39.95, $16.95 pa.

Justice in the Sarladais is a useful, thoughtful addition to a growing number of local studies of crime, justice, and society in southwestern France in the late eighteenth century. Indeed, it fits itself consciously into the existing corpus of work by Yves and Nicole Castan, Iain Cameron, and Julius Ruff. A natural response is to question the need for another study of crime and justice in an area already so intensively studied, but to the author's credit he creates a useful dialogue with these closely related works and shows readers the singular value of his own chosen region. The Sarladais was more remote than the Languedoc or the Guyenne, yet not quite as isolated as the Auvergne, and so offers an area touched by many currents of modernity but not dominated by them. What emerges is a cautious, measured portrait of a region typical of its times.

Justice in the Sarladais may draw criticism from some quarters for indecisiveness, but this would be to mistake a weakness for a strength: Reinhardt weighs his sources very carefully, for much of the book at least, and builds a careful analysis around their limitations. His evidence is confined to runs of cases that seldom amount to sixty and can be as few as a handful; it is greatly to his credit that he does not lose sight of this until the conclusion. By far the strongest, most valuable part of this study is the three central chapters on the nature of the disputes themselves, which are marked by an admirable sensitivity to evidence. Reinhardt has a keen awareness of the complex mixture of social and economic motives that condition legal procedures in the rural world of the late ancien régime, as witnessed by a well-chosen series of archival examples in these chapters. The Sarladais is an especially useful area of this kind of study; it is isolated from large cities, unlike the Languedoc of the Castans or Ruff's Libourne, and is even more closed than Cameron's Auvergne. In such a setting, the full social ramifications of a *société blocquée* are observed in their natural habitat.

Reinhardt's study makes important contributions to several important aspects of local life of meridional society in the decades before the Revolution. His close analysis of the workings of seigneurial justice adds to a growing picture of administrative indifference towards the enforcement of criminal justice in this period, not only in southern France, but in northern Italy as well. The emerging pattern of readier recourse to royal justice is equally interesting and useful, yet it is also here that the book's innate caution regarding the limitations of its sources seems to slip away. The author equates recourse to royal justice with the process of modernization, specifically with an emerging bourgeoisie, but this stands at odds with his own, carefully argued conclusion that any recourse to law—seigneurial, paralegal, or royal—must be seen as but one option in a complex web of strategies. Indeed, much of the evidence produced points to a rural bourgeoisie still as prone to violence as the lower orders or the nobility—a theme present throughout the book but never fully addressed despite the wealth of evidence presented for it.

Similarly, the evidence presented in the conclusion of a new discourse on Enlightened language in some *plaintes* may have been interpreted in too-straightforward a manner. The use of such language may indicate less an acceptance of the values it embodies than an acute awareness of what the authorities concerned would most readily respond to. Although there is much in its general conclusion that fails to convince, *Justice in the Sarladais* is an important contribution to our knowledge of rural society and its preoccupations in a vital period of European history. As a local study, it is a fine model of the genre and a timely advertisement for its continued life.

M. G. Broers
Leeds University

Jean-Marc Berlière, *La Police des moeurs sous la IIIe République*. Paris: Éditions du Seuil, 1992. 125 Fr frs.

Early in May 1903 there occurred an arrest that seemed likely to bring to an end the notorious *police des moeurs*, the French system for regulating prostitution. The Forissier scandal, as it came to be called, involved the seizure (by two police agents, one of them obviously drunk) of two young bourgeois women who were the sister and the fiancée of a journalist. As it happened, the journalist worked for *La Lanterne*, the paper of the longtime anti-*police des moeurs* activist Yves Guyot.

The official response to the outrage was a clumsy attempt at a cover-up. The arresting agents and their immediate superior bullied two genuine prostitutes into claiming that they, and not the Forissier females, had been the real objects of the arrest. The police claimed that the journalist Forissier himself, apparently in a state of delirium or temporary insanity, had mistakenly believed his own women in peril and had attacked the officers, which had led to the arrest and detention of all three of them. Two days later, Prefect of Police Louis Lépine, furious at the crude deception (which had temporarily deceived him), fired the agents.

But the damage was done: The old issues that had surrounded the *police des moeurs* since its inception in the early years of the nineteenth century—the absence of a law against prostitution and the complete "discretion" of the Prefecture of Police in a matter that involved the liberty and dignity of thousands of working class women—came to the surface once again. (It did not help that this affair was followed shortly thereafter by the *affaire des brossiers* in Rennes, in which striking female brushmakers, their incomes stopped and savings exhausted as their work-stoppage continued, were arrested for having no visible means of support and examined for syphilis, a form of strikebreaking that seemed to reach a new low.)

Critics pointed out that the *régime des moeurs* was particularly anachronistic during the Third Republic, as the imprisonment without trial and due process of women on the grounds of prostitution (the "judges" who sent them to prison were police officers, their courtroom a bureau in the Prefecture) seemed reminiscent of the *lettres de cachet* of the old regime. The grounds of arrest were often fearfully flimsy and subjective ("provocative glances" could subject women to brief stays in jail); and the morals agents themselves were regarded with some horror, as "men that we would not want our sisters to marry," in the words of an editor of the *Gaulois* (p. 118). In response, the proponents of the regime, largely abandoning the old justification of morality, now stressed the need for regulation on the basis of order and public health. Lépine himself frequently mocked the often-overheated rhetoric of abolitionists, as the "antis" were called, commenting that "between the women and the police functionaries, all these *moeurs* issues, forced inscription, coerced examinations, imprisonment at Saint-Lazare, are all just *affaires de famille*" (p. 60).[1] In short, the forces of the status quo drew themselves up in good order; and as in earlier *affaires*, all of them equally egregious, the police control of prostitution survived the Forissier Affair intact. Why did the system prove so resilient?

Jean-Marc Berlière's *La Police des Moeurs sous la IIIe République* focuses on the political debate over prostitution control up to 1914. (The last years of the Third Republic, as well as postwar legislation, are briefly summarized in the last few pages.) The early chapters of this book cover familiar ground, focusing on the legal evolution of prostitution control in France and then on the arguments put forward by activists on both sides of the issue—the terms of the decades-long struggle perhaps by now as wearisome to twentieth-century social and political historians as they must have become to the participants in the debates.

A more significant contribution is the author's careful recounting of the role of prostitution control within the police force itself. This issue perhaps indicates why the police defended their control so strenuously, even with all its attendant problems. Those caught up in the system were valuable sources of information; the reputation of the prestigious *Sûreté*, Berlière suggests, owed at least as much to its ability to extort information from prostitutes, madams, and pimps as it did to good detective work. The control of prostitution also could be used politically: The office of Prefect of Police, under the Minister of the Interior, was a political appointment; and the *maisons de luxe*, attractive to prominent men, sometimes entrapped adversaries of the regime. During the 16 May crisis in 1876, the future cabinet minister and Republican deputy Maurice Rouvier, an opponent of the regime, found himself accused of sexual assault against a minor; her father brought the charge, and the police leaked it to the press. Rouvier relinquished his parliamentary immunity, went on trial, and was acquitted. Three years later it was discovered that the child's father had been an informant and secret operative of the *brigade des moeurs*, under their control because of his own homosexuality (pp. 107–8).

All these controversies are covered competently. Those who have read some studies of nineteenth-century prostitution in other countries as well as in France will not find much that is new here and may also wish that the author had chosen to engage some of the other students of prostitution in debate. Alain Corbin's work, which covers much the same ground (though Corbin deals more extensively with the interwar period), has put forward the provocative thesis that the form of prostitution control was tailored by male consumer demands. This thesis seems, at least to this reader, to offer some contradiction to Berlière's assertion that the changes in the system were shaped by the needs of the police administration.

Still, those who are new to the subject will find this book a competent, thorough introduction to the subject, with copious quotations from archival and printed sources. All readers will find very useful the fifty pages of appendices in the back of the book that include some of the major legal and administrative documents that governed the regime.

NOTE

1. " 'entre femmes et fonctionnaires de police, toutes les choses de moeurs, in-scription forcée, visite coercitive, emprisonnement à Saint-Lazare, tout cela ne sont qu'affaires de famille.' "

Jill Harsin
Colgate University, Hamilton, New York

Jacques Laplante, *Prison et ordre social au Québec*. Ottawa: Les Presses de l'Université d'Ottawa, 1989. 211 pp. $28. pa.

Jean-Marie Fecteau, *Un nouvel ordre des choses: la pauvreté, le crime, l'Etat au Québec, de la fin du XVIIIe siècle à 1840*. Outremont: VLB Editeur, 1989. 287 pp. $22 U.S. $20. pa.

Corrections is one of the most important components of the growing field of Canadian criminal justice history. Given the amount of ink spilled in the last fifty years on this subject by academics, this is rightly so. Two French-language monographs published in Quebec in 1989 fill important gaps in both the Quebec and Canadian literature on penal reform. The two studies overlap in terms of their focus and time periods; they also adopt a similarly broad view of state management of social deviancy. Although one author is an historian and the other a criminologist, they both make liberal use of Marxist theory (no pun intended) in their analysis.

Historian Jean-Marie Fecteau has produced an ambitious study of the relationship among crime, poverty, and the state in Quebec from the end of the Old Regime until the aftermath of the 1837–38 Rebellions. The influence of Foucault's 1975 *Surveiller et punir* is strongly evident in his analysis of this relationship.[1] According to Foucault, the social policies of the past 150 years have been dedicated to disciplining, classifying, educating, and resocializing "prisoners" or clients. Institutional reforms in penal and charitable circles were motivated by elite fears of social disorder. Fecteau, in a pared-down version of his University of Paris doctoral dissertation, employs "official" sources: government reports, newspaper accounts of criminal justice and social welfare issues and, to a lesser extent, judicial archives. Chapters are devoted to Lower Canadian charity prior to 1815, the repression of illegality in the same period, the reform discourse between 1815 and 1840, and the realities of social regulation in the same period.

Under France, Quebec's social welfare was attended to largely by the Catholic Church, and lay initiatives were subject to royal supervision. The colony's social control institutions consisted of three *hôtels-Dieu*, two *hôpitaux generaux*, and a *bureaux des pauvres*. Under the English administrative system that was grafted onto Quebec after the Conquest, the emphasis in social policy shifted to the local community and a variety of experiments in social control inspired by Britain, France, and the United States. The Catholic Church was preeminent in the social field by 1810. After 1763, and particularly by the late eighteenth century, Crown-appointed justices of the peace and the poor law were instrumental in controlling vagabonds and mendicants. Famines and epidemics were other challenges to the social order that attracted both state and private charity.

Fecteau summarizes the major components of the English legal system as it developed in Quebec/Lower Canada after 1760. These included the court system, constables in Montreal and Quebec, magistrates exercising summary jurisdiction, and criminal prosecutions conducted by a *procureur général*. Quebec's prisons prior to 1815 were not thought of as preventive or rehabilitative institutions. Court records, Fecteau warns us, represent a conservative level of true crime because they are largely urban in nature and because of the weakness of the oppressive apparatus.

French Canadian nationalists think of 1791–1840 as a period of budding but fragile nationalism constrained by an oppressive British presence. Yet as Lord Durham later reported, the "state" that developed in Lower Canada, with its large French Canadian population, aggrandizing Catholicism, economic dependency on Britain, and anglophone commercial class, was limited in power. Although Lower Canada was touched by international currents of institutional reform after 1810, the contrast between reform discourse and practice was striking. Prior to the 1830s, constitutional issues kept spending on public works such as prisons to a minimum. Montreal's House of Industry, which opened in 1819, housed several dozen pauper families before closing four years later. As late as 1836, the colony had but seven jails.

After 1800, the colonial government began to support philanthropic institutions dedicated to assisting abandoned children, the mentally ill, and the infirm poor. In this period reformers supported new institutions such as the hospital, the asylum, and the house of industry. Plans for a penitentiary modelled on the institution at Auburn, New York, were begun for Upper Canada in 1832. In 1834 Quebec legislators studying theories of penal reform endorsed the Philadelphia model penitentiary. Reformers also called for professional police and municipal institutions. Public discussions of social policy were informed by notions of class and morality, particularly with the arrival of impoverished British immigrants in the 1820s and 1830s. Yet economic, ideological, and political constraints contributed to a persistent "institutional blockage" in the colony. The Lower Canadian state, subject to political strife between the anglophone-dominated executive and the French Canadian assembly, proceeded from one crisis to the next in the years leading up to the 1837 Rebellion. Lower Canada's institutional development would expand with the Union of the Canadas in the 1840s. By 1859 the colony had twenty-one prisons in operation or under construction, professional police in urban centers, municipal institutions, a growing state bureaucracy, and a host of voluntary organizations dedicated to moral and social reform. The conclusion to *Un nouvel ordre des choses* is almost anticlimactic in its depiction of a hobbled colonial Leviathan c. 1840.[2]

The central argument of *Prison et ordre sociale au Québec* is that penal policy since the nineteenth century has served as a form of managing poverty. The criminologist author traces the evolution of penal policy from the era of New France (1608–1760) through the British colonial period (1760–1830), the period of penal repression starting with the advent of the penitentiary (1830–1930), and the shift to a less coercive yet more comprehensive corrections system aided by the modern social and medical sciences. According to Laplante, the rise of the prison both reflected and made possible the development of the modern state, with its wide range of controls over individual behavior. It did not develop, as older chroniclers assumed, as a response to crime so much as to changing social, economic, and ideological conditions. In this analysis, prison reform and the expansion of imprisonment for petty offenses coincided with the Industrial Revolution.

Penal policy was affected by various trends, but the underlying goal was the criminalization of the dependent classes. St. Vincent de Paul (1873) reflected the "fortress" period of Canadian corrections, when the emphasis was on discipline. The rule of silence was not abolished in federal penitentiaries until 1945. Laplante also generalizes about the larger field of social policy. In this century scientific practices replaced charity in the management of the poor, accomplished through overtly coercive mechanisms such as the prison as well as more discrete but nonetheless intrusive practices such as social welfare and mental health intervention. For Laplante, Bentham's Panopticon, a self-financing prison where both inmates and custodians would be under scrutiny is a metaphor for the rise of state power in the social realm. Rejecting liberal (formerly mainstream) criminology, the author sees each step in the evolution of "la defence sociale" as increasing justification for a more active and intrusive state.

The book's most important chapter is "Le maintien de la prison: la répression et la traitement scientifique, 1930-," which examines the modernization of corrections theory and practice. Innovations within correctional institutions included classification, segregation, prevention, and new education programs. Particularly after the 1940s, the decade when academic criminology first appeared in Quebec, there was an increased reliance on probation, parole, pre-sentencing reports, medium- and minimum-security institutions, pardons, supervision within the community, and community service. In the early 1980s the federal Young Offenders Act removed the outdated status offenses of earlier juvenile legislation. By the late 1950s, the theory that criminality was a form of illness was allowing psychiatrists and social workers to engage in "professional imperialism." By the 1970s, according to Laplante, despite the hopes of 1960s reformers, prisoners had simply "changed jailers"; the medical and social science communities had become part of the state's apparatus of control.

Prison et ordre social condemns penal policy in Quebec on two grounds: for failing to accomplish its official or public goals and for masking oppression in the guise of humanity and public welfare. Laplante agrees with Foucault and a number of government studies that, in terms of its original mandate, the penitentiary has been a spectacular failure: it has not led to decreased levels of crime, but in fact contributed immeasurably to recidivism. Despite the avowed commitment to rehabilitation, penitentiaries are still designed for security. A convict's time in prison does not prepare him for "normal" living, and his release is merely a continuation of punishment, as he has been branded a social misfit. Citing a federal government study, the author suggests that fifty to eighty percent of persons jailed in Quebec in a given year should not be there. Many are jailed for minor offenses or for the inability to pay fines. Laplante does not spare the behavioral sciences for their complicity in furthering state surveillance of the lower classes. Allegedly humane, rationalistic "treatment," even in mental health clinics, is in actuality a more sophisticated form of control and repression. Psychiatric and social services contribute to the construction of deviance and criminality.

Lost from much of Laplante's discussion are the very people with whom he sympathizes, the actual clients of the penal system. Aside from aggregate data on recidivists, young offenders, and other categories, the "victims" of the system usually are referred to as poor or disadvantaged. Second, there is little discussion of prison culture—were inmates able to resist "treatment," or were they simply overwhelmed by Quebec's penal juggernaut? Has the prisoners' rights movement of the last twenty-five years made no difference? Third, there is little acknowledgment of broader societal views of corrections and treatment. The public, despite the utterances of nineteenth-century penal reformers, mid-twentieth-century Quebec social scientists and social workers, and more recently criminologists, psychologists, and psychiatrists, probably never regarded prisons and penitentiaries as institutions for rehabilitation. Although Canadians have exhibited a degree of compassion for the plight of young offenders, penal institutions commonly were viewed as mechanisms of punishment, deterrence, and containment. Working-class Canadians support the police, and public opinion polls indicate considerable support for capital punishment. Victims of crime (the majority of them working class) and members of the public concerned with perceived crime waves have never subscribed to official versions of corrections policy—a fact that realist criminology recognizes. As Fecteau realizes, it is imperative to differentiate between the rhetoric and ideology of reform movements and social policy and its actual accomplishments. A final observation applies to the writings of many theoretical criminologists on corrections and the police: Laplante illustrates how criminal justice reflects class structure but offers no alternatives to prisons and police. The notion that the social welfare system has become a vast prison without walls is intriguing. It is difficult to refute the author's claims that prisons developed as a strategy of managing poverty and that most clients of the disciplinary state are of humble origins. But it is equally problematic to expect the abolition of the prison and penitentiary.

NOTES

1. M. Foucault, *Surveiller et punir: naissance de la prison* (Paris: Gallimard, 1975).

2. The phrase is borrowed from Allan Greer and Ian Radforth, eds., *Colonial Leviathan: State Formation in Mid-Nineteenth Century Canada* (Toronto: University of Toronto Press, 1992).

Greg Marquis
St. Francis Xavier University, Antigonish

Alf Lüdtke, ed., *"Sicherheit" und "Wohlfart": Polizei, Gesellschaft und Herrschaft im 19 und 20 Jahrhundert*. Frankfurt am Main: Suhrkamp Verlag, 1992. 394 pp. $64.95.

As the editor, Alf Lüdtke, states in his foreword to this collection of essays, the history of policing in Germany to date has largely focused on its institutional and bureaucratic aspects or has been devoted to restricted themes or periods, making it difficult to gain an overview of policing developments and their connection with the evolution of the modern state. This collection by thirteen different contributors, while making no claim to fill the gap, presents a useful step in that direction. The essays are of a high standard, mostly based on primary research material, and together cover a broad spectrum of issues ranging from early nineteenth-century resistance by South German community-controlled police authorities to encroachment by the state (Albrecht Funk/Norbert Pütter and Bernd Wirsig respectively) to the implementation of a policy of expulsion and exclusion of gypsies from the last decades of the nineteenth century to the present day (Michael Zimmerman). Lüdtke also comments on the general lack of comparative policing studies and includes an essay by Clive Emsley comparing English and American policing of strikes in his collection (although an Anglo/German comparison might have been more to the point).

Inevitably in such a book, what is lacking is a closer sense of the interplay between politics and policing policy over the whole period. We are nevertheless offered a view of the ambiguities inherent in the police idea as it evolved from a preindustrial conception of "Polizey" with its broad-based regulatory and order-maintaining functions, through the revolutionary and industrial struggles of the second half of the nineteenth century to a modernized policing system as it operated in the Weimar and Nazi periods. The essays show how the emphasis swung between a regulatory social service and a militarized and crime-busting model of policing, as well as between a local and a state-controlled system—the dominance of one or the other depending less on any straight evolutionary path than on the outcome of power struggles between opposing electorates and social groups as well as on the exigencies of the developing state. Such alterations do not, however, distinguish German policing systems from those of other Western states.

Germany's distinguishing feature, according to Lüdtke, is the German emphasis on order maintenance, and several of the essays emphasize this theme in one form or another. The struggle between local and central or private and public authorities over policing functions and policy incorporates a strong desire on the protagonists' part to retain control for this purpose. Thus Ralph Jessen shows in his excellent essay how employers in the Ruhr mining industry at the end of the nineteenth century took over responsibility for public and private in the effort to tame their immigrant workforce and restore order within their enterprises, after the traditional policing service failed them. Equally, Herbert Reinke, in his paper on policing in the Rhineland around the time of World War I, explains how despite state insistence that the police confine their activities to the prevention and prosecution of crime, municipal policy was still focused primarily on keeping order on the streets, largely at the behest of the citizens.

From a very different perspective, Peter Becker and Martin Leuenberger in their separate essays concentrate on police perceptions—the former in a Foucauldian piece that develops the idea of the "controlling gaze" within a German context, in the hope of being able to recognize and separate the criminal from the noncriminal; the latter on the police's power to define the meaning of everyday actions by juveniles as nonconforming and therefore punishable. The essays by David Crew and Ursula Nienhaus emphasize this aspect of repressive control and authoritarian judgements in the work of family welfare agencies that sought to mold their clients' behavior to conform with an expected "orderly" norm, as did that of women police officers in their work with women and children. But resistance to these expected norms is equally documented and discussed, whether by Crew's welfare recipients who demanded their rights or as in Karin Hartweg's paper on the looting and food riots after World War I by an impoverished local working class who resisted the police and were able to impose a reduction in food prices despite middle-class calls for tough police action.

The study of support from below for the Nazi policies of exclusion of alien elements and for the restoration of order has also been neglected to date, according to Robert Gellately's largely historiographical essay that criticises historians for ignoring the way in which this support greatly facilitated the way in which the regime functioned. The police themselves may be seen as a case in point: Here, police resistance to their overwhelming concentration on bureaucratic, order-maintaining, and regulatory tasks in the mid-Weimar period is one reason attributed by Richard Bessel to the police's easy adaptation to the Nazi regime, where what they saw as their professional role of fighting crime was given much greater precedence. The contradiction between Gellateley's and Bessel's viewpoints, however, is more apparent than real, as the restoration of order through terror converged only too readily with the view that the opponents of the new order were criminals. An overriding concern with order and intolerance of nonconformist behavior is thus implicated in the slide into the Nazi terror and the implementation of eugenic policies. This explanation seems to me questionable and too much influenced by hindsight. The fear and distrust of criminal, outcast, or deviant groups and the effort to segregate them from the rest of society if and when the reformist enterprise faded, bourgeois concern with public order, and the social Darwinism and eugenic concepts on which racial theories were built have all been common influences on policing policies and practices in most developed countries. What distinguishes the German case much more is the nature of German politics and the political structure, rather than any other supposed distinguishing cultural traits.

Barbara Weinberger
University of Warwick

David J. V. Jones, *Crime in Nineteenth Century Wales*. Cardiff: University of Wales Press, 1992. £25.

Since the late 1970s, David Jones has played a major part in bringing the history of the working class in Wales alive; and it is a pleasure to find his many interests, from Rebecca rioters to poachers and vagrants, brought together in this admirable examination of the main contours of Welsh crime in the nineteenth century.

Basically, this book is a sustained investigation of the meaning of the Welsh criminal statistics. The difficult and maligned national figures, their pitfalls exposed by Gatrell and Hadden, can still reveal much when effectively handled in conjunction with other sources, as they are here. The main fascination of the criminal statistics is simply the number of puzzles and the range of possible explanations they present. If they give no conclusive result on the "real" extent of crime, they can still offer insights into the nature of criminality and social attitudes towards it.

The outline of crime in Wales was roughly similar to that of England, with the familiar rise in the early nineteenth century of "serious" crime, which did not begin to decline in Wales until the mid-1850s, a little later than in England. But in comparison with the English figures, Jones argues, the Welsh were apparently a law-abiding people. On paper, at any rate, Taffy was far less a thief than his English counterpart, and well behind the Irish, who swelled the crime statistics for the Welsh seaports. Jones explores the background to these figures, and particularly the reluctance in the earlier nineteenth century for rural communities to bring offenders before a formal court. Many village offenders probably never reached the official record because they were dealt with by informal means, including the humiliating *ceffyl pren*, the Welsh counterpart of the English "rough music." In the early Victorian years, the targets of the *ceffyl pren* included not only minor criminals, but "prosecutors, informers, witnesses ... bailiffs, keepers and land-grabbing farmers, as well as the more common targets of adulterers, wife-beaters and deserters ... " (p. 12). Lest this all sound too high-minded, Jones also emphasizes the violent attacks, until late in the century, on Catholics, Jews, and even the English. But certain groups of outsiders were more likely than local residents to be targets for prosecution, as shown in the higher rates of arrest for the Irish and vagrants.

It is difficult to find an organizing principle for a history of crime over a relatively long period, and this work reads more as a series of essays on the central theme than a sustained narrative. Jones concentrates first on the types of offense such as crimes of violence and property crime. The results do not differ markedly from the pattern established by Gatrell and Hadden, though Jones, working on a smaller scale, can offer insights into regional differences, not only on the varying incidence of crime, but its seasonality. As with other parts of Britain, one is struck by the sheer banality of most crime and the petty amount of property involved: Some gangs of professional criminals did exist, but for most, crime offered little in the way of prizes, and no great prospect of an increase in the standard of living. Turning to the category of "other offences," Jones offers a variation of Gatrell's arguments on the rise of the policeman-state. While "serious" crime declined, the tightening of urban regulations, combined with the growth of police, brought growing numbers of citizens into conflict with the law through drunkenness and highway offences, hawking, dog-ownership, cruelty to animals, sanitation, or truancy. This effectively handed over much of the judicial process to magistrates, a speedy, effective, but inevitably class-distorted system of justice.

Later chapters analyze the criminals themselves, the growth of policing, and the nature of punishment. Jones rejects the simple polarity of seeing the police either as the welcome protectors of the working class or repressive agents of the elite. He settles instead for an ambivalent working-class view of the constabulary. Although certain villages resisted any recourse to the police, the increase in reporting minor offenses indicates a more regular relationship between public and police—though here Jennifer Davis's investigation of London prosecutions and the possibility of malicious reporting might be taken into account. In the end, Jones reveals a nostalgia for an older, self-policed society, before the expansion of urban regulation that brought ever more families into contact with the law.

This is an attractive and readable book, with the rare bonus of being reasonably priced. It brings the statistical account to life, though it is sensitive to the problems of any statistical approach. For the student, it would have to be read in conjunction with a standard guide such as Radzinowicz, as its thematic nature tends to disguise the cumulative effect of legislation on crime. At the risk of offending national sentiment, it might also be argued that the Welsh evidence does not argue for the separateness of Wales, but rather for its assimilation into the mainstream of European patterns of crime. Jones's work on the Rebecca riots opened up a world of very specific pain and grievance: but the examination of crime over a longer period, with its divisions into agricultural and mining villages, towns and seaports, offers a Welsh reflection of national events.

M. A. Crowther
University of Glasgow

George Robb, *White-Collar Crime in Modern England: Financial Fraud and Business Morality 1845–1929*. Cambridge: Cambridge University Press, 1992. 250 pp.

In the perception of the Victorians, crime in England was something committed by the criminal and/or dangerous classes. The notion continued well into the twentieth century, while many historians working on crime in England since the eighteenth century have, in some respects, continued the idea by focusing almost entirely on the working-class offender. To the extent that poor members of the working class constituted the majority of the offenders processed by the police and the courts, this focus has some validity. But if the historian were to shift the angle of vision from the thousands of petty thefts to the offenses involving thousands of pounds, a very different image of criminality would emerge. Of course, historians have not been oblivious to this fact, but George Robb's *White-Collar Crime in Modern England* is the first detailed published historical monograph on the problem.[1]

Victorians were not unaware of business and financial fraud and, given the sheer scale of such fraud, this is not surprising. In 1856 Leopold Redpath, the Registrar General of the Great Northern Railway, was exposed as having defrauded the company out of £240,000. Writing in the aftermath of the Great Crash of 1929, the economist H. A. Shannon estimated that as many as one in six of the companies promoted during the nineteenth century were fraudulent. Novelists drew on contemporary scandals to create their own swindlers; thus Dickens transformed John Sadlier into Mr. Merdle for *Little Dorrit*, and Trollope modelled Augustus Melmotte on Alfred Grant for *The Way We Live Now*. Yet these individuals never became either bogeymen or romantic rogues with the respective appeal of Dickens's Bill Sikes or Harrison Ainsworth's Dick Turpin.

Following a brief survey of the transformation of finance and public borrowing in the eighteenth century, Robb plunges the reader into a catalogue of fraud beginning with the Railway Mania of the 1840s and running on through chapters focusing on banking and credit fraud, stock fraud, and fraud in both the promotion and the management of companies. There is a gallery of appalling rogues. John Sadlier, a director of the Tipperary Joint-Stock Bank, embezzled £200,000 and issued £150,000 of fictitious shares in the Swedish Railway. Millions passed through Alfred Grant's hands as he promoted company after company; much of the money went into his pockets, enabling him to build a luxurious house near Kensington Gardens and to enter Parliament, from which he was eventually unseated for election bribery. Twenty years after Grant, Ernest Terah Hooley, "the Napoleon of Finance," blazed an even more illustrious trail to ruin on other people's money. The problem was that people with money to invest had so little information on where to invest and on the validity of most ventures, while the experts professing to advise and guide them were often involved with or duped by the fraudsters.

Two questions immediately spring to mind out of this sorry chronicle: Why was so little done to prevent it? If the London money market was so rotten with fraud, how was it able to attain and maintain its position as the financial capital of the world before 1914? Robb makes a significant stab at the first question. Things were done. Scandals prompted parliamentary enquiries and legislation; they also prompted a degree of professionalization involving training and examinations for accountants and bankers. But both the parliamentary enquiries and the legislation were hampered by the prevailing ideology of laissez faire, while the powerful business lobby in Parliament was vigorously opposed to interference in its affairs. The relations between the old landed elite and big business were, Robb insists, much closer than has been popularly argued. "Expert" witnesses to select committees on company law and fraud could be chosen by members of those committees who were themselves businessmen or company directors. The second question about Britain's financial primacy is not really explored, but then it falls outside criminal justice history. Robb briefly explains some of the differences between the financial markets in Britain and parts of continental Europe; the British system appears to have been much less regulated. In the light of Robb's analysis, the issue deserves some reconsideration.

This is an illuminating book. Well researched in parliamentary papers and the financial literature of the Victorian and Edwardian periods, it is well argued and convincing. In sum, it makes a valuable and novel addition to the literature on offending and justice in nineteenth- and early twentieth-century England. The parallels with the more recent past and the present are almost too painful.

NOTE

1. See also R. S. Sindall, "Aspects of Middle-Class Crime in the Nineteenth Century" (M. Phil. thesis, University of Leicester, 1974); idem, "Middle-Class Crime in Nineteenth-Century England," *Criminal Justice History* 4 (1983): 23–40; Philip Jenkins, "Into the Upperworld? Law, Crime and Punishment in English Society." *Social History* 12 (1987): 97–102; and Clive Emsley, *Crime and Society in England 1750–1900* (London, 1987), pp. 6–7 and 120–21.

Clive Emsley
The Open University, Milton Keynes

Hai-Huey Liang, *The Rise of Modern Police and the European State System from Metternich to the Second World War*. Cambridge: Cambridge University Press, 1992. xiii + 345 pp. £30/$49.95.

This book presents the results of an ambitious project, a study of the emergence of contemporary forms of policing in Europe through a comparative analysis of individual country experience over more than a century. As the history of policing is hardly an overworked field, the appearance of such a work must be welcomed, especially as it is based upon extensive research in the primary sources. Indeed, one of the merits of this book is its demonstration of the scholarly potential of police archives for social and political historians generally. The text includes numerous extracts from the files of long-forgotten surveillance operations in Vienna and Paris, which make entertaining and often instructive reading.

For all the richness of the material, however, it must be said that the author's overall thesis remains obscure and, insofar as it can be reconstructed, questionable. The very title indicates a range of conceptual difficulties. As this is a book about the relationship between the emergence of modern policing and the evolution of the European state system, at least three questions need to be answered: First, what does the author mean by "modern police"? Second, what is lost and gained by focusing exclusively on Europe (and on only part of Europe at that, as Britain, for example, is not discussed at all)? Third, what sort of relationship between policing and politics is proposed?

So far as the first point is concerned, Liang seems to have adopted a rather unusual sort of modernization thesis. Modern police, we read on page 229, are found in societies that are "politically educated, down-to-earth rationalist, and individualistic in motivation." So far this is standard modernization fare, though it has a resolutely old-fashioned sound. Liang describes his study as charting "a period of one hundred years of progress toward more civilian police rule in Europe and better police collaboration among its various nations" (p. 309). This too has the Whig teleology characteristic of such modes of historical explanation.

It is just here, however, over the matter of periodization, that doubts set in. For Liang regards "modern police" as a historical phenomenon that comes to an end in 1939 (p. 3). Or does it? His concluding remarks imply that this phenomenon continues into the postwar world. But Liang does not appear to think that the political role of the "modern police" is an ideological matter; the police forces he describes apparently existed in a pre-ideological era. This bizarre view causes him serious difficulties in analyzing developments in the 1920s and even worse problems in accounting for the impact of Nazism or professional policing.

Liang's assumption that a professional police force must be immune to ideology leads him to express astonishment at the "difficulty of modern police officers to [sic] apply their professional ethics of individual judgement and legal objectivity to social situations" (p. 19)—this of those Viennese police officials in the 1920s whom he rates highly from the professional point of view. But recent work on racial science and criminology in the Third Reich has made it clear that scientific racism was widely espoused. Thus there is no reason to be surprised that Johann Schober, for example, was both a rabid anti-Semite and an accomplished police reformer. Liang's concept is what leads him to this fix.

The focus on Europe also requires justification. A footnote informs us that "modern police" did not appear in the European colonies in Africa and Asia. Indeed not. However, Liang does not admit the possibility that the colonial experience exerted a formative influence upon European policing. At one point he quotes a revealing comment by an Austrian policeman in Bosnia in 1914 who likened imperial rule to "a punitive expedition . . .

an expedition of the kind so-called cultured states launch against obstreperous natives in their colonies" (p. 183). He does not, however, consider the impact of policing Algeria upon French police methods generally. Nor, as he fails to discuss Britain at all, can he take account of the critical importance of the Irish question in British political policing. The relationship between Europe and the wider world was surely not all one way, and Europeans did not merely export their own policing methods overseas.

Finally we come to the key issue of the relationship between the rise of "modern police" and the European state system. I have to confess that to me at least the nature of this relationship is never made clear. At some points it seems that Liang is trying to show that international cooperation was gradually increasing over this period. At others, he seems simply concerned to show what role the police played in such major turning points as the Franco-Prussian War and the Sarajevo assassination. Occasionally he argues that the police could be used as spies or for counterespionage in the interests of one state or another. But while the narrative is shaped by shifts in European politics, the author does not manage to demonstrate any obvious connection with trends in policing.

Sources dominate and distort the argument. There are strange unexplained leaps (for example, in the discussion of the Austrian police we jump suddenly from the 1820s to 1848) or lengthy discussions of peripheral topics (such as Franco-Swiss relations in the mid-nineteenth century). The key first chapter surveys the experience of five countries seriatim and ends abruptly with no attempt to provide a comparative overview or to tell the reader what the comparision has shown.

An enormous amount of research has gone into this book, and numerous insights dot its pages. It raises important issues, and we should be grateful to the author for that. But it is difficult not to feel disappointment at the confused nature of the analysis and the ill-digested manner of presentation. We can perhaps at least learn that, if we are to explore the political history of policing, we shall do well to abandon the assumptions of modernization theory and Eurocentrism upon which this book is based.

Mark Mazower
University of Sussex, Brighton

Eleanore Bushnell, *Crimes, Follies, and Misfortunes: The Federal Impeachment Trials*. Urbana and Chicago: University of Illinois Press, 1992. x + 380 pp. Illustrations, notes, bibliography, index. $39.95.

In this accessible study, Eleanore Bushnell provides a welcome introduction to impeachment and a welcome assessment of the fourteen impeachments and trials in America's history. Professor emerita of political science at the

University of Nevada, Bushnell provides the first history to survey all federal impeachment trials and to identify the key elements common to all. Although the bulk of her study stresses the twelve federal impeachment trials—from the first in 1799 of Senator William Blount of Tennessee for conspiring with the British to gain control of Florida and Louisiana from Spain to the impeachment and conviction of federal district Judge Harry E. Claiborne for federal income tax evasion in 1986—Bushnell uses her epilogue to review the impeachments of Alcee L. Hastings and Walter L. Nixon, Jr., in 1989, for a total of fourteen impeachment trials. Just over fifty other federal officials, such as President Richard Nixon in 1974, have avoided impeachment and trial by resigning from their offices.

Organized chronologically, with a chapter devoted to each impeachment, Bushnell's study isolates trends and characteristics. Using Edward Gibbons's definition of history as "little more than the register of the crimes, follies, and misfortunes of mankind," Bushnell convincingly groups the targets of impeachment. Her first category includes five men who had been accused of crimes for which they could have been or were convicted of in court. Into this category Bushnell places Blount, William W. Belknap (Secretary of War in Grant's first administration), and the most recent three impeachments of Claiborne, Hastings, and Nixon. Under the second category, "follies," defined as "unfitness to remain in office because of breaches of judicial propriety or chronic inability or unwillingness to perform their duties" (p. 320), Bushnell places five others: federal district judge John Pickering (for alcoholism and possible insanity), the imprudent Associate Justice of the United States Supreme Court Samuel Chase (the only Supreme Court justice to be impeached by the House, although the Senate failed to convict), federal district judge West H. Humphery (who abandoned his federal bench to support the so-called Southern Confederacy), and federal district judges Charles Swayne and Robert W. Archbald (who abused their offices for personal enrichment).

Lastly, Bushnell brings four men together under the category "misfortunes," labelling them "misfortunes" because all were "political orphans, unsupported by the dominant forces of their time" (p. 321). In this grouping are federal district judges James H. Peck and Harold Louderback, who were impeached but found not guilty and therefore were not removed by the Senate, and the only president to be impeached, but also not removed, Andrew Johnson. With them are federal district judge Halsted L. Ritter, whom the House impeached and whom the Senate removed in 1936 (in the process becoming the only person the Senate convicted on a cumulative article of impeachment after having failed to convict him on one of the more specific articles of impeachment).

Bushnell's case-study approach allows careful and thorough analysis, but over the course of fourteen studies it has a tendency toward redundancy and tediousness. Nevertheless, she distills from each biography the characteristics common to all. For example, eleven of the fourteen impeached (and all of those impeached in the twentieth century) belonged to the federal judiciary (the others were one senator, one cabinet officer, and one president). For the most part, all the men impeached had become "alienated from the political mainstream," they had performed their duties in an "unacceptable fashion," which included their unofficial actions, and they repeatedly behaved in an unacceptable fashion (p. 323).

The most recent impeachments have suggested several other trends. Bushnell points out that executive or judicial action, not congressional initiative, started the procedures against Claiborne, Alcee, and Judge Nixon. Bushnell rightly worries that Congress is abandoning its traditional centrality in impeachment, and certainly her work is an strong argument for Congress to reaffirm its role and its responsibility for policing the federal judiciary and executive officer holders. Further, recent impeachments have occurred after the judges had been convicted of crimes. If those judges had not been removed from their life-tenure offices, then the country could have faced the spectacle of a federal judge, after having served his time in federal prison, retaking his seat on the federal bench. Although this scenario has not occurred, Bushnell describes the possibility as "an outcome too grotesque for serious contemplation" (p. 320).

In yet another trend, the Senate has altered traditional impeachment procedure by appointing a special committee to hear the evidence of the House of Representatives on their articles of impeachment and to report to the full Senate on their findings. Although the constitutionality of this procedure has been challenged by accused officeholders, it is likely to be used again, because the traditions and customs of the Senate rely heavily on the committee system and because it saves the time and effort of the full body.

Bushnell's plan to make impeachment more effective hinges on a congressional statute defining "good behavior." As she demonstrates in her review of the impeachments, impeached federal officials have rarely committed crimes while in office, but many of them have engaged in behavior that embarrassed the official or brought the government and law into disrespect. Yet, that behavior did not fall into the vague constitutional clause of "high crimes and misdemeanors." Ethical violations, alcoholism, and absenteeism have proven to be consistent problems, and it is debatable whether such behaviors are high crimes and misdemeanors. If Congress passed a statute defining the "good behavior" referred to in Article III, §1, of the Constitution to cover such behaviors, then impeachment would become a more efficient and effective device to treat the "crimes, follies, and misfortunes" of federal officeholders.

Recommended for all undergraduate, graduate, and law libraries, this volume contributes significantly to the growing body of literature on impeachments and their role in maintaining the accountability of officeholders. Here is political science written in an accessible style with a program worth the attention of Congress. Perhaps the University of Illinois Press ought to send copies of this monograph to each member of the House and Senate Judiciary Committees for their information and action—and soon.

Thomas C. Mackey
University of Louisville

Nancy Leys Stepan, *"The Hour of Eugenics": Race, Gender, and Nation in Latin America.* Ithaca and London: Cornell University Press, 1991. viii + 210 pp. Index. $31.50.

Nancy Leys Stepan, author of several important contributions to the history of science and medicine, seeks in *"The Hour of Eugenics"* to examine the story of this idea and movement from its nineteenth-century roots in Europe to its twentieth-century spread to Latin America, especially in Brazil, Argentina, and Mexico. To European eugenicists the problem was thus: The advance of civilization now provided humane protection for the weak—humans beings previously weeded out in a cruel, if essential, process of natural selection. Now, the eugenicists lamented, the "unfit" were breeding, sabotaging the efficiency of Darwinian law.

Not just for Nazis, eugenics during its "hour" spawned quite a following: In the late 1920s eugenic sterilization became law in Switzerland and Denmark; Sweden operated on some 15,000 mental patients in the 1930s and 1940s; and the United States, from 1907 to 1945, selected 70,000 from asylums (nearly all African Americans) for forced sterilization in the name of eugenics. At length, the terrifying eugenical extremism of the Nazis, including the forced sterilization of fully 1 percent of the German population (as well as other well-known horrors in the name of "racial purity") rightly brought discredit on this project of human engineering. By the 1940s it was over; even the term "eugenics" disappeared from use.

Traditional scholarship in the history of ideas has focused on Europe and the developed world, and study of eugenics has similarly centered on the regions where the movement went the furthest: the United States, the United Kingdom, and Germany. However, previous historians have too often acted as if Latin America (and indeed the whole of the less-developed world) could be safely ignored, supposing, it would seem, that scientific ideas could be but dimly understood there, that no significant advances ever came from there, and that, in a word, nothing intellectually interesting or important ever happened in Latin America. Stepan challenges these assumptions, arguing that an examination of how eugenics were understood and employed in Latin America will lead us to a different conceptualization of all eugenics.

Stepan takes what she terms a "constructivist" approach: scientific ideas are never true in the abstract but only as considered within their social and political time and place. Social claims are cloaked in scientific jargon in order to *appear* objective, neutral, and apolitical.

Eugenics was above all about race, but, as Stepan shows, the whole idea of "race" is really little more than a social construct, within which reside further socially based notions: judgments about beauty and ugliness, intelligence and stupidity. What eugenics sought to do was elevate these collections of utterly subjective, cultural prejudices to the level of scientific fact. Stepan adeptly peels away the scientific pretensions of racial classification, exposing its cultural, political, and usually racist suppositions.

Stepan's work represents a thoughtful contribution to the study of the consumption of ideas. In Europe, eugenics were generally understood to mean that the socially successful had superior genetic attributes; the less successful, a more impoverished inheritance. Moreover, human character was immutable; no amount of reforming do-goodism could do any good. Clearly, for Latin America this European view posed problems. For one thing, it negated the mission of public health officials, declaring that such efforts had no value. But more to the point, European and United States eugenics insulted Latin Americans. Blacks, Indians, and swarthy southern Europeans it labeled as obviously inferior; and in miscegenation it saw the blending of the vile.

So for eugenics to build any following in Latin America, enthusiasts usually had to turn to a minority interpretation of genetics, one that allowed for the extragenerational transfer of characteristics acquired in life. In Brazil, eugenic-oriented reform joined with the call for sanitation, just the reverse of the situation in Europe. But this "Lamarckian" approach to eugenics (after nineteenth-century French scientist Jean Baptiste Pierre Antoine Lamarck) grew increasingly suspect and was finally disproven in the 1940s. However, Latin American acceptance of these ideas must not be seen as proof of the region's scientific illiteracy, Stepan insists. Rather, one must consider how adherence to Lamarckian views stemmed from Latin America's social, cultural, and political realities.

On miscegenation, Latin American eugenicists had to innovate. Mexico's Jose Vasconcelos created "counterracial mythologies," proclaiming the virtuousness of Mexico's mestizos, his "cosmic race." Still, it turned out that what Vasconcelos thought was good about racial mixing was that it improved "inferior" breeds, at least to some degree, by blending in "superior" European blood. Similarly, racist white eugenicists in Brazil saw miscegenation as hopeful because of the long-term tendency of the "inferior"—the blacks and mulattoes—to mix and "whiten," one scientist brashly predicting that by the year 2012 Brazil's racial "improvement" would be complete, its color bleached out.

There are some problems with this book. Trendy phraseology sometimes burdens the text. (Precious few pages pass safely by without the word "discourse" being summoned for duty. If words could be granted early retirement from the English language in recognition for extended service, this is surely one so deserving.)

Another difficulty is Stepan's somewhat forced gender analysis. Repeatedly she asserts that eugenicists took a particular interest in defining and restricting women's reproductive role. However, Stepan's own evidence seems instead to suggest that women were not singled out for special treatment. Proposed eugenical prenuptial registration laws referred to both women and men. And drunk, sexually undisciplined men, she notes, aroused the most attention and concern from Latin American eugenicists.

Finally, although Stepan discusses many eugenicist proposals for Latin America, she can only rarely demonstrate that these were taken seriously, let alone acted upon. It is difficult to see where Latin American eugenicists caused important changes in social conduct or, failing that, where they at least dominated the public debate. Indeed, one is hard pressed to see where eugenicists even significantly informed the debate. As a result, one cannot help but wonder why we should not just regard the Latin American eugenicists as a not-very-influential group of extremists. And if this is so, why should we care very much what they thought?

Ronn F. Pineo
Towson State University

Nigel Walker, *Why Punish?* Oxford and New York: Oxford University Press, 1991. ix + 168 pp. $45, $14.95 pa.

Philosophers and penologists who have considered the justification of punishment have not usually taken account of one another's findings. This has produced a certain shallowness in penological writings and a certain lack of realism in philosophical ones. Nigel Walker thinks that penology and philosophy can provide complementary kinds of illumination, and he regrets what has become a very sharp division of labor. Accordingly, he has tried to write a book that will engage philosophical questions at the same time as it brings to bear relevant empirical research. *Why Punish?* goes a considerable way toward achieving his aims. It contains some telling criticisms of philosophical theories that try to justify punishment by its supposed effects, in particular the supposed effects of deterrence and social cohesion. It is less good at confronting theories that say that justice itself requires transgressors to pay for taking liberties. It is less good, that is, at confronting theories that are sparing in their empirical assumptions. The book occasionally criticizes theories for being too distant from and ignorant of actual penological practice when this criticism is out of order, that is, when a theory, for good reasons of its own, employs idealizations.

Walker's strongest chapters are the first five. These make up Part One, on the supposed effects of punishment according to utilitarianism. Walker objects that these effects are often not achieved or are often not known to be achieved. For example, a statistical investigation in England and Wales reveals that the rate of violent crime decreases as conviction is more likely, but not according as the term of imprisonment following conviction is longer (p. 17). Yet utilitarians often assume that the longer the sentence, the lower the rate of offense. Another striking finding bears on the idea that by expressing public disapproval of crime, punishment satisfied the law-abiding majority, who dislike lawbreakers and lawbreaking. What survey evidence in a number of jurisdictions shows is that members of the public often think that sentences are more lenient than they (the members of the public) would pass (pp. 31–32). This finding suggests that punishment does not satisfy the law-abiding majority, because it is not thought to be severe enough. More useful empirical data and interpretation is brought to bear on the utilitarian aims of rehabilitation and correction (chap. 5).

The twelve chapters following Part One are devoted to moral objections to utilitarianism (chaps. 6 and 7), retribution (chaps. 8–14), and attempts to compromise between utilitarianism and retributivism (chaps. 15–17). Walker is hostile to retributivism. He thinks that there are problems with thoroughgoing versions of the theory, versions that imply that it is obligatory to inflict punishment (chap. 9), and that even less-demanding forms of the theory fail to guarantee that the punishment will fit the crime (chap. 12). He even suggests that retributivism punishes the innocent, as it stigmatizes and otherwise imposes foreseeable suffering on innocent people connected with convicted criminals (chap. 13). Occasionally retributivist justifications of punishment are criticized for their lack of realism, as when punishment is said to express penitent understanding and to restore the offender's ties to the community. Walker points out that in practice many offenders are unrepentant (p. 79). But this no more discredits the suggestion about the point of punishment than people's lack of interest in voting discredits the suggestion that democracy is for maximizing people's say in public affairs.

Walker discusses, but finds unsatisfactory, Kant's account of the obligatoriness of punishment (p. 76). He recognizes that Kant justifies punishment by reference to a social contract, but does not see how the social contract justifies retributive punishment, as Kant wants it to, rather than utilitarian punishment. I should have thought that considerations of justice made the difference. According to the *Metaphysics of Morals*, justice demands "equality" of crime and punishment, while utilitarianism justifies opportunistic departures from equality if the benefits are great enough.

Not finding an adequate justification for retributive punishment in the writings of the main proponents of retributivism, Walker provides what he takes to be a novel justification of his own (chap. 10), according to which any code of rules contains specifying that violations of rules need to be penalized. Another general justification is latent in the social contract theory of Kant. That justification makes use of the idea of freedom. According to Kant, maximal freedom depends on each person's having an incentive not to encroach on the next person's freedom, and this incentive is provided by the penal law. Whichever approach, Walker's or Kant's, is taken, it seems that retributivism can meet the first of the objections that Walker levels against it: that it fails to ground the obligation to punish. The second objection, to the effect that retributivism urges the punishment of dependents of offenders, seems less weighty to me than the first. The unpleasant side effects on those related to offenders are just as convincingly traced to the offender and the offense as to the publisher of the offender. As for the last of the objections—that retributivism fails to specify a criterion for a fitting punishment—this is admittedly less easy to meet. But it is not always clear whether the challenge is to provide punishments that intuitively are equal to the crime or whether it is to spell out, systematically and in full generality, what makes any crime equal to any punishment. Kant was not being evasive when he said that the proportioning required the use of judgment: he was making the point that not all requirements of equality can be reduced to algorithms.

When Walker takes up compromises between retributivism and utilitarianism, he is mainly concerned with the theoretical costs. Retributivists, he thinks, have to make greater concessions than utilitarians. That may be, but it matters only if a compromise is really forced on them. Walker has not convinced me that an unreconstructed retributivism, along Kantian lines, has no future.

Tom Sorell
University of Essex

Index

Contributors

M. G. BROERS is a lecturer in history at Leeds University, England. He has written several papers on the history of war, law, and crime in Modern Europe. His current speciality is Napoleonic Italy, some of the results of which will be published in Volume 15 of *Criminal Justice History*.

M. A. CROWTHER is a lecturer in history at the University of Leeds, England. He is currently completing a manuscript on Napoleonic Italy.

CLIVE EMSLEY is professor of history at the Open University, Milton Keynes, England. He has published numerous books and articles on the French Revolution, the history of policing, and crime and society in modern Britain. His most recent study is *The English Police: A Social and Political History* (Oxford, 1991).

JILL HARSIN is professor of history at Colgate University, New York. She has published in modern French history, and her most recent book is *Policing Prostitution in Nineteenth-Century Paris*.

PETER KING is senior lecturer at Nene College, Northampton, England. He has published seven articles on aspects of crime and justice in England, including more recently "Gleaners, Farmers and the Failure of Legal Sanctions in England 1750–1850," *Past and Present* (1989); and currently is completing a book on *Crime, Justice and Discretion: Law and Society in South-Eastern England 1740–1820* (Oxford University Press).

LOUIS A. KNAFLA is professor of history at the University of Calgary, Alberta, Canada. He has published books and articles on the legal history of early modern England and of nineteenth-century and Western Canada. He currently has two books in press: *Law, State and Society: Essays in Modern Legal History* (University of Toronto Press) and *Kent at Law 1602* (Her Majesty's Stationery Office).

KATE LOWE is a lecturer in modern history at the University of Birmingham, England. A scholar of Renaissance Italy, she has held lectureships at the universities of Hong Kong, London, and Cambridge. Her most recent book is *Church and Politics in Renaissance Italy* (Cambridge, 1993), and she has in press *Crime and Disorder in Renaissance Italy* (Cambridge University Press).

THOMAS C. MACKEY teaches at the University of Louisville, Kentucky. He is a specialist in American legal history and the author of *Red Lights Out: A Legal History of Prostitution, Disorderly Houses, and Vice Districts, 1870–1917.*

GREG MARQUIS is an assistant professor of history at St. Francis Xavier University, Antigonish, Nova Scotia, Canada. He has written numerous articles on Canadian legal history and policing, and is the current author of *Policing Canada's Century: A History of the Canadian Association of Chiefs of Police* (Toronto, 1993).

MARK MAZOWER is a lecturer in international relations at the University of Sussex, Brighton, England.

JOHN McELDOWNEY is reader in law at the University of Warwick, England. He has published widely on the criminal justice system and on the working of the law in nineteenth-century Ireland.

EUGENE McLAUGHLIN is a lecturer in criminology and social policy at the Open University, Milton Keynes, England. He has held lectureships at Manchester University and the University of Hong Kong. His most recent books are *Out of Order? Policing Black People* (London, 1991) and *Social Problems and the Family* (London, 1993).

JOAN NOEL was a research assistant at Nene College, Northampton. She suffered a sudden and tragic death in the summer of 1992.

RUTH PALEY is an editor at the Public Record Office, Chancery Lane, London, England, where she is engaged on a calendar of select cases on the crown side of the court of King's Bench. She has published several articles on the history of English policing and is currently preparing a book on policing Hanoverian London.

STEFAN PETROW is law librarian and honorary research associate in the department of history at the University of Tasmania, Hobart, Australia. His research interests include the legal history of England and Australia from 1800. He has published "The Legal Enforcement of Morality in Late-Victorian and Edwardian England" in the *University of Tasmania Law Review* (1992) and has in press *Policing Morals: The Metropolitan Police and the Home Office 1870–1914* (Oxford University Press).

RONN F. PINEO is an assistant professor of history at Towson State University, Maryland. He has authored two articles in the *Hispanic American Historical Review* and is presently completing a book on the urban social consequences of rapid economic growth and the political process of reform.

BERNARD PORTER is professor of history at the University of Newcastle-upon-Tyne, England. He has worked extensively on aspects of imperialism and nineteenth-century policing in Britain. His most recent books are *The Lion's Share* and *The Origins of the Vigilant State*.

XAVIER ROUSSEAU is Research Fellow at the Belgian National Fund for Scientific Research at the Catholic University of Louvain, Department of History, and at the University of Saint Louis, Brussels, Faculty of Law. He has published several articles on criminal justice history in the Netherlands, and most recently he co-authored "Etats, justice pénale et histoire, bilan historiographique et relecture," *Droit et Société 20/21 (1992)*. He is currently working on state formation and criminal justice in North-West Europe 1750–1850.

J. A. SHARPE is senior lecturer at the University of York, England. He has published extensively on crime, criminal justice, and punishment in early modern England, including *Crime in Early Modern England 1550–1750* and a recent history of punishment. His current research project is a study of witchcraft.

TOM SORELL is reader in philosophy at the University of Essex, Chelmsford, England. His publications in this area include *Moral Theory and Capital Punishment*.

JONATHAN SWAINGER is a lecturer in history at the University of Northern British Columbia, Prince George, Canada. He has recently published an article on the judiciary of Quebec and is currently writing on the criminal law in central Alberta and capital crimes in nineteenth-century British Columbia.

RICHARD VOGLER is solicitor and lecturer in law at the University of Sussex, Brighton, England. His most recent book is *Reading the Riot Act*, and he is currently researching the development of the jury in France.

BARBARA WEINBERGER is senior research fellow in the Center for Social History at the University of Warwick, England. Her most recent book is *Keeping the Peace? Policing Strikes in Britain 1906–1926* (Oxford, 1991), and she is currently completing a comparative study of policing in Manchester and Wuppertal in the late nineteenth and early twentieth centuries.

Submissions

Notes on Submissions:

The general rule guiding authors and editors is that submissions should follow as closely as possible the formats of the most recent publication. Therefore, the previous volume of *Criminal Justice History* should be consulted for guidance. The basic format used is the University of Chicago Style Manual.

Editorial correspondence and submissions:

Professor Louis Knafla
Department of History
University of Calgary
Calgary, Alberta
Canada T2N 1N4
FAX 403–289–8566

Books for review, proposals to review, and reviewer registrations should be sent to the appropriate review editor:

U.S.A. and Canada

Professor Julia Kirk Blackwelder
Department of History
University of North Carolina
Charlotte, NC 28223
U.S.A.

Other areas and transnational:

Professor Clive Emsley
European Centre for Policing
The Open University
Milton Keynes MK7 6AA
England